Ethnic Cues

THE POLITICS OF RACE AND ETHNICITY

Series Editors Rodney E. Hero, University of California, Berkeley
Katherine Tate, University of California, Irvine

Politics of Race and Ethnicity is premised on the view that understanding race and
ethnicity is integral to a fuller, more complete understanding of the American
political system. The goal is to provide the scholarly community at all levels with
accessible texts that will introduce them to, and stimulate their thinking on,
fundamental questions in this field. We are interested in books that creatively
examine the meaning of American democracy for racial and ethnic groups
and, conversely, what racial and ethnic groups mean and have meant for American
democracy.

*The Urban Voter: Group Conflict and Mayoral Voting Behavior in
American Cities*
Karen M. Kaufmann

Democracy's Promise: Immigrants and American Civic Institutions
Janelle S. Wong

Mark One or More: Civil Rights in Multiracial America
Kim M. Williams

Race, Republicans, and the Return of the Party of Lincoln
Tasha S. Philpot

The Price of Racial Reconciliation
Ronald W. Walters

Politics in the Pews: The Political Mobilization of Black Churches
Eric L. McDaniel

*Newcomers, Outsiders, and Insiders: Immigrants and American
Racial Politics in the Early Twenty-first Century*
Ronald Schmidt Sr., Yvette M. Alex-Assensoh,
Andrew L. Aoki, and Rodney E. Hero

Ethnic Cues: The Role of Shared Ethnicity in Latino Political Participation
Matt A. Barreto

Ethnic Cues

The Role of Shared Ethnicity in Latino Political Participation

MATT A. BARRETO

The University of Michigan Press

Ann Arbor

First paperback edition 2012
Copyright © by the University of Michigan 2010
All rights reserved
Published in the United States of America by
The University of Michigan Press
Manufactured in the United States of America
♾ Printed on acid-free paper

2015   2014   2013   2012   5   4   3   2

A CIP catalog record for this book is available from the British Library.

Library of Congress Cataloging-in-Publication Data

Barreto, Matt A.
    Ethnic cues : the role of shared ethnicity in Latino political
participation / Matt A. Barreto.
        p.   cm. — (The politics of race and ethnicity)
    Includes bibliographical references and index.
    ISBN 978-0-472-11709-3 (cloth : alk. paper)
    ISBN 978-0-472-02185-7 (e-book)
    1. Hispanic Americans—Politics and government.   2. Hispanic
Americans—Suffrage.   3. Hispanic America—Ethnic identity.
4. Political participation—United States.   5. United States—Race
relations.   6. United States—Ethnic relations.   7. United States—
Politics and government.   I. Title.
E184.S75B366   2010
323.1168'073—dc22   2010007939

ISBN 978-0-472-03495-6 (pbk. : alk. paper)

To my parents
Kathy and Guillermo
Thank you for all your love and support

Contents

Acknowledgments

This book was completed with support from the Ford Foundation Minority Fellowship, the University of California Office of the President Fellowship, and the University of California MEXUS Fellowship, which provided me with the resources I needed to finish this project in a timely manner. In addition, support from the University of California at Irvine's Center for the Study of Democracy and Chicano/Latino studies program were crucial to the early stages of this research.

At the University of Washington, I received financial and research support from a variety of sources. Most important was the Washington Institute for the Study of Ethnicity and Race, then under the leadership of Gary Segura. In addition, the Diversity Research Institute, headed by Luis Fraga, and the Institute for Ethnic Studies in the United States, under the leadership of William George, provided important research assistance that allowed me to revise this manuscript. Feedback from Christopher Parker greatly improved this manuscript.

My mentors—Bernie Grofman, Louis DeSipio, Katherine Tate, and Carole Uhlaner—provided helpful ideas and suggestions, and I could not have completed this project without their support. In particular, Bernie Grofman provided thoughtful and intelligent critiques that undoubtedly strengthened this book as well as my other research projects. Uncle Wuffle also shared helpful advice, a keen editorial eye, and his terrific sense of humor, all of which benefited me in a profession that sometimes takes itself too seriously. It was also a pleasure and a wonderful learning experience to serve as a research assistant for Katherine Tate, Louis DeSipio and Bernie Grofman, and I am confident that their tutelage helped prepare me for my career as a research professor. Carole Uhlaner's advice at an academic conference was a primary reason why I enrolled at Irvine, and I am indebted to her.

I am also grateful for the support and guidance I received from other faculty members at Irvine: Russ Dalton, Etel Solingen, Marty Wattenberg, Willie

Schoenfeld, Shawn Rosenberg, and Hans-Dieter Klingemann. On the long list of other notable scholars who have provided valuable assistance, no one stands out more than Gary Segura. In addition, Ricardo Ramírez, Adrian Pantoja, José Muñoz, Gabe Sanchez, Yishaiya Abosch, Chris Parker, and especially Nathan Woods have provided unwavering support, advice, and friendship. I am also thankful for the opportunities provided by Harry Pachon, president of the Tomás Rivera Policy Institute, and Fernando Guerra, director of the Center for the Study of Los Angeles. My experience as a researcher at these institutes has dramatically improved my scholarship. Other scholars who have helped me along the way include Kristin Johnson, Jongho Lee, Mara Marks, Shawn Bowler, Ken Meier, Luis Fraga, Rodney Hero, Rudy Espino, Karthick Ramakrishnan, Matt Streb, Natalie Masuoka, Stephen Nuño, Janelle Wong, Miko Son, John Bretting, Sylvia Manzano, and Elsa Macias.

Finally, and most important, I could not have completed one page of this book without the love and support of my family. My parents, Kathy and Guillermo, and my sisters, Natascha and Renata, listened to early versions of this project and provided some of the most relevant feedback. My father double- and triple-checked translations, making crucial corrections. I am most thankful for my wife, Julie, who has endured countless conference, dinners, and research presentations and keeps me going. My son, Daniel, reminds me when it is time to take a break and play.

CHAPTER 1

Assessing the Role of Shared Ethnicity in Latino Political Behavior

In 1960, Henry B. Gonzalez was elected to the U.S. Congress from a heavily Hispanic district in San Antonio, Texas. As the only elected official of Hispanic or Latino descent in the House of Representatives,[1] Gonzalez had both enormous and little influence. Within the Chicano community, he was the key voice on Mexican American politics and gained immediate prominence, but in Washington, D.C., he was but 1 of 435 representatives and found it difficult to make himself heard. Gonzalez was soon joined by Edward Roybal, elected to Congress in 1962 from California; Eligio "Kika" de la Garza, elected from Texas in 1964; and Herman Badillo, elected in 1970 from New York. With these four men from three different states,[2] Latino politics and Latino politicians were born in the United States, although it was still too early to identify "Latino politics" per se. In 1976, the Congressional Hispanic Caucus (CHC) was formed, which led to the creation of the nonpartisan CHC Institute two years later. The National Association of Latino Elected and Appointed Officials (NALEO) was founded in 1980, and by 1990, the number of Latinos in Congress had grown to seven. During these formative years, practitioners and scholars of Latino politics focused more on the modes of Chicano representation in the political system than on the consequences of Latino candidates on the ballot (see, e.g., F. C. Garcia and de la Garza 1977; Rocco 1977). With fewer Latinos running for office than African Americans in the 1970s and 1980s, research on ethnic candidates, ethnic voters, and shared ethnicity has not flourished within Latino politics as it has within studies of African American politics (see, e.g., Tate 1993; Dawson 1994; Swain 1995; Gay 2001a).

Scholars interested in American racial and ethnic politics may not have foreseen the growth in the Latino population and Latino political participation. With the passage of the Voting Rights Act of 1965, millions of African Americans registered to vote for the first time, and research on Black voting and Black candidates burgeoned during the 1970s and 1980s. Issues of civil rights, housing discrimination, busing, and affirmative action dominated not only the Black-White racial agenda but also political science scholarship. However, another historic piece of legislation passed the same year, the Immigration and Nationality Act, fundamentally changed the course of American racial and ethnic politics. Writing about ethnic politics in 1965, Wolfinger noted the persistence of national-origin identity among European ethnics but reminded us that "mass immigration ended more than fifty years ago" (896), suggesting that even European ethnics might eventually assimilate into Anglo America. Instead, the 1965 Immigration Act abolished national-origin quotas, provided visas for family reunification, and resulted in a sharp increase in the number of Asian and Latin American immigrants, adding new facets to the Black-White race debate. Most notably, the Latino population in the United States grew from about 3.5 million people (about 2 percent of the total) in 1960 to more than 45 million (15 percent) in 2007. While this growth has been fueled by immigrants, the number of naturalized Latino citizens has also grown considerably over the past thirty years (Pachon 1987, 1999). Moreover, the fastest-growing segment of the American electorate is Latino registered voters, estimated to top 10 million in 2008. There is no question that the dynamics of race and politics have changed in this country, and scholarship and research must keep pace.

In the 1930s and 1940s, scholars including Gosnell (1935), Myrdal (1944), and Key (1949) began to examine the impact of race relations on America's politics and future well-being. These researchers examined the extent to which Black political participation differed from that of Whites and noted the significance of a voter's race in models of political behavior (Alt 1994). Dahl (1961) took up the question of ethnicity, and scholars of racial and ethnic politics began to examine its effect on political behavior. Distinct from Dahl's or Wolfinger's research on "ethnic politics," research on race was prominent among political scientists interested in African American political incorporation. Empirical research on Black politics found that race significantly affects voting behavior; however, the impact of ethnicity—particularly with regard to Latinos—has been less conclusively documented.

Before the rise in studies of Latino politics, research prior to the 1965 Voting Rights Act typically examined dissent or protest in light of the fact that African

Americans lacked full voting rights. Carmichael and Hamilton argue that "solidarity is necessary before a group can operate effectively from a bargaining position of strength in a pluralistic society" (1967, 44), a statement consistent with Piven and Cloward's (1979) argument that race provided an important linkage for poor blacks who felt alienated by the status quo and organized protest movements around their shared racial experiences. More recently, work by Tate (1993), Dawson (1994), and Walton (1994) has made the case that beyond protest, racial attitudes and issues are a significant factor in understanding Black voting trends. Simply put, race identification "significantly shapes Black political behavior" (Tate 1993, 165), and "racial group politics remains salient for African Americans" (Dawson 1994, 11).

Rather than focusing only on research in Black or Latino politics, this book builds on broader studies of identity politics and in-group identification. Mansbridge (1986) and Cook (1994) have found that female voters are more interested in campaigns when female candidates or issues (e.g., the Equal Rights Amendment) are present. Work in comparative politics has determined that ethnic minorities in Canada (Landa, Copeland, and Grofman 1995), Australia (Jupp 1997), the Netherlands (Rath and Saggar 1992), and Romania (Shafir 2000) are often persuaded by ethnic appeals and vote as a bloc for ethnic candidates. Even nonethnic interest groups such as labor unions have been well documented as playing an important role in mobilizing their members as a cohesive bloc when labor-friendly candidates emerge (Uhlaner 1989a). While research on African American and other group voting trends has found that ingroup identification can matter to voting behavior, work on Latino voting has generally not concurred. In fact, some observers have argued just the opposite—that shared ethnicity is not a key mobilizing force in Latino political behavior—instead focusing on partisanship as the dominant factor (Cain and Kiewiet 1984; Graves and Lee 2000; Michelson 2005; de la Garza 2005). Most notably, in a summary of Latino political behavior, de la Garza states, "As was true in 1990, in 2004 Latinos do not behave as a political group united by ethnicity. Latinos do not see themselves as united politically and they report that they will not vote for a candidate because of shared ethnicity" (2005, 16).

This book examines the question of whether ethnic identification affects Latino voting behavior. Specifically, does the presence of Latino candidates mobilize the Latino electorate, resulting in elevated turnout and strong support for the co-ethnic candidates? While some scholars—most notably, Hero (1992)—have provided a strong theoretical basis for such a claim, no comprehensive body of empirical evidence has suggested that ethnicity is salient for Latinos, and no coherent theory exists for separating out the role of co-ethnic candidates and the role of party affiliation. Indeed, de la Garza states that ethnicity has no influence whatsoever even though numerous case studies available in court transcripts of expert witness testimony strongly support the idea that Latino voters are mobilized by Latino candidates (see, e.g., *Garza v. Los Angeles County; Ruiz v. Santa Maria; Martinez v. Bush*).

In an extensive review of research on Chicano voting behavior, J. A. Garcia and Arce argue that no consensus exists about whether ethnicity affects voting patterns, suggesting that more research is needed. They write that "strong cultural attachments have been found to be associated with either political isolation and distance, or heightened ethnic group consciousness and politicization[, and] current research efforts are still sorting out their directional effects" (1988, 130). However, in the twenty-first century, two significant developments have changed the way we think about Latino political participation. First, the 2000 presidential election marked the first time that both political parties conducted extensive outreach to Latino voters. Second, many high-profile Latino candidates ran for political office across the nation and demonstrated an even stronger commitment to Latino voter outreach.

In 2001, Latino mayoral candidates in the several of the nation's largest cities ran vigorous and competitive campaigns that seemed to generate political excitement among Latino voters. In New York, Los Angeles, Miami, and Houston, "Democrats and Republicans got a reminder that Hispanic voters are a fast-growing and crucial swing vote tied more closely to ethnic than party loyalty" (Lester 2001). Viable Latino candidates garnered national media attention in the fall 2002 New Mexico and Texas governors' races as well as the 2003 California gubernatorial recall election. Elsewhere, Latino mayoral candidates surfaced in cities not traditionally considered to have significant Latino influence, including Bloomington, Indiana; Las Vegas; and Wichita, Kansas, and Latinos were elected for the first time to city councils and state legislatures in Georgia, North Carolina, and North Dakota. In 2006, the number of Latinos in the U.S. Senate jumped from zero to three. According to NALEO, nearly one thousand more Latinos held public office in 2008 than in 1998, and thousands more had run for office and lost. Simply stated, cities and states across the nation are witnessing increases in both Latino candidates for office and Latinos who are winning election (see table 1.1). The growth in Latino candidates creates a political environment that may result in higher rates of voting and strong support for Latino candidates by Latino voters. This volume does not seek to explain the success of Latino candidates for office but rather to assess these candidates' impact on the behavior of Latino voters.[3]

TABLE 1.1. Time Line of Latino Political Representation in the United States

1822	Joseph Marion Hernández is the first Latino to serve in Congress, as a territorial delegate of Florida.
1853	José Manuel Gallegos is elected as New Mexico's territorial delegate to Congress.
1866	Cristobal Aguilar is elected first Latino mayor of Los Angeles.
1876	Romualdo Pacheco becomes the first Latino governor of California.
1876	Romualdo Pacheco is the first Latino elected to Congress from a state, California.
1897	Miguel Antonio Otero is elected the first Latino governor of the territory of New Mexico.
1912	Ladislas Lazaro is elected to Congress from Louisiana in the year it becomes a U.S. state.
1928	Octaviano Larrazolo becomes the first Latino elected to the U.S. Senate, from New Mexico.
1936	Dennis Chavez of New Mexico is the first Latino to serve a full term in the U.S. Senate.
1949	Edward Roybal is the first Latino since 1881 to win a seat on the Los Angeles City Council.
1957	Raymond Telles is the first Latino elected mayor in El Paso, Texas.
1960	Henry B. Gonzalez is the first Latino from Texas elected to Congress.
1962	Edward Roybal is the first Latino elected to the U.S. House in California since 1882.
1964	Joseph Manuel Montoya is elected to the U.S. Senate from New Mexico.
1970	Herman Badillo is the first Puerto Rican elected to Congress, from New York.
1974	Raúl Castro is elected first Latino governor of Arizona.
1981	Henry Cisneros is the first Latino elected mayor of San Antonio.
1987	Robert Martinez is the first Latino elected governor of Florida.
1989	Ileana Ros-Lehtinen, Cuban American, is the first Latina elected to Congress from Florida.
1990	Ed Pastor is the first Latino elected to Congress from Arizona.
1992	Luis Gutiérrez, Puerto Rican, is the first Latino elected to Congress from Illinois.
1992	Robert Menédez, Cuban American, is the first Latino elected to Congress from New Jersey.
1992	Nydia Vasquez is the first Puerto Rican woman to be elected to Congress from New York.
1996	Cruz Bustamante is elected the first Latino Speaker of the California Assembly.
1996	Bill Richardson is first Latino U.S. ambassador to the United Nations.
2002	Bill Richardson is elected governor of New Mexico.
2004	John Salazar is the first Latino elected to Congress from Colorado
2004	Mel Martinez is first Cuban American elected to the U.S. Senate from Florida.
2004	Ken Salazar is the first Latino elected to the U.S. Senate from Colorado.
2005	Antonio Villaraigosa is elected first Latino mayor of Los Angeles since 1872.
2006	Robert Menendez is the first Latino elected to the U.S. Senate from New Jersey.
2007	Bill Richardson announces he is running for Democratic nomination for president.

Latino Representation in the United States, January 2007

U.S. House	28 Latino members (6.4%)
U.S. Senate	3 Latino members (3.0%)
Governor	1 Latino governor (2.0%)

Studies by Ambrecht and Pachon (1974) and Garcia and de la Garza (1985) demonstrate that previous research on Latino political behavior has downplayed the role of shared ethnicity in models of participation and vote choice. Ambrecht and Pachon note that "the oversight of ethnicity in American life over recent decades has been primarily attributed to the assimilationist ideologies present in this society vis-à-vis its ethnic groups" (1974, 500). Despite the prominence of the assimilationist approach as a theory, they argue against it and call for more research on the topic of ethnic politics in the Mexican American community. While claims emerged that ethnicity might be salient, it has not yet been thoroughly investigated. For example, J. A. Garcia and Arce note that "ethnicity in its various dimensions . . . should prove to be very important in explaining the extent of Chicano political participation" yet conclude that "these orientations do not translate into higher rates of participation" (1988, 126, 148). Thus, attempts to understand the lower rates of turnout among Latinos have often focused on lower levels of resources (DeSipio 1996a) and lower levels of civic skills (Verba, Schlozman, and Brady 1995) within the Latino community, leaving much room for improvement in explaining the Latino vote. This book presents two improvements in modeling Latino political behavior: (1) controlling for the presence of Latino candidates; and (2) accounting for shared ethnicity as a mobilizing factor. I argue that the electoral context surrounding the campaign of a Latino candidate creates a mobilizing force, resulting in higher rates of Latino voting and strong levels of support for the co-ethnic candidate. This electoral context may include endorsements by prominent Latino leaders, more in-depth coverage of the election by Spanish-language media, registration and mobilization drives by Latino civic organizations, and campaign appearances by Latino candidates at Latino churches, union halls, and schools. Further, the effect should hold after controlling for standard predictors of political participation and partisanship.[4] How Latino candidates change the larger electoral context is underexplored in the current literature. Figure 1.1 addresses this deficit and depicts the relationship between ethnic candidates and ethnic voters, an important foundation for examining Latino voting behavior. Simply stated, voters encounter two types of elections, those in which a Latino candidate does and does not appear on the ballot. While our previous understanding of Latino participation relies heavily on elections with no Latino candidates, the future of American politics is much more likely to witness elections with viable Latino candidates.

In fact, the bulk of research on Latino political behavior emanates from an era in U.S. politics in which very few viable Latino candidates ran for office; thus, the general findings with respect to Latino political engagement downplayed the role of shared ethnicity. Latino politics takes on a new perspective in the twenty-first century: prominent Latino candidates for public office are increasingly commonplace, yet Latinos continue to face discrimination and underrepresentation.

The basic argument in this book rests on two theories: first, ethnic candi-

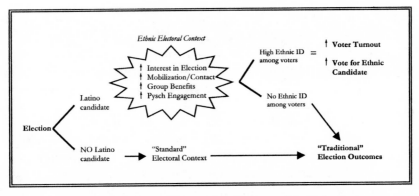

FIG. 1.1. Ethnic candidate model of Latino political behavior

dates increase the level of psychological engagement and interest in the election among ethnic voters (Dahl 1961; Parenti 1967; Tate 1993, 2003); and second, ethnic candidates direct more resources to mobilize voters in ethnic communities (Guerra 1992; Leighley 2001). While not all ethnic candidates publicly run "ethnic campaigns," the popular media are quick to report candidacies through racial or ethnic lenses, leading minority and White voters to assess the election in racial terms even if the candidates do not (see, e.g., Reeves 1997). In instances where candidates and campaigns make strong ethnic appeals, the argument is quite clear; yet even when ethnicity is not on the front page, Latino candidates are still likely to reach out to co-ethnic voters and are likely to promote issues that resonate with Latino voters. If anything, these phenomena may bias the data against my findings, making it more difficult to find mobilizing effects without knowing the exact details of every Latino candidate's campaign for office. However, if Latino voters are more likely to vote when Latino candidates are running for office and are more likely to support Latino candidates, it is reasonable to conclude that the theoretical assumptions are accurate.

However, the effect may not be the same for all Latino voters, and we should therefore try to include a measure of the degree of ethnic identification among voters. Building on theories of minority empowerment and racial incorporation, I make the case that for Latino voters with higher levels of ethnic identification, co-ethnic candidates increase the level of political awareness and interest in the election, increase the opportunity to be contacted and asked to vote, generate a sense of psychological engagement with the political system, and strengthen feelings of shared group consciousness (see, e.g., Miller et al. 1981; Uhlaner 1989a; Leighley 2001).

While a handful of studies have examined the connection between ethnicity and political participation, they have repeatedly concluded that no direct link exists for Latino voters. Both Cain and Kiewiet (1984) and Graves and Lee (2000) show that partisanship, not ethnicity, explains candidate preference for Latinos. DeSipio observes that "ethnicity will come to play less of a role in [Latino] political decision-making than will other societal divisions" (1996a, 8). In contrast, Hero's overview of Denver mayoral elections in the 1980s provides some evidence that Latinos will "vote for their own" (1992, 129) in a racialized political environment (see also Muñoz and Henry 1990). This book brings a variety of new evidence to bear on this question.

ETHNIC IDENTIFICATION AND LATINO VOTING

Why might Latinos have a sense of shared ethnic identity? Why is ethnicity more likely to matter in future elections? Individuals employ multiple forms of identification but nevertheless typically have groups of people with whom they have overlapping identities, such as language, cultural practices, religion, and race. Gordon argues that peoplehood is roughly "coterminous with a given rural land space, political government, no matter how rudimentary, a common culture in which a principal element was a set of religious beliefs and values shared more or less uniformly by all members of the group, and a common racial background ensuring an absence of wide differences in physical type" (1964, 23). The notion of peoplehood that Gordon describes can also be seen as an individual's ethnicity (from the Greek *ethnos*, meaning "people") and may encompass his or her race, religion, national origin, language, and more. Although ethnic identity is fluid, societies often develop fixed categories for identification that reinforce each identity as separate and unique and reinforce group members' attachment to their ethnic identity. For two hundred years, the U.S. census asked individuals to choose only one identity, despite many Americans' rich multicultural and multiracial history. Not until 1970 was the category "Spanish origin" added to the census, and not until the 2000 census did the federal government permit individuals to check more than one box, thereby allowing multiple identities to emerge (Masuoka 2008). The social constructions of group identification, whether real or not, guide individuals to take their places in groups and to act as group members. Miller et al. (1981) have found that group consciousness causes subordinated group members to join their group identity with a political awareness regarding their group's status, resulting in elevated levels of participation. This volume considers the extent to which Latinos act congruently on political issues.

Four characteristics describe the roots of all Hispanic Americans regardless of their background: (1) Latin American heritage; (2) the immigrant experience; (3) Spanish language; and (4) Spanish colonial influence. For some Latinos, these traits may be stronger; in other cases, they may be altogether dormant. In any event, their existence cannot be easily refuted. In addition, the experience of ethnic discrimination augments the relationship of these four characteristics. When any one of these components of ethnic identity comes under cultural attack, Latinos are likely to draw together around their common heritage. This argument about shared ethnic identification provides the foundation for this book—that is, the idea that ethnicity is an important component of Latino political behavior, especially given the current state of underrepresentation of Latinos and growing discrimination against Latino immigrants. Although distinct differences exist between Latinos of Mexican, Puerto Rican, Cuban, Dominican, and Salvadoran ancestry, they share a common Latin American heritage that brings them together (Padilla 1985). Further, patterns of residential geography make national-origin differences less relevant because Latinos of different countries of origin are somewhat concentrated in different cities and states.[5] Second, the confluence of several factors provides the opportunity for shared ethnicity to emerge as an important predictor of Latino voting behavior. These factors include the decline of party control over campaigns and candidate-centered elections (Wattenberg 2002), a growing interest in candidate qualities over issues (Popkin 1991), and the reliance on ethnic-based outreach and mobilization by candidates of both major parties (Segal 2003; DeFrancesco Soto and Merolla 2006).

In particular, this research builds on the theories advanced by Uhlaner (1989a), Leighley (2001), and Bobo and Gilliam (1990), among others. Uhlaner advances a theory of group relations to demonstrate that political participation is rational despite high costs because in-group members receive additional benefits from a sense of shared group consciousness. She argues that groups with more unified support for a candidate or issue have a stronger sense of group identity, which they can use as a bargaining chip to collect additional in-group benefits. Leighley proposes a new model for examining Latino and Black political participation that takes into account shared group consciousness, minority empowerment, and geographic racial context to improve on traditional socioeconomic models. In particular, she argues that ethnic candidates direct more resources to mobilizing ethnic communities and deserve more attention in understanding Latino voting behavior. According to Bobo and Gilliam, minority elected officials empower minority communities, resulting in higher levels of voting and bloc voting. Above all, Black mayors are found to empower Black voters through feelings of shared group consciousness and in-group benefits. Bobo and Gilliam provide a framework that envisions minority candidates and officeholders as instrumental in explaining minority participation. Tate's (1993) analysis of Jesse Jackson's presidential campaigns concurs. I expand this examination to Latino voters and Latino candidates for public office to test whether co-ethnic candidates cue ethnic voting.

Finally, from a practical perspective, Sosa, a media consultant and presidential campaign adviser, notes that in his experience conducting national surveys, studying small focus groups, and targeting Latino voters, positive ethnic identification with the candidate is an important factor. Specifically, Sosa argues that "issues also work, but only *after* Hispanic voters like and trust the candidate" (2004). Although he served as a major media consultant for President George W. Bush in 2000 and 2004, Sosa joined the presidential campaign team of New Mexico governor Bill Richardson in 2007, stating that "if his name was Bill Garcia, then every Latino would have been focused on him already" (quoted in Kornblut 2007, A4). Sosa also noted that in thirty years of campaign experience, he had observed that Mexican American voters bore a strong affinity for Mexican American candidates.

In Los Angeles's 2001 municipal election, for example, Latino candidates sought the city's top two posts, mayor and city attorney. In the mayoral contest, Antonio Villaraigosa, a Democrat, ran a "liberal" campaign that focused on labor and working-class families; his opponent, James Hahn, also a Democrat, ran as a moderate who embraced increasing business development in the city, among other issues (see figure 1.2). In the city attorney race, Rocky Delgadillo, who attended Harvard Law School and worked as a staff attorney for the previous mayor, Republican Richard Riordan, ran a centrist campaign emphasizing his record as tough on crime; his opponent, Mike Fuerer, ran a more liberal campaign, including a stance against racial profiling. The differences between the candidates were borne out in exit polls—a majority of voters identified Villaraigosa as more liberal and Delgadillo as more centrist. Despite their varying backgrounds and ideologies, however, both Latino candidates received more than 80 percent of the Latino vote in an election where Latinos outvoted all other groups of registered voters. Why did Latinos have the highest rates of voting, and why did they overwhelmingly prefer the more liberal Villaraigosa in

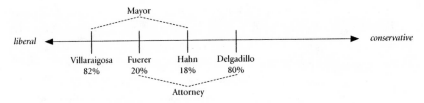

FIG. 1.2. Candidate ideology and percentage vote won among Latinos, Los Angeles, 2001

the mayoral election and the more centrist Delgadillo for city attorney? One possible explanation centers on the mobilizing effect of Latino candidates.

Critics commonly contend that the Latino community is too diverse—too heterogeneous to demonstrate shared group identity—and New York City is perhaps the most diverse of any city with a large Latino population. New York's 2001 Latino population of 2.2 million was 39 percent Puerto Rican, 23 percent Dominican, 14 percent South American, 10 percent Mexican, and 7 percent Central American. In 2001, Puerto Rican candidate Fernando Ferrer reached the Democratic runoff for mayor, where he faced Mark Green. Ferrer was well known in the Puerto Rican community and campaigned heavily throughout the city's Latino neighborhoods. Although Ferrer lost the election by a few percentage points, he received strong support from Puerto Rican, Dominican, and other Latino groups. Ferrer won 86 percent of the vote in heavily Puerto Rican Latino precincts, 80 percent in heavily Dominican precincts, and 79.5 percent in mixed Latino precincts where neither Puerto Ricans nor Dominicans were the majority. (Most often, Mexicans or Colombians are the largest Latino group in these precincts.) In contrast, he won only 15 percent of the vote in majority-White precincts.

TABLE 1.2. Percentage Vote for Fernando Ferrer, New York, 2001

Precinct Type	n	Percentage
Majority Latino	457	84.3
Puerto Rican	180	86.0
Dominican	192	80.3
Neither Puerto Rican nor Dominican	85	79.5
Majority White	691	15.1
Majority Black	520	65.6

These examples illustrate Latino candidates' potential mobilizing effects on Latino voters—across ideology and across national origin. In this study, I test the ethnic-mobilization hypothesis with several new and previously underanalyzed data sets. In addition, I utilize an alternative mechanism for measuring shared ethnicity that may account for its lack of relevance in previous research. Earlier attempts to include ethnicity in a model of Latino political behavior considered it an all-or-nothing issue in which all Latinos had the same level of ethnic identification. Instead, I rely on a scale of Latino ethnic identification similar to the measure of party identification. This scale includes both direct and indirect measures of political ethnic identification. Direct evaluations may include questions such as "Is the candidate's ethnicity or partisanship more important in deciding your vote?" and "Do you find yourself more interested in an election when Latino candidates are running for office?" Indirect evaluations may include questions such as "Is it important to elect more Latinos to public office?" and "Is it important for Latinos to stick together on political matters?" More accurate assessments of degree of shared ethnicity demonstrate that for Latinos with higher levels of ethnic identification, ethnicity plays a central role in political decision making.

RESEARCH DESIGN AND CHAPTER OUTLINE

The book is organized into four main sections: first, an introduction and overview of the question under consideration; second, a review of the literature and exploration of the concept of ethnic identification; third, empirical data analysis; and fourth, a discussion of the findings and their implications for our understanding of political behavior, followed by a brief conclusion.

Following this introduction, section 2 consists of two theory-building chapters that lay the foundation for the empirical analysis. Chapter 2 brings together a review of the relevant literature within the subfields of political behavior, African American politics, Asian American politics, ethnic group politics, and Latino politics. It is important to examine what has been written—and, more important, accepted—about voter turnout and vote choice from a broad perspective and then to compare these writings to the current scholarship and theories within minority politics to disentangle the state of ethnic Latino politics. In particular, I take up the question of whether Latinos will follow a model of immigrant-based ethnic politics, comparable to the path followed by Irish and Italian arrivals, or a model of discrimination-based racial politics, similar to African Americans. In addition, chapter 2 explores the origins and basis for shared ethnic attachment among Latinos today and proposes a new approach to quantitative studies of racial and ethnic politics.

Building on this theoretical review and discussion, chapter 3 then incorporates a real-world perspective through interviews with Latino elected officials and candidates for public office. I present findings from interviews with Latino elected officials and campaign operatives in California, Texas, New York, and Colorado to determine the extent to which theory meets reality in campaigning for Latino votes. These states are important because they parallel the analysis of mayoral elections in each state and provide the necessary context for the election results discussed later. The interviews were conducted with Latino candidates for mayor in Los Angeles, San Francisco, Houston, New York City, and Denver as well as their campaign managers and relevant staff. Speaking directly with Latinos who have run for office and organized get-out-the-vote campaigns strengthens my argument by adding practical examples that both confirm and challenge the theoretical arguments and assumptions. For example, in Houston's 2001 mayoral election, Republican Orlando Sanchez received more than 70 percent of the Latino vote; in 2000, however, the same precincts voted overwhelmingly for Democrat Al Gore. What explains this discrepancy? Talking to key actors inside the Sanchez campaign and other campaigns clarifies the connections among shared ethnicity, partisanship, and voting patterns among Latinos.

In the third section, I analyze the relationship between Latino candidates, shared ethnicity, and political participation using various data sources, including official precinct-level vote results, county registrar vote records, election surveys, and hypothetical candidate evaluations. The section includes three chapters covering both local and state-level elections in California, Texas, New York, and Colorado to determine what geographic and Latino national origin patterns may exist.

As a starting point for the empirical section, I examine public opinion data to gauge what Latino voters are saying about ethnic politics and ethnic candidates. In chapter 4, public opinion surveys conducted in California and New York by the Latino Issues Forum and the Tomás Rivera Policy Institute are used to explore theoretical candidate matchups and crossover voting tendencies among Latino voters after controlling for partisanship and issue preference. The Latino Issues Forum survey asks voters to decide between two fictitious candidates, Smith and Hernandez, and presents the voter with an issue platform for each candidate. The Tomás Rivera Policy Institute survey asks the specific question of whether Latino voters prefer Latino candidates of the opposing party or non-Latino candidates of the same party. For both surveys, I assess whether, after controlling for issue congruence and party strength, people with strong ethnic identities are likely to prefer the ethnic candidate or whether ethnicity has no effect on vote choice. While I do not anticipate that all Latinos will prefer the Latino candidate, I do find a positive and significant effect for degree of ethnic attachment and ethnic voting, which provides grounding for my theory that ethnicity influences political participation. While the data are hypothetical in nature, the findings provide an important starting point for examining the salience of ethnicity for Latino voters, setting the stage for analyses of election results involving Latino candidates.

Building on the public opinion data, chapter 5 examines precinct-level election results from the 2001 Los Angeles, New York, and Houston mayoral elections and the 2003 San Francisco and Denver mayoral elections to determine the relationship between high-density Latino precincts and voter turnout and vote preference for Latino candidates. While the hypothetical candidate data in chapter 4 suggest that Latinos are mobilized by co-ethnic candidates, the actual election results bring real data to bear on this issue from a variety of cities and contexts. These mayoral contests represent both nonpartisan and partisan examples where the Latino candidates come from a variety of backgrounds. Los Angeles featured a Latino Democrat versus an Anglo Democrat; New York featured a Democratic primary election with a Puerto Rican running against a Jewish candidate; in Houston, the Latino candidate was a Cuban American Republican who faced an African American Democrat; in San Francisco, a Latino Green Party candidate ran against an Anglo Democrat; and in Denver, Latino and non-Latino Democrats faced each other in the runoff. This analysis effectively neutralizes the role of partisanship because the elections are nonpartisan in nature (although one is a partisan primary) and the Latino candidates represent three different political parties. None of the five elections studied pitted a Latino Democrat against a non-Latino Republican, a situation in which the Democratic leanings of Latino registered voters would make it exceedingly difficult to separate the impact of ethnicity from that of partisanship. Each of these elections provides a unique view of Latino candidates and Latino voters. Ecological inference, ecological regression, and multivariate regression analysis are performed to estimate Latino turnout and Latino vote preference in each city. Further, because the demographic data provide information on the percentage of White, Black, and Asian American adults within each precinct and across all five cities, I offer some conclusions about the impact of Latino candidates on all segments of the American voting public.

Chapter 6 investigates additional real data: validated vote records from Los Angeles and Orange Counties, California, for elections in which Latino candidates ran for office. While the analysis in chapter 5 is at the aggregate level, county vote records merged with ethnic surname lists permit individual-level analysis of Latino and non-Latino voting patterns. For the 2002 general election in California, I examine the probability of voter turnout for voters in districts where Latino candidates ran for office. If Latino voters are more psychologically engaged in elections with Latino candidates, and if Latino candidates are more likely to mobilize Latino voters, we should see higher rates of voting for Latinos as the number of Latino candidates for office increases. This chapter focuses on all offices on the ballot featuring Latino candidates, including lieutenant governor, insurance commissioner, U.S. Congress, state senate, and state assembly. While some voters had the opportunity to elect one or two Latinos, other voters lived in jurisdictions where seven or more Latino candidates appeared on the ballot. Here, multivariate probit regression reveals that Latino candidates have a mobilizing effect on Latino voters, with different effects for different levels of office. Again, because I employ all voter records for Southern California, I can estimate the impact of Latino candidates on the likelihood of turnout by Latino and non-Latino registered voters and then compare the results. Although it is not possible to know for whom voters cast their ballots, the data reveal that Latinos were significantly more likely to turn out and vote in jurisdictions with more Latinos running for state-level office.

Chapter 7 examines the presidential candidacy of Bill Richardson to determine whether his campaign resonated with Latino voters. Richardson was hailed as the first Latino candidate for president, providing the first opportunity to extend the analysis of co-ethnic candidates to the nation's highest office. Tate's (1993) research on Jesse Jackson demonstrates that co-racial candidates can have a significant mobilizing effect in presidential elections, a trend again observed with respect to Barack Obama and Black voters in 2008. However, nothing is known about the possible mobilizing effects of the presence of a Latino candidate during a presidential run. Using two preelection surveys, I estimate the effect of shared ethnicity or ethnic cues on Latino support for Richardson in the early stages of the 2008 presidential election. The data reveal that although Richardson had low name recognition, he received strong support from Latinos who follow ethnic cues. Taken together, the election results, official registrar records, and hypothetical candidate data present a full picture of the potential and reality of ethnic cues in Latino political participation and behavior. Analysis of each data set provides support for the idea that Latino candidates mobilize Latino voters, irrespective of partisanship, national origin, or locality.

The data analysis in chapters 4–7 suggests that these hypotheses are well founded. Latino candidates are mobilizing agents who result in (1) higher levels of Latino voter turnout and (2) higher levels of support for the candidate than would have been predicted had the candidate not been Latino. In both sets of models, the inclusion of ethnicity-related variables greatly improves the results.

Finally, in chapter 8, I take up the broader question of the degree to which

TABLE 1.3. Overview of Data to Be Examined

Data Set	Sample	Geography	Election	Hypotheses Tested	Chapter
Elite interviews	$n = 10$	CA, TX, NY, CO	2000–2003 mayoral elections	Interviews examine if and how Latino candidates mobilize Latino voters	3
LIF survey	$n = 800$	CA	2000, hypothetical campaign	Ethnicity vs. issues in vote choice of hypothetical candidates	4
TRPI survey	$n = 800$	CA, NY	2002 congressional midterm	Crossover voting for co-ethnic candidate	4
Precinct returns	$n = 1,730$	Los Angeles, CA	2001 Los Angeles mayoral runoff	Impact of mayoral Latino candidate on turnout and vote preference	5
Precinct returns	$n = 3,449$	New York City, NY	2001 New York mayoral primary	Impact of mayoral Latino candidate on turnout and vote preference	5
Precinct returns	$n = 614$	Houston, TX	2001 Houston mayoral runoff	Impact of mayoral Latino candidate on turnout and vote preference	5
Precinct returns	$n = 561$	San Francisco, CA	2003 San Francisco mayoral runoff	Impact of mayoral Latino candidate on turnout and vote preference	5
Precinct returns	$n = 422$	Denver, CO	2003 Denver mayoral runoff	Impact of mayoral Latino candidate on turnout and vote preference	5
Registrar of Voters records	$n = 5$ million	Los Angeles, Orange Counties, CA	2002 congressional midterm	Impact of State Legislative and congressional Latino candidates on turnout	6
LPC survey	$n = 1,000$	Nationwide	2008 presidential	Impact of presidential Latino candidate on vote choice	7
Latino Decisions survey	$n = 400$	NV	2008 presidential	Impact of presidential Latino candidate on vote choice	7

Latinos will vote on the basis of their ethnic ties. Following the empirical analysis, I explore the implications of ethnic Latino politics for American politics as a whole. While much of the data primarily focus on Latino registered voters, they should not be viewed in isolation or as distinct from the larger American electorate. Latinos represent the fastest-growing segment of voters in the country, increasing by more than 28 percent from 2000 to 2004 (de la Garza, DeSipio, and Leal 2010). In comparison, the entire American electorate grew by less than 5 percent during the same period (Current Population Survey 2006). In addition, both political parties are actively courting the Latino vote. In states such as New Mexico and Florida, Latino voters provided the winners with their margins of victory in the 2000 presidential election, and in 2004, Latino voters proved critical in swing states such as Nevada, Colorado, New Mexico, Florida, and even Pennsylvania. Thus, as Latinos are increasingly integrated into the mainstream American electorate, it is important to understand the motivations behind their political participation. In addition, the analysis of Latino voters and candidates offers insight into racial and ethnic politics as a whole. I explore how Latinos' experiences both resemble and differ from those of African and Asian Americans. Many questions remain: Will racial and ethnic minorities form political coalitions? Will intragroup differences create a competitive environment? Latino politics is no longer a regional matter of interest only in the southwestern United States. Latinos have already won election to the state legislatures in thirty-six states, and more Latino candidates will be running for and winning elected office. The increasing diversity within campaigns and elections necessitates new perspectives on the influence of ethnic candidates and ethnic voters. In particular, Latino politics represents an integral component for understanding the new American voter and increasingly the new American candidate.

CHAPTER 2

Latino Politics in the Twenty-first Century:
A New Theory of Latino Political Behavior

In 1980, the decennial census first used the term *Hispanic* to count persons of Latin American ancestry living in the United States. That census revealed that almost 15 million Americans were Hispanic or Latino,[1] accounting for roughly 6.5 percent of the overall U.S. population. The politics of Black and White that was present during the 1960s and 1970s was now being forced to make room for a new minority group, although few people were equipped to address "Latino" concerns. At the national level, most policymakers were unaware of or out of touch with the Latino community, and they were even more at a loss to address policy issues of concern to the Latino community.[2] Much of the work of doing so thus fell on the shoulders of the few Latinos in Congress.

The same year, Latino elected officials agreed that they were not getting enough institutional backing to support Latino candidates running for office. During the Democratic National Convention, Congressmen Edward Roybal (D-California) and Robert Garcia (D–New York) and California assemblyman Ruben Ayala met and discussed the formation of the National Association of Latino Elected Democrats. In 1981, after a few years of recruiting Latino candidates, the organization expanded into the nonpartisan National Association of Latino Elected and Appointed Officials (NALEO) and created the nonprofit NALEO Education Fund (Pliagas 2005). The organization promotes citizenship drives, voter mobilization, and Latino candidates for office. As a part of this effort, NALEO began to document the number of Latino elected and appointed officials and to create a network of elected Latinos. In its early years, when the number of Latino officials was few, NALEO conducted opinion surveys to create a sense of a Latino agenda and provide non-Latino policymakers with a framework for addressing the needs of their Latino constituents. The number of Hispanic or Latino elected officials has subsequently grown exponentially, increasing the difficulty of surveying every elected official but easing the process of promoting a Latino viewpoint on important policy issues. In 2007, NALEO estimated that 4,853 Latinos held public office across the country.

This chapter lays out the framework for an ethnic-candidate paradigm of American politics in the twenty-first century. As the U.S. Latino population grows and more Latino candidates run for the mayor's office, the state legislature, and the U.S. Senate, scholars and pundits alike will need a firm understanding of the dynamics at play within the Latino community and between the Latino and non-Latino communities. It is not enough to simply state that co-ethnic candidates matter. We need a sound theory for understanding why they matter so that we can identify cases and sort out results. Co-ethnic candidates are salient to Latino voters for two reasons. First, by definition, people who self-identify as Latino are members of a common ethnic group,[3] and for a variety of reasons, ethnicity is a salient political cue for Latino voters. Second, campaigns increasingly emphasize and voters are increasingly concerned with candidate characteristics. The convergence of a growing Latino electorate and a campaign system that focuses on candidate traits provides the foundation for exploring the impact of shared ethnicity and co-ethnic candidates.

ETHNICITY AS A SALIENT ISSUE

While this book ultimately takes up the issue of Latino candidates and their effect on Latino voters, we should be careful not to put the cart before the horse. That is, before we can examine the importance of co-ethnic candidates, we must demonstrate that ethnicity is a salient political identity for Latino voters. If ethnicity matters, then we can move forward to examine the role that candidate ethnicity plays in explaining Latino voting behavior. If the concept of shared ethnicity is immaterial to Latino voters, co-ethnic candidates should have no impact on voting calculi. Shared ethnicity is an important component of Latino political incorporation for five reasons: (1) Latinos share a Latin American heritage and culture, including the prevalence of Spanish; (2) they draw on a shared immigrant experience; (3) continued discrimination against Latinos highlights their commonality; (4) ethnic candidates typically focus on co-ethnics as their base, reinforcing the bond; and (5) the presence on the ballot of a candidate with a Spanish surname cues known traits. In this section, I explore these five points and demonstrate that ethnic attachment is relevant to Latino political participation; first, however, I examine why group identification is so rooted in our social and political culture.

Social Group Identification

According to Gordon, the first social question of human civilization was asked when a Pleistocene hunter roamed too far away from the safety of his home and encountered a person he had never seen before: "That question is 'Who are you?'" And how does the hunter respond? According to Gordon, "He places himself in a group which is a political unit, which is culturally uniform, and which occupies a definite geographical place, and within this group he occupies more specific relationships of kinship" (1964, 19). Since this first encounter, the world has evolved, and the simple question of self-identification has now become quite complex. While individuals may have multiple identities, they may share many characteristics—language, cultural practices, religion, and race—with a group of people. Gordon calls this social group "peoplehood" and equates it with ethnicity. Throughout the world, the concept of peoplehood has provided an important basis for social grouping and community. As nation-state boundaries came into clearer focus during the nineteenth and twentieth centuries, national identities became salient; in addition, the idea of peoplehood or ethnicity grew stronger, especially in the United States as predominantly White immigrant groups from Europe arrived and struggled to form a national identity. Ethnic identity became the overriding social group in America, and the original thirteen states were somewhat divided or even settled based on patterns of ethnicity. In particular, the middle colonies of British North America were filled with pockets of religious and ethnic settlements. Bonomi reminds us that through religious and linguistic differences, ethnic diversity and ethnic identity dominated the political and social development of the mid-Atlantic states and ultimately the entire country. She brings her discussion of ethnic communities at the founding of this country forward three hundred years to reflect on the importance of social group identity today: "This history of group tensions in the Middle Colonies can serve as a springboard for discussion about the pros and cons of group identity, a subject that has gained renewed attention in recent American discourse and practice. Is it better for Americans to play down their ethnic, religious, and racial differences in order to nurture an overarching national identity? Or should we cling to those differences as valuable attributes that enrich our society, and also amplify each group's voice in politics?" (2008). Despite all the rhetoric about the American melting pot, this country has perhaps the strongest tradition of ethnic group identity: different peoples have come together for common political and social ideals yet maintain their own distinct cultures and communities. This process held true in 1709 and continues to do so in 2009.

Although ethnic identity is fluid, a society may develop seemingly fixed categories for identification that serve to reinforce each identity as separate and unique. According to many social psychologists, societal pressures influence people to fit neatly into one identity or another (Tajfel and Turner 1979; Turner et al. 1987; Hogg and Vaughn 2002). Twentieth-century research on religious identity found that in America, people must be categorized as Protestant, Catholic, or Jewish, regardless of their formal connection with any religion (Herberg 1955). Further, during the 1950s, when Herberg was writing, racial status was usually limited to "White," "Negro," or "Chinese"; no other options were available.[4] As Herberg notes, "The way in which one identifies and locates oneself ('Who, what, am I?') is closely related to how one is identified and located in the larger community ('Who, what, is he?')" (25). Although he is referring to religious cleavages, Herberg's description of "belonging" and group association applies equally to ethnic groups: "To be 'something,' to have a name, one must identify oneself to oneself, and be identified by others, as belonging to one or another of the three great religious communities in which the American people are divided" (54). More broadly, Herberg advances a theory of self-identification:

> Everyone finds himself in a social context which he shares with many others, but within this social context, how shall he locate himself? Unless he can so locate himself, he cannot tell himself, and others will not be able to know, who and what he is; he will remain "anonymous," a nobody—which is intolerable. To live, he must "belong"; to "belong," he must be able to locate himself in the larger social whole, to identify himself to himself and to others. (24)

Thus, individuals face strong internal pressure to identify themselves as well as external pressure to be identified as belonging to one group or another. If a group does not appear large enough or salient, it loses its identity and falls into a category where "all other forms of self-identification and social locations are either peripheral or obsolescent" (Herberg 1955, 53). Gordon agrees with this assessment and finds that group categorization is a powerful societal force: "Group categorization, then, has its own social momentum once it is set in motion and is by no means purely a matter of individual volitions acting in concert" (1964, 29). The social constructions of group identification, whether real or not, guide individuals to take their place in and act as members of groups.

The factors that motivate or contribute to group identity or group consciousness have received considerable attention in sociology, psychology, and political science scholarship. While group consciousness is often reserved for research on African Americans, many scholars have contributed to the development of a broader concept of social-group-based identity and political behavior. In their seminal work on American political behavior, Campbell et al. (1960) devote an entire chapter to the question of social group identity and political socialization. Using data from 1952 and 1956, the authors assess the strength of group attachment among Catholics, Jews, Blacks, women, and union members, finding that social group identity constitutes an important factor in partisanship and voting behavior: "Shared membership provides a focus and direction for behavior that is lacking among nongroup members" (304). Scholars during the 1960s explained this finding by arguing that group voting increased the chances of group benefits, an argument that was later refined by Browning, Marshall, and Tabb (1984) and Bobo and Gilliam (1990) as the minority-empowerment thesis, which assessed the extent of group cohesion in cities that had elected Black or Latino mayors.

From a rational-choice perspective, Uhlaner (1989a) has argued that intermediary group leaders motivate group members to act cohesively on political matters and increase the consumption benefits to group members when they do so. Candidates, who want to maximize their vote share and turnout among members of favorable groups, promise to reward the groups with beneficial policy and patronage. Uhlaner applies this theory to the social group of a labor union. From my perspective, the connection is even stronger when applied to an ethnic minority group and a co-ethnic candidate because the candidate is the key link to motivating group behavior. Wouldn't we expect the group to behave more cohesively and participate at higher rates when the candidate is a group member? Uhlaner notes, "The process can be seen most easily in those situations in which groups claim a special relationship between their political support and the behavior of a politician" (1989a, 392). A key to Uhlaner's theory is the intermediate group leader, who mobilizes the group and conveys the group unity to the politician. However, when the politicians themselves are members of the social group, the intermediary may be less necessary as the politicians can directly mobilize the group through speeches, advertisements, and ethnic outreach. Still, the point that receipt of group benefits motivates a stronger sense of group action is clearly relevant to this discussion.

Other studies have attempted to explain group behavior by focusing on group members' psychological underpinnings. Scholars such as Uhlaner and Bobo and Gilliam observed cohesive group action but did not determine what motivated group identity. Important theoretical and empirical contributions came from Gurin, Miller, and Gurin (1980), Miller et al. (1981), and Dawson (1994). All of these works examine the factors that contributed to cohesiveness among groups—based on age, class, occupation, and race. Gurin, Miller, and Gurin argue that important differences exist between group identification and group consciousness: "Identification refers to the awareness of having ideas, feelings, and interests similar to others who share the same stratum characteristic. Consciousness refers to a set of political beliefs and action orientations arising out of this awareness of similarity" (1980, 30). Given this valid distinction, Latino group identity is high and will manifest itself politically when co-ethnic candidates cue the ethnic identification. Looking at data from 1972, the authors point to subordinate-group status as a motivating factor for group identity and ultimately group consciousness. Today, it is easy to argue that Latinos are a subordinated group. Whether we measure this position by socioeconomic attainment, occupational status, discrimination against immigrants, or political underrepresentation, Latinos are disadvantaged with regard to Whites along almost every social and political marker. Miller et al. refine the idea of group consciousness and note that while group identity is often correlated with less power or deprivation, such does not have to be the case. Other factors contribute to a politicized group consciousness. In addition to group identity, members must view the "group as relatively lacking in societal influence" and "attribute their deprived condition to social barriers" (1981, 500). Finally, both of these studies remind us that group identity needs to be politicized for group consciousness to serve as a mobilizing force. Latinos have the bases for group identity and disadvantaged status, and the presence of a vibrant and viable Latino candidate is the source of politicization. Pantoja, Ramírez, and Segura (2001) have found ballot measures, particularly in California, to be a source of ethnic politicization among Latinos. Shaw, de la Garza, and Lee (2000) point to co-ethnic mobilization—that is, being asked to register or vote by another Latino—as a source of politicization. Thus, our understanding of Latino politics is beginning to conclude that a fairly strong sense of group identification does exist; however, it may not always be politicized.

Dawson (1994) argues that African Americans' individual interests cannot be separated from their group interests. His concept of linked fate explains that many individuals view their opportunities for success as depending on how the overall African American community fares. Even controlling for socioeconomic status, Blacks have demonstrated a strong attachment to group identity and group consciousness. In particular, Dawson points to the economic subjugation of Blacks and the experiences of White domination via slavery as dominant forces in racial group interests. According to Dawson, "Both components were forged during the historical experiences that linked a general subjugation of black life with economic domination of blacks by whites" (48). During Reconstruction, as Blacks attempted to enter the political system, they faced widespread discrimination that sought to deprive them of political, economic, and social rights. Thus, racial group interests became inherently tied to Black politics. Strict residential segregation ensued, along with lynchings and Jim Crow legislation that rendered African Americans powerless in the South. However, a sense of linked fate, group identity, and group consciousness developed and strengthened.

While these scholars establish important principles in group consciousness that we can adapt to Latino politics, none of these authors has written explicitly about Latinos. Although Latinos and Blacks and Latinos and Jews have many similarities, many differences remain. Most notably, Latinos do not have a single entry point into the U.S. political system that defines their history or their future development as a minority group. Dawson clearly points to the institution of slavery for African Americans as a basis for the concept of linked fate in the twentieth century. For Hispanic Americans, no single historical event, institution, or migration creates a shared group experience. Instead, the process of becoming a minority group—and now the largest minority group—has been slow and steady. Some Hispanics have historical experiences dating back to the Mexican-American War and the 1848 Treaty of Guadalupe Hidalgo, while others are first-generation immigrants from El Salvador who arrived in 1980. Some Puerto Ricans may trace their family ancestry in the United States back to 1898 and the Spanish-American War, when Puerto Rico became a U.S. territory and thousands of island residents migrated to the North American mainland. But Dominicans, the fastest-growing Latino national-origin group, did not arrive in the United States in significant numbers until nearly one hundred years later, during the 1980s and 1990s. The 1959 Cuban Revolution pushed many people to flee the island for Florida, with subsequent waves arriving in 1972 and 1980. Finally, since 1990 alone, approximately 10 million new Latino immigrants—more than one-fifth of the current U.S. Latino population—have arrived in the United States from twenty different Latin American countries. Thus, Latinos' historical community and discrimination experiences differ greatly from those of African Americans. Yet we still rely heavily on theories of Black political participation and group consciousness to explain Latino group identity and political behavior. To some extent, doing so makes sense—perceived discrimination as a contributing factor to group identity applies equally well to Blacks' and Latinos' political experiences. But none of these earlier authors has discussed other factors, such as acculturation and the immigrant experience, that we know greatly shape Latino group identity (Masuoka 2006; Sanchez 2006; Branton 2007).

Racial and ethnic identities are important for a number of reasons. Primarily, they provide a psychological foundation for group identification and are central to an intimate sense of peoplehood. In a more practical sense, such identity is important because it provides a patterned network of associations, organizations, businesses, and institutions that allows members to define their primary relationships within their racial or ethnic group. Finally, the overarching cultural patterns and values are absorbed and reflected through the group's unique cultural heritage (Gordon 1964). While many differences exist, Mexicans, Puerto Ricans, Cubans, Dominicans, Peruvians, Salvadorans, and Argentineans also have shared cultural traits that are important to their group members' identity. Beyond the social value associated with group identity, it is now well known that social group identity among minorities in the United States directly influences patterns of public opinion and political participation. "The social implications attached to a racial identity influence the individual's worldview that frames that individual's political perceptions" (Masuoka 2008, 254). Masuoka has recently assessed the formation and impact of racial identity among U.S. Blacks, Latinos, Asians, and multiracial persons, finding that "those individuals who have strong perceptions of racial group consciousness are more likely to adopt political interests that take into consideration the issues of the racial group as a whole" (255).

Shared Ethnic Identity among Latinos

With a population of 44 million, more than 15 percent of the U.S. total, Latinos surpassed African Americans as the country's largest minority group in 2000. However, many political analysts argue that Latinos lack the same strength in numbers as the Black community because they have no strong collective sense of ethnic identity as a consequence of their origins in more than twenty countries. Indeed, Highton and Burris state that "analyses that combine Latinos of all national origin groups in a single group and thereby implicitly assume that they are all similar will likely conceal important differences" (2002, 289). While national-origin-based identities may remain dominant, shared group or pan-Latino identity might play a significant role in Latinos' political behavior for two reasons. First, overlapping ethnic and cultural bonds may unite Latinos of different national origins, providing the basis for the emergence of a shared ethnic identity. Second, national-origin groups tend to be geographically segregated in the United States, making pan-Latino identity less politically vital in elections where, for example, a Mexican American candidate is running for office. Political districts are geographically bounded and consequently are likely to include Latinos of the same national origin, even when the state as a whole (e.g., Florida) is diverse. Pachon concludes in a series of articles that ethnic identity has increased in California, emerging as a mobilizing force in the political participation of Latinos (Pachon 1998, 1999; Pachon, Barreto, and Marquez 2004).

However, we should not assume that ethnic identification is equally strong among all Latinos. In fact, one of the main objectives of this chapter is to provide a range of ethnic identification for Latinos and to determine if those with high degrees of ethnic attachment are more likely to vote along ethnic lines. As stated earlier, there are five aspects of a common ethnic experience among Latinos.

1. *Latinos share a Latin American heritage and culture, including the prevalence of Spanish.* Shared group identity for Latinos is strongest at the national-origin and generation levels, but shared identities can cross these boundaries (Masuoka 2006). The North, Central, and South American territories occupied by Spain provide a shared homeland and thus a common cultural heritage for virtually all Latinos living in the United States. In addition to linguistic ties, important cultural, religious, and social similarities provide Latinos of different national origins with a common point of reference. The strong role of the family, in particular as it relates to holidays and traditions, is shared throughout Latin America (Moore and Pachon 1985; Williams 1990; Santiago and Davidow 1998). Latinos overwhelmingly support and follow Catholicism and its practices and often embrace the community ahead of the individual. While differences exist from country to county, the shared aspects of Latin American heritage are highlighted for Latinos living as a minority in the Anglo-Christian U.S. environment.

2. *Latinos draw on a shared immigrant experience.* According to the 2000 Census, 44 percent of all Latinos were born in Latin America and migrated north to the United States, and an additional 30 percent are the children of foreign-born parents. Thus, three-quarters of the Latino population shares this immigrant experience and its accompanying social and cultural issues. About

15 percent of the Latino population has immigrant grandparents, leaving only about 10 percent of Latinos without an immediate family connection to the immigrant experience.

As Jones-Correa (1998) notes, immigrant families confront unique challenges in interacting with the public sphere and rely on immigrant-based community networks for assistance. Whether facing challenges related to naturalization, visa status, employment, housing, access to health care, or public education, the common experiences and struggles of immigrants provide bridges for Latinos of different nationalities (Portes and Rumbaut 1996).

In addition, regardless of Latinos' country of ancestry, the Spanish language provides them with a collective communication resource. While not all Latinos are completely fluent in Spanish, a nationwide survey by the Kaiser Foundation (*National Survey* 2000) found that only 5 percent of Latinos speak no Spanish at all, and nearly nine of ten Latinos speak and understand Spanish well. While some U.S.-born Latinos may overstate their Spanish proficiency, the connection to the language is nevertheless clear. DeSipio maintains that even for "non-Spanish dominant Latinos, Spanish offers a different sort of cultural link—the experience with language-based discrimination is a part of the Latino experience in the United States" (1996b, 179). With the growth of the Latino community, Spanish media outlets have become important advertising venues for both Latino and non-Latino candidates for public office.

Although the Spanish colonial experience is less tangible than other pan-Latino characteristics, it is nonetheless important because it represents an underlying psychological attitude within the Latino community. While the Spanish colonial occupation occurred almost two centuries ago (one century for Puerto Rico and Cuba), it left a lasting legacy of domination, oppression, struggle, and liberation. For two hundred years, Spanish occupation led to constant conflict between the colonizer and the colonized. Descendants of Spain's empire in Latin America, the Southwest, and the Caribbean have endured savage conquest and domination and have had to fight for freedom and respect. While hard to pinpoint, shared historical traits are considered important components of shared identity among minority groups (Linz and Stepan 1996; Robinson 1999). Just as there is an enduring "American spirit" 225 years after the American Revolution, the Spanish colonial influence remains present, to some degree, among Latinos.

3. *Continued discrimination against Latinos highlights their commonality.* Perceived discrimination against the group can strengthen and solidify the group identity (Dawson 1994; Tate 1993). Racial or ethnic identity is shaped not

only by group members but also by the larger American society. African American scholars have noted that Black identity is in large part influenced by the core American society and institutions and that focusing solely on internal community identity building is naive (Appiah 1994, 155). Discrimination against the Latino community has come in both structural and attitudinal varieties. While the legal discrimination is not as widespread or severe as against African Americans during the post-Reconstruction and pre–civil rights eras, discrimination has and does exist based on language and immigration rights (e.g., California's Propositions 187 and 227). In addition, attitudinal discrimination against Latinos has existed for many years. Latin American immigrants have been blamed for job loss and economic problems and have been considered a drain on social welfare programs. Latinos are often associated with drug trafficking, crime, gangs, and the general deterioration of inner cities. With these stereotypes has come discrimination in the workplace, in public schools, and in the political arena (e.g., gerrymandering and polarized voting). Latinos perceive themselves as victims of group-based discrimination. In the National Survey on Latinos in America (2000), 82 percent of Latinos responded that discrimination against "Latinos" is a problem in society. Further, 40 percent of Latinos reported that they or their families had personally experienced discrimination because of their ethnicity. While this figure is lower than the 54 percent of Blacks who claim to have felt discrimination, it is considerably higher the 14 percent of Whites who did so.

In their investigation of "racial formation" in America, Omi and Winant (1989) argue that the Otherizing of people of color reproduced by social, economic, and political forces negatively affects the individual and collective psyche of minorities but also strengthens group consciousness and in-group identity. The official and political classifications of ethnicity by the state have serious consequences for people of color. Indeed, "racial minorities pay a heavy price in human suffering as a result of their categorization as 'other' by the dominant racial ideology" (67). Taylor agrees that "our identity is partly shaped by recognition or its absence, often by the *mis*recognition of others" (1994, 25).

Thus, the ingredients for pan-Latino identity exist. In the National Survey of Latinos in America (2000), 84 percent of respondents reported that all Latinos would be better off if various Latino groups worked together politically. Dawson has called this connection between race and identity "linked fate" and argues that it is an important heuristic for the political participation of African Americans (1994, 75). The main contention of the "black utility heuristic is that the more one believes one's own life chances are linked to those of blacks as a group, the more one will consider racial group interests in evaluating alternative policy choice [and] evaluating candidates and parties" (75). Similarly, studies of Latino politics can be improved by borrowing Dawson's idea of linked fate as it relates to decision-making shortcuts in the political arena. Latinos who tie their self-interests to ethnic group interests should be expected to use ethnicity as a heuristic device when they find themselves in the polling booth deciding between Hernandez and Smith. Dawson concurs that a strong sense of ethnic identity goes far in influencing minorities' political behavior, calling this group consciousness the "political building blocks for analyzing perceptions of racial group interests," such as party and candidate preference (84).

Published research has found that Latinos' perceptions of discrimination increase their sense of ethnic identity and group consciousness. According to Masuoka, who has explored predictors of panethnic group consciousness among Latinos and Asian Americans, "For Latinos, those who understood discrimination against Latinos to be a problem in society have a strong sense of group consciousness" (2006, 1008). Likewise, Sanchez (2006) has concluded that perceived discrimination is an important contributing factor to "Latino commonality." Sanchez further argues that discrimination not only contributes to group identity but also promotes collective action. In his model exploring ethnic group participation, he notes that "individuals who believe that discrimination directed toward Latinos is a big problem are significantly more likely to indicate that Latino collective action leads to an improved situation for Latinos" (2008, 435).

4. Ethnic candidates typically focus on co-ethnics as their base, reinforcing the notion of shared ethnicity. Parties, candidates, and campaign managers have for decades ignored Latino voters during elections. When push comes to shove, a typical candidate wants to mobilize likely voters, not bring new voters into the electorate. Latino communities have often been viewed as rife with noncitizens, nonregistrants, and nonvoters, resulting in few phone calls and mailers and little door-to-door canvassing (de la Garza, Menchaca, and DeSipio 1994). However, when Latino candidates run for office, they are much more likely to view Latino voters as part of their base and to conduct voter mobilization in Latino communities (de la Garza, Menchaca, and DeSipio 1994; Leighley 2001). A study of voter mobilization during the 2000 election revealed that Latinos with at least one Latino representative were more likely to report that they received voter mobilization efforts (Barreto et al. 2003). Further, Latino candidates are more likely to conduct Spanish-language outreach, connecting with Latino voters on a more personal level. If the primary interaction with the political system is via ethnic channels (i.e., Latino candidates), Latino voters are more likely to rely on shared ethnicity as a political cue. Indeed, Ramírez (2007) establishes that California Latinos who first registered to vote between 1994 and 1996, when the contentious statewide Propositions 187 and 209 appeared on the ballot, were more likely to respond to ethnic-based voter mobilization in subsequent elections.

Coupled with a high sense of ethnic attachment, a sense of political underrepresentation rather than issue alignment may drive Latinos to follow ethnic cues when voting, especially if Latinos are more likely to be contacted and mobilized by Latino candidates. DeSipio maintains that for ethnicity to become a salient mobilizing force, a link beyond mere culture must exist to unite Latinos politically (1996a). While he points to a distinct perspective on policy issues, the presence of a viable Latino candidate may be one such condition.

5. *A candidate with a Spanish surname on the ballot cues known traits.* Voters do not like casting ballots for candidates about whom they know very little (Jacobson 1987), and most voters continue to know very little about candidates for public office (Popkin 1991; Tate 1993; Delli Carpini and Keeter 1996). To help make decisions about often complex campaigns and elections, voters rely on information shortcuts. Lupia (1994) has found that voters are likely to take electoral cues from trusted organizations and spokespersons when casting ballots. When signal providers are thought to be credible, voters are more likely to trust and side politically with the signalers. Latino voters who read campaign signs, political advertisements, or newspaper articles about co-ethnic candidates are likely to infer some things about those candidates based on their names. For example, voters may infer that the candidates are Latino, speak Spanish, are Catholic, had parents who immigrated, have family living in Latin America, and understand Latino culture, values, and political needs. Among African Americans, Tate (2003) has found that voters who had co-ethnic representatives were more familiar with those representatives. Similarly, Pantoja and Segura (2003a) have found that Latinos who are represented by Latino elected officials are more trusting of government and have higher levels of political efficacy.

These arguments are theoretical reasons to expect ethnicity and group identity to matter to Latinos. But does it? Public opinion data from the 2006 Latino National Survey (LNS) highlight the extent to which ethnicity is salient to Latinos. Ninety percent of registered Latino voters have a strong ethnic identification, a trend that holds across national-origin group and immigrant generation (Barreto and Pedraza 2009). Among Latinos of Mexican origin, 63 percent report very strong ethnic identification, and 27 percent indicate somewhat strong ethnic identification, compared to 61 percent and 24 percent among Cubans and 73 percent and 19 percent among Puerto Ricans. Foreign-born Latino registered voters have virtually the same rate of ethnic identity as U.S.-born second-generation registered Latinos. Even a majority of Latinos who speak no Spanish at all have very strong ethnic identities. Further, the LNS finds a relatively high level of Latino group commonality and linked fate. Seventy-five percent of Latino registered voters report some or a lot of group commonality with other Latinos. The survey asked respondents a variant of Dawson's linked fate question: "How much does [national origin group] 'doing well' depend on other Hispanics or Latinos also doing well? A lot, some, a little, or not at all?" Sixty-nine percent of Latino registered voters answered "some" or "a lot." Finally, getting directly to the issue of candidate traits and the importance of co-ethnic candidates, the LNS asked Latinos about the importance of a candidate's Hispanic or Latino ethnicity in their vote choices. Fifty percent of the sample said that co-ethnicity was "very important," and 23 percent said "somewhat important." Theories about the importance of candidates' co-ethnicity thus appear to be rooted in the realities of the Latino political experience. By almost any metric, an overwhelming majority of Latinos see ethnicity as a significant and prominent factor in their lives (Fraga et al. 2006).

WHY CANDIDATE TRAITS MATTER

Shared ethnicity and ethnic attachment are only half of the story. To show that co-ethnic candidates influence Latino voting behavior, we must demonstrate that candidate characteristics—not just policy statements or partisanship—matter to voters. Among the earliest explanations of vote preference, Downs (1957) argues that voters evaluate competing candidate policy positions, leaving little room for affect or candidate appeal. However much has changed in campaign practices over the past fifty years, candidate traits continue to play a major role in voting behavior for five reasons: (1) the diminishing role of political parties; (2) the rise of candidate-centered elections; (3) candidate appeals for groups of voters; (4) media focus on ethnicity of candidates; and (5) the continuing lack of minority representation. Before delving into each of these five points, I will review some of the foundations for understanding vote preference.

Early Voting Preference Models

In an information-rich environment, each voter identifies the policy platforms of all candidates and picks the candidate who best represents the voter's political interests. In this model, candidates can be placed at various points along an ideological spectrum, and voters are expected to select the candidate who is closest to their personal views. The first modern application of this spectrum can be found in Hotelling's (1929) economic analysis of business competition. Adapting this model to politics, Hotelling contemplated political parties to better understand why Democrats and Republicans often align themselves near the center of the left-right spectrum to attract votes. Downs (1957) later expanded this model of one-dimensional political competition, arguing that voters have ordered and stable preferences that allow them to be placed on a one-dimensional issue spectrum. In fact, Downs conceptualizes a "linear scale running from zero to 100 in the usual left-right fashion" and "assume[s] that the political preferences can be ordered from left to right in a manner agreed upon by all voters" (115). These early attempts to describe voter preference characterize voters as rational decision makers for whom issue positions serve as the key determinant of vote choice.

While the single-dimension structure is theoretically sound, scholars have rejected it as too simplistic. The linear economic model is based on assumptions that the political environment is stable and that voters have well-ordered preferences. In politics, parties and voters' locations along a linear dimension are often unclear. As Stokes explains in his critique of one-dimensional spatial models, "The ground over which the parties contend is *not* a space in the sense that Main Street or a transcontinental railroad is. Treating it as if it were introduces assumptions about the unidimensionality of the space, the stability of its structure, the existence of ordered dimensions and the common frame of reference of parties and electorate that are only poorly supported by available evidence from real political systems" (1963, 369–70). Stokes's main argument is that the decision to cast a ballot for one candidate or another is not as simplistic as the economic theory of voting suggests. Instead, voters may consider multiple issue and candidate-related dimensions. These five criteria are essential to formulation of an ethnic-candidate model of vote preference.

1. *The diminishing role of political parties.* Scholars have long contended that partisanship is a critical predictor of vote choice (see esp. Campbell et al. 1960). Similar to issue position, this theory suggests that voters will sometimes overlook misaligned issues and support the candidate of their same party. At

least since *The American Voter,* this theory has been accepted, and party identification remains one of the best indicators of vote preference today. However, some research suggests that a voter's partisanship may not be as stable as previously thought and that the role of the party is on the decline.

Tedin and Murray (1981) argue that with respect to state elections, voters are not static and that considerable instability exists in voter preference regardless of candidates' partisanship. This finding contrasts with those of studies conducted by Lazarsfeld and Berelson (e.g., Berelson, Lazarsfeld, and McPhee 1954) that concluded that because of strong party ties, voters made their minds up early and did not waver. However, political parties have been losing steam in American politics for quite some time. Arguably the biggest blow to parties was the transition to democratic primaries, giving nominating power to voters rather than party bosses. The result was less organizational control over the nominees and more variance in the issue positions of partisan candidates. At the same time, scholars have noted an increase in split-ticket voting (Rusk 1970; Wattenberg 1996) and in the number of voters registering as independents (Dalton 2002). According to data from the National Election Study, 12 percent of voters split their tickets between president and Congress in 1952, whereas 28 percent split their votes in 1980. Similarly, these data show that the percentage of respondents who identify as independents has doubled from 19 percent in 1958 to 40 percent in 2000 (see National Election Study 1952, 1958, 1980, 2000). The days of the party machine are long gone, and voters are now more independent thinkers, paying attention to a host of issues and concerns when choosing candidates. While partisanship remains a powerful predictor of vote choice, it is not the only game in town.

2. *The rise of candidate-centered elections.* While political parties are declining in importance, candidates themselves are increasingly becoming the focus of elections. Although previous scholarship suggested that individuals' voting practices rarely waver between elections, Tedin and Murray find that voters can indeed be persuaded by campaign appeals and that the media's focus on candidate characteristics does matter. They find that ideology and issue position are influential but that candidates can overwhelm these factors in persuading voters. "The declining importance of party cues, coupled with the absence of salient issues that divide the electorate along stable lines create opportunities for candidates to gain or lose sizable elements of the electorate in their campaign. . . . [S]uch being the case, electoral success thus comes to depend more than ever on the personal attributes of the candidates" (1981, 455).

Additional support for candidate-centered elections comes from Wattenberg (1987, 1994) and Abramowitz (1989), who argue that voters pay attention to candidates, not parties. While Abramowitz describes voters as rational utility maximizers who vote for the candidate closest to their own ideology and with the best shot at winning, Wattenberg views candidates as central because of a larger decline in partisan attachment and the diminishing role of party organizations. Despite their differences, the two scholars agree that voters are now paying more attention to candidates, providing an opportunity for the race and ethnicity of the candidate to play a central role. With regard to minority voters, Abramowitz finds such strong support for Jesse Jackson among Blacks that they do not conform to his other theories of vote preference (as does Tate 1993). The same may hold true for Latino voters.

3. *Candidate appeals for groups of voters.* Candidates seek to capitalize on voter calculations of personality and symbolism. Popkin (1991) has argued that savvy candidates know the importance of symbolic politics and will often make religious, racial, and ethnic appeals during campaigns. Popkin extends Dahl's (1961) theory of "ethnic politics," which found immigrant communities beleaguered by home-country campaign appeals in Italian and Irish boroughs as far back as 1900. Popkin notes that campaign strategists try to insert their candidate into high-profile cultural events, fitting in comfortably with ethnic voters, so the candidate appears in touch with the minority electorate. In 1976, President Gerald Ford was photographed eating tamales at a Mexican American festival to gain support of Latino voters in San Antonio, Texas. However, his appearance won him jeers, not cheers, because he neglected to remove the corn husk from the tamale and attempted to eat the entire thing (Popkin 1991). In their 2000 contest for the U.S. presidency, George W. Bush and Al Gore spent millions of dollars on Spanish-language advertising and tried to one-up each other in wooing Latino voters with broken Spanish and symbolic gestures. Gore announced to a crowd of Latinos in Denver, "My first grandson was born on the Fourth of July, and I hope that my next is born on Cinco de Mayo" (National Association of Latino Elected and Appointed Officials 2000). Candidates seek to appeal to groups of voters by highlighting personal connections to those groups. For example, in 2004, Democratic presidential candidate John F. Kerry routinely noted the immigrant story of his wife, Theresa Heinz-Kerry, when speaking to Latino crowds. In 2008, Hillary Clinton talked about the summer she spent working on a Hispanic voter registration drive in Texas, when she became "addicted to Mexican food."

Non-Hispanic candidates take such actions because voters may rely on candidates' demographic characteristics, such as race, ethnicity, gender, religion, and social origin, as information shortcuts—that is, as ways to predict candidates' policy stands in the absence of concrete information. Similarly, in her analysis of Blacks' evaluations of their representatives in the U.S. Congress, Tate has drawn our attention to the power of officeholders' and voters' shared ethnicity using the analogy of athletics: "Is the race of the players salient and important to the many Black spectators in the stands?" (2003, 20). She has found that legislators' racial group membership matters and is one of the most important factors (along with party identification) in candidate evaluations. As Popkin notes, voters may be more likely to head to the polls wondering, "How does he look to me lately?" rather than "What has he done for me lately?" (1991, 97). A reality of twenty-first-century elections is that candidate characteristics are important, especially for racial and ethnic minorities, as Barack Obama's 2008 candidacy clearly demonstrated.

4. Media focus on candidates' ethnicity. Unless a minority group comprises a clear majority in the geographic voting area—city, state, or legislative district—minority candidates need the support of nonminority voters. Thus, not all ethnic candidates will make clear ethnic appeals during the campaign. Independent of the level of ethnic campaigning undertaken by ethnic candidates, however, the media will no doubt sensationalize the candidacy through an ethnic lens. A quick review of news headlines from across the country reveals that most major newspapers continue to call attention to the ethnicity of Latino candidates for public office:

"Hispanics Ken Salazar and Mel Martinez Win Senate Seats"—*Salt Lake Tribune*

"Latinos Go for Brass Rings"—*New York Daily News*

"Hispanic Candidate Just a Dream"—*Denver Post*

"West Becomes Board's 1st Hispanic"—*Milwaukee Journal-Sentinel*

"Hispanic Candidate to Test GOP Voters"—*Houston Chronicle*

"Latino Aldermen Press Daley to Select Hispanic for Top Cop Spot"
—*Chicago Sun-Times*

"2 Hispanic Candidates Battle It Out"—*New York Times*

"Hispanic Candidate, Incumbent Compete for Minority Votes"
—*Washington Post*

"Hispanic Candidate Is Pitching Herself as People's Choice"—*Boston Globe*

"The Latino Candidate: Yours, Mine or Ours?"—*New York Times*

"Big Lead for Latino in Council Race"—*San Francisco Chronicle*

"Latino Candidates: Victories Signal Growing Clout"—*Atlanta Journal-Constitution*

"Latino Candidates Running Strong in Salem"—*Boston Globe*
"Latino Candidates See a Bright Future in Mass."—*Boston Globe*
"Latino Pols Building Dream Machine"—*Chicago Sun-Times*
"Latino Candidate in Tossup Race for L.A. Mayor"—*Boston Globe*
"A Latino Mayor for Los Angeles?"—*San Diego Union-Tribune*
"Latino Mayor Is First in Region"—*Milwaukee Sentinel*
"Latino Leads Race to Be Los Angeles Mayor"—*Financial Times*
"L.A.'s Runoff Could Elect a Latino Mayor"—*USA Today*[5]

These headlines clearly demonstrate the media's reliance on ethnic adjectives to describe ethnic candidates. A search for the terms "White candidate" or "Anglo candidate" turned up no results in the Lexis-Nexis database. In fact, an Associated Press headline during the 2004 Senate race between Peter Coors and Ken Salazar read, "Beer baron, Hispanic lawyer in tight Colorado Senate race" (Kohler 2004), drawing attention only to Salazar's ethnicity. Another headline in the *Washington Post* did not label the candidate as an ethnic but instead suggested the connection between a Spanish surname and Hispanic voters: "GOP Picks Gonzalez to Run in 49th: Newcomer to Politics and District Targets Mostly Democratic Hispanic Vote" (O'Hanlon 2001). Without commenting on the normative implications of such practices, the point is simply that the media focus on Hispanic/Latino candidates as ethnics, potentially reinforcing the connection for Latino voters even if the candidates do not publicly do so. During the 2008 presidential election, the media never referred to Republican John McCain as the "White" candidate, while his opponent, Democrat Barack Obama, was referred to almost exclusively as the "Black" candidate. The only time McCain was labeled as the "White" candidate was when pundits openly speculated whether the "Black" Obama could win over White voters. The historic nature of Obama's candidacy certainly provided an extra incentive for the media to hype his race, but it was clearly a one-sided affair.

5. *Continuing lack of minority representation.* A final ingredient in the recipe of co-ethnic politics is the continued underrepresentation of minorities at all levels of government. Given the rising U.S. Latino population, Latino political representation is receiving a great deal of attention. Although Latinos currently comprise 15 percent of the U.S. population, they hold just 31 of the 535 seats in the House and Senate (5.8 percent). Low levels of Latino representation are nothing new. F. C. Garcia notes that "one of the political disadvantages of Latinos through U.S. history has been that they have been inadequately represented by their own co-ethnics in decision-making capacities" (1988, 269). Since

the early 1980s, many scholars have focused on the implications of inadequate Latino representation (see, e.g., Welch and Hibbing 1984; de la Garza 1988; Pachon 1988) with "the assumption being that Latino representation will make more decisions which are favorable to the Hispanic community" (F. C. Garcia 1988, 269). Advocacy groups such as NALEO, the National Council of La Raza, LULAC (League of United Latin American Citizens), and the Mexican American Legal Defense Fund call attention to Latinos' underrepresentation and make a point of promoting the candidacy of Latinos in elections across the United States. Civic groups, redistricting experts, and the media tend to advance the message that only Latino voters can help elect Latino representatives. However, when Latino public service reaches parity with its population, less attention is likely to be paid to candidates as Latinos. For the foreseeable future, however, Latino candidates will continue to garner attention from the media, civic groups, and Latino voters. As Latino candidates compete for higher-level office, they will draw more attention, not only to themselves but also to all Latino elected officials and candidates. In 2008, Rafael Anchia ran for the U.S. Senate from Texas; a victory would have made him the first Latino senator in the state's history. Not only was the campaign a major story in the Texas Latino community, but as Anchia campaigned with other Latinos running for the U.S. House, the state legislature, or even for city councils, the issue of Latino representation was emphasized.

SHARED ETHNICITY AND LATINO POLITICAL PARTICIPATION

While the number of articles investigating Latino political behavior has grown somewhat, relatively few works have dealt directly with the impact of Latino candidates. Most studies of Latino politics continue to focus on the perceived low levels of participation among Latinos vis-à-vis non-Latino voters (J. A. Garcia and Arce 1988; Hero 1992; de la Garza, Menchaca, and DeSipio 1994; Verba, Schlozman, and Brady 1995; Arvizu and Garcia 1996; DeSipio 1996a; Shaw, de la Garza, and Lee 2000; Pantoja, Ramírez, and Segura 2001; Cassel 2002). The conventional wisdom in political science holds that Latinos are less interested in politics and register and vote at low rates relative to other groups. According to J. A. Garcia and Arce, "Chicanos tend to vote 10–20 percent less than their Anglo counterparts" (1988, 129). Similarly, Portes and Mozo note that "the data indicate that the Spanish-origin population of voting age has much lower registration and voting rates than the U.S. population as a whole" (1985, 35). Salces and Colby concur: "The primary reason for the political weakness of

Spanish-Americans in Chicago is that so few of them participate in elections" (1988, 195). A Houston study conducted by MacManus and Cassel concluded that "the data show that even among registered voters, Mexican-Americans are less interested in politics than Anglos or blacks" (1982, 57). This foundation, however, is based on a history of elections that typically featured two Anglo candidates who ignored the Latino community. How might our understanding change given the presence of a viable Latino candidate?

A handful of studies specifically address theories of Latino vote choice and candidate preference. DeSipio (1996a) contends that although ethnicity had no statistically significant impact in his model of vote choice, such an impact could emerge under "unique circumstances" or in response to "ethnic-based discrimination." Based on existing data sets at the time, he concludes that such a scenario is unlikely as Latinos achieve greater assimilation into society.

Most recently, Graves and Lee (2000) tackle the issue of Latino candidates head-on in their examination of voting preference in the 1996 Senate election in Texas. Cain and Kiewiet (1984) had previously examined the relationships among ethnicity, issue positions, and candidate evaluations in a 1982 congressional election in Los Angeles. Despite literature showing evidence of distinct patterns of voting behavior by Latinos (Grofman and Handley 1989; Engstrom 1992; Grofman 1993; Engstrom and Brischetto 1997), academic journal articles other than those by Graves and Lee and Cain and Kiewiet have devoted little empirical attention to theories of ethnic voting.

Graves and Lee (2000) have found that ethnicity played a key role in the Texas senatorial election but that its influence was mediated by partisanship. Building on the theories advanced by Kinder and Sears (1985), Graves and Lee argue that ethnicity influences the primary determinants of vote choice—partisanship, issue positions, and candidate evaluations—but not vote choice outright. Latino identity may influence the "manner in which individuals are brought into and engage the political system" by placing them in a particular social and cultural milieu that shapes their worldview (229). Graves and Lee's findings go far to support these claims. While being Latino is not a significant predictor of candidate evaluation, it is significant in models accounting for partisanship and issue position. In the final model predicting vote choice, Latinos do not behave significantly differently from Anglos, but partisanship is the best predictor of vote preference for Morales (the Latino Democrat), and being Latino is the best predictor of Democratic partisanship. Thus, Graves and Lee conclude that "ethnicity exerts a substantial *indirect* influence on [Latinos'] voting preference" (234).

Much of what Graves and Lee have found is based on a similar analysis conducted by Cain and Kiewiet (1984), whose study of Mexican American voting preference found that ethnicity is associated with party identification and perceptions about the candidates but not directly with vote choice. Controlling for party identification, Cain and Kiewiet found no statistical support for the proposition that ethnicity affects vote choice. While both of these analyses point to a role for ethnicity in the political behavior of Latinos, they ultimately rely on traditional models of vote choice, in which partisanship, issue position, and candidate evaluation hold the true keys (Aldrich, Sullivan, and Borgida 1989). This finding is consistent with DeSipio's (1996a) argument that conventional predictors of participation and behavior are important in understanding Latino voting and that ethnicity may play only a minor role. However, both Cain and Kiewiet's and Graves and Lee's studies examined voting preference in a general election that pitted a Latino Democrat against an Anglo Republican. Because of this scenario and Latinos' historic ties to the Democratic Party, Latino voters can be expected to prefer a Latino Democratic candidate in such a contest. However, the findings might differ in nonpartisan or primary elections, in which partisanship is less relevant, or in an election in which the Latino candidate is a Republican.

Ethnicity may have a more direct impact on vote choice for Latinos after controlling for issue congruence and party identification. In addition, while previous analysts have speculated that ethnicity is all or nothing, it more likely has varying degrees of salience for different voters. Thus, while all Latinos may not share a strong attachment to their ethnicity, it is likely to serve as a guiding force in the political behavior of those who have such an attachment, equal to or possibly surpassing traditional factors, such as issue position and party identification, that may explain vote preference.

John Garcia and Arce (1988) have noted that the ingredients for political participation exist among Chicanos yet did not find consistent participation in politics among respondents in the 1979 Chicano Survey: "It would seem that Chicanos have developed strong predispositions to active political participation in a group manner. With this pattern of political orientations, one might expect active levels of political participation. . . . [P]articipatory attitudes are conducive to actual political behavior. Yet . . . the participation rates are rather low" (137). They may have conducted their study too early in the political development of Chicanos and Latinos. Twenty years later, the Latino electorate is much more developed. Both parties actively court Latino voters, Latino civic groups promote citizenship and voter registration drives, and Latino elected officials have empowered the Latino community.

Finding evidence of racial group consciousness among Asian Americans and Latinos, Masuoka has argued that scholars should shift their attention to shared ethnicity as an independent variable in models of participation: "Scholars on Asian-American and Latino political participation hesitate to apply a group-based model of behavior given the speculation that these individuals do not feel attached to others in their panethnic group. However, given evidence presented here, I am optimistic about the application of group-based behavior models to Asian-American and Latino political behavior" (2006, 1009). The concepts of shared ethnicity and candidate-centered elections provide a new theoretical framework for examining Latino political participation based on the mobilizing potential of co-ethnic candidates. While Latinos' level of group political solidarity or shared political consciousness might be less strong than that of Blacks, there are many reasons to suspect that Latino voters will rely on ethnic cues. A new model of American politics should view Latinos as actively engaged where ethnic candidates are present. In contrast to earlier research that argued that "since language may be a barrier to politics, it is possible that Mexican-Americans will remain less politicized than blacks for some time to come" (MacManus and Cassel 1982, 65), I believe that Latino voters can be expected to participate at rates equal to the American public as a whole when the mobilizing potential of Latino candidates is realized.

CHAPTER 3

Theory Meets Reality: Elite Perspectives on Latino Mobilization

"The city's looking for leadership that can bridge communities in the most diverse city in the country. I think I have a fresh perspective. . . . The mayor should be someone who can speak in many languages, who understands diversity, who is comfortable with it and can communicate to the city that it's an asset. . . . But I'm not running as a Latino mayoral candidate. The Latino agenda is the American agenda."

—ANTONIO VILLARAIGOSA, October 19, 1999,
    announcing his bid for mayor of Los Angeles

"The Latino agenda is the American agenda" was the most popular refrain that Latino candidates for mayor and their top-ranking campaign staff declared when interviewed about their campaigns in 2005. They obviously had prepared this opening statement for my interviews about shared ethnicity and the mobilizing effects of Latino candidates on Latino voters. "I did not run as a Latino; I was a candidate who happened to be Latino," each mayoral candidate said, using almost identical language. However, a little digging revealed that a Latino agenda indeed existed, including all issues on the "American" agenda as well as the unique perspective of descriptive representation, awareness of issues in the Latino community, sensitivity to the story of immigration, and the sincere desire to elevate Latinos to an equal stature with all Americans. While the campaigns and candidates insist that they have no ulterior "Latino agenda," in some ways they clearly do: they put more energy and respect into mobilizing Latino communities, they refuse to scapegoat or demonize immigrants, and most important, they can connect with and motivate Latino voters during the election. While much of the rest of this book focuses on Latino voters and their experiences with Latino candidates, this chapter explores how Latino candidates approached, interacted with, and ultimately mobilized Latino voters. As part of my theoretical argument, I argue that ethnic cues are a two-way street. Latino voters respond to ethnic cues, shared ethnicity, and ethnic messages; however, Latino candidates for office must send out those ethnic cues—sometimes implicitly, sometimes explicitly. This chapter examines closely five Latino campaigns for mayor, discovering that voters do not imagine the elevated ethnic appeals; indeed, all five candidates discussed here conducted extensive Latino outreach campaigns that played heavily on their shared ethnic experiences with Latino voters.

Electoral outcomes are not the sole evidence for or against shared ethnicity. The poor performance of Latino candidates, such as Cruz Bustamante in 2003 and Bill Richardson in 2008, and seemingly low levels of Latino turnout, as in the 2005 San Antonio mayoral election, do not indicate that co-ethnic candidates do not mobilize Latino voters and that shared ethnicity matters very little. Final election results do not tell the full story of the political campaign. In 2004, for example, Benigno "Benny" Diaz, a Peruvian immigrant who had lived in the United States for twenty-four years, ran for the city council in Garden Grove, California. A city council election in a small Los Angeles suburb would not normally have gotten my attention, but Garden Grove is just thirteen miles from Irvine, where I was writing. Diaz's election would make him the first Latino elected to office in Garden Grove, a bedroom community in Orange County that borders Disneyland and is typically conservative but where 30 percent of the population and 20 percent of registered voters are Latino. After he filed his candidacy paperwork and paid his fees to the county registrar of voters, Diaz's first stop was the local LULAC office, where he sought volunteers for his campaign. With no previous campaign experience, Diaz next turned to Latina congresswoman Loretta Sanchez for political advice, an endorsement, and campaign money. Diaz routinely held political meetings and brokered deals at a local Peruvian restaurant and was the only candidate to send bilingual campaign mailers to Latino households. In the end, Diaz finished fourth out of six candidates for two council seats. The city council election, a down-ballot office during the 2004 presidential contest, drew little attention, and Diaz's defeat meant that Latino politics had not yet arrived in Garden Grove. Looking at the election results, most watchers of Latino politics might conclude that ethnic politics was irrelevant in the 2004 Garden Grove city council election. However, a closer look at the campaign—rather than the election results—reveals that Diaz's candidacy reinforces the notion of shared ethnicity within Latino politics: he viewed Latino voters as his base, relied on other Latino incumbents for advice and money, campaigned heavily in Spanish and English, and had the most yard signs in heavily Latino precincts. Although he raised less money than all five of his opponents, Diaz finished second in the eighteen majority-Latino precincts. Conversations with candidates such as Diaz, their campaign staff, and other Latino politicos illustrate new layers of the electoral process that help shape our understanding of Latino politics and co-ethnic candidacies.

In this chapter, I present findings from interviews with Latino candidates for mayor in five cities (Los Angeles, Houston, New York, San Francisco, and Denver) in four states to determine the extent to which theory meets reality in campaigning for Latino votes. These states are important because they parallel the analysis of elections in each city and state and provide the necessary context for the election results and focus on Latino voters discussed in chapter 5. In addition to the Latino candidates themselves, I interviewed at least one of each of their campaign managers, consultants, or top advisers. Speaking directly with Latinos who have run for office and organized get-out-the-vote campaigns provides considerable insight into the reality of Latino politics and adds practical examples to my theoretical arguments and assumptions. While the candidates, as public figures, were open in their interviews and allowed me to attribute quotations directly to them, the campaign managers, consultants, and advisers generally requested anonymity to discuss the inner details of their campaign strategies and observations about their candidates and the opponents. All interviews were conducted in person, in the city where the candidate ran for office, and ranged in length from 45 to 180 minutes. In most cases, supplemental correspondence was conducted via e-mail following the interviews.

I begin with a brief biographical sketch of each of the five mayoral candidates based on the personal interviews as well as news accounts of their campaigns. Each candidate is a unique individual, and it is important not to lump them all together as merely "Latino candidates." Details about the candidates and their campaigns strengthen the ethnic-candidate theory of Latino political participation by illustrating the diversity among Latino candidates for public office. Following the description of candidates and their campaigns, I present the results of the in-depth interviews, which show a clear pattern of ethnic cues during the 2001 and 2003 mayoral elections.

ETHNIC POLITICS IN ACTION: THE CANDIDATES

Antonio Villaraigosa, Candidate for Mayor, Los Angeles, 2001

Antonio Villaraigosa was born in East Los Angeles and raised there by a single mother. Like other working-class Chicanos in Los Angeles, Villaraigosa began working and contributing money to the family at a young age, selling newspapers downtown by age seven. He started high school in the late 1960s, when the Chicano movement was taking hold in Los Angeles. He dropped out of tenth grade, joined a gang, and got a tattoo that read "Born to Raise Hell." After getting kicked out of a second high school, Villaraigosa got himself back on the right path with help from a teacher, Herman Katz, who tutored Villaraigosa and paid for him to take college entrance examinations. After graduating from the University of California at Los Angeles, he played an active role in the Chicano movement and served as a union organizer, making many important friends and future political allies. He subsequently headed up the Los Angeles chapter of the American Civil Liberties Union, expanding his network of friends and colleagues. In 1990, California voters passed a term-limits initiative that created many new opportunities in the state legislature. In 1994, Villaraigosa was elected to the State Assembly from Los Angeles's heavily Latino Forty-fifth District. Four years later, Villaraigosa was elected speaker of the assembly, becoming the second Latino to hold the post (after Cruz Bustamante). In 2000, term limits forced Villaraigosa out of the assembly, and he decided to run for mayor of Los Angeles. Although he had a strong record as assembly speaker, he lacked the city-level experience of his challenger, James Hahn, who had served as Los Angeles's city auditor and city attorney for sixteen years. As the election neared, many in the English- and Spanish-language media saw the promise of Villaraigosa being the first Latino mayor of Los Angeles—the city with the country's highest percentage of Latino residents. Indeed, Villaraigosa was a popular figure within the Latino community, and he attracted overflow crowds at events in predominantly Mexican neighborhoods, where he campaigned bilingually. Coverage of his candidacy took place almost entirely though an ethnic lens, which mobilized Latinos but may have worried some non-Latinos. Villaraigosa asked the media to stop referring to him as the "Latino candidate" and insisted that he would be a mayor for all residents of Los Angeles. In the final weeks of the election, the Hahn campaign unveiled an attack ad that portrayed Villaraigosa as supportive of a convicted drug dealer. In fact, the shadowy images and drug paraphernalia in the ad created the impression that Villaraigosa had been filmed with drug users and dealers (like the sting tape of Washington, D.C., mayor Marion Barry). As with similar commercials in other cities, this negative ad weakened Villaraigosa's support among moderate Whites.

Many pundits compared Villaraigosa's candidacy to that of the first African American candidate for mayor of Los Angeles, Tom Bradley, who ran in 1969. Bradley faced incumbent Sam Yorty, who used negative racial attacks to portray Bradley as a leftist Black militant. Bradley lost that election but mobilized the

Black community and defeated Yorty four years later with record high Black turnout.

Los Angeles's 2001 mayoral contest featured no incumbent and several well-qualified candidates, including two viable Latinos. As of 2000, Latinos comprised 47 percent of the city's residents, with Whites comprising 30 percent, Blacks comprising 11 percent, and Asians comprising 10 percent.

The April 10 primary included fifteen candidates, with the top two finishers facing each other in a runoff election. Among the favorites were Republicans Steve Soboroff and Kathleen Connell and Democrats Hahn, Joel Wachs, Villaraigosa, and Xavier Becerra. Soboroff and Hahn were seen as the front-runners: Soboroff had received the endorsement of outgoing mayor Richard Riordan, and Hahn was a two-term city attorney and the son of a renowned former member of the Los Angeles County Board, Kenneth Hahn. Despite the city's large Latino population, both Villaraigosa and Becerra were seen as long shots for the runoff. Important political endorsements, including those of Governor Gray Davis, the state Democratic Party, and labor unions, helped Villaraigosa to a surprise primary victory, garnering 30 percent of the vote. Hahn finished second with 25 percent, while Soboroff was third at 21 percent.

Since both Villaraigosa and Hahn were Democrats, the general-election campaign focused on racial and ethnic divisions rather than political or ideological differences. Hahn, whose father had been very popular among African Americans, quickly galvanized Black support, while Villaraigosa unified Latino voters. Many observers commented on the Black-Brown divisions the campaign highlighted, and the racial animosity reached its high point when a commercial sponsored by the Coalition to Elect Jim Hahn implied that Villaraigosa supported drug use and gang violence. According to exit polls, this ad caused some moderate and conservative White voters to leave the Villaraigosa coalition. However, it strengthened and mobilized his base among liberal and Latino voters, who saw the commercial as an attack on Latinos as a group. As the election drew near, the buzz surrounding the possibility of Los Angeles's first Latino mayor garnered national press attention and mobilized several organized get-out-the-vote drives by organizations such as the Southwest Voter Registration and Education Project and the National Association of Latino Elected and Appointed Officials. Further, Villaraigosa tapped into Los Angeles's political, economic, and media resources to bring unprecedented legitimacy to his campaign in a manner that resembled Henry Cisneros's first run for mayor of San Antonio, Texas. Endorsements from the *Los Angeles Times,* Davis, and Riordan, coupled with millions in fund-raising, helped Villaraigosa.

Although Villaraigosa ultimately lost the election, his candidacy highlighted new possibilities in political behavior that could reverse more than four decades of established results. Registered Latinos voted at higher rates than non-Latinos, and ethnicity was a strong predictor of candidate choice, as evidenced by *Los Angeles Times* exit polls and precinct-level results from the Los Angeles city clerk. Latino turnout was the highest of any of the city's racial or ethnic groups, and more than 80 percent of Latinos voted for Villaraigosa. In addition, in nearly all precincts with more than 50 percent Latino voters, the turnout rates exceeded the citywide average, and Villaraigosa received strong support.

Orlando Sanchez, Candidate for Mayor, Houston, 2001

Orlando Sanchez was born in Havana, Cuba, and fled the country with his parents as a young child following the Castro-led revolution. Unlike many Cuban refugees, however, the Sanchez family headed not for Miami but for Venezuela, where Sanchez's father was employed as a radio announcer. In 1962, Major League Baseball's newly founded Houston Colt .45s launched a Spanish-language broadcast and hired the elder Sanchez. Orlando Sanchez attended Houston's public schools, where he did not receive bilingual education. After graduating from high school, Sanchez attended the University of Houston and became increasingly interested in local politics. Sanchez had long been surrounded by politicos—most notably, the Colt .45s' owner, Roy Hofheinz, who served as the city's mayor from 1952 to 1960. In 1997, Sanchez decided to run for an at-large city council seat, forcing him to interact with voters citywide rather than in a particular area. He won reelection to the council in 1999, when Lee Brown, an African American Democrat, was elected to his first term as mayor. Sanchez found that many Houston residents—mostly a mix of working-class Latinos and wealthy Whites—were unhappy with Brown's leadership. As a Latino Republican, Sanchez saw an opportunity to reach out to both constituencies. When he announced his candidacy for mayor, Sanchez received considerable attention from Spanish-language media. He regularly spoke Spanish at events and made a point of walking through heavily Mexican neighborhoods and introducing himself to residents. At the same time, Sanchez attended fund-raisers sponsored by the Houston Chamber of Commerce and by development interests. While he received no official endorsements from Houston's elected Latino officials (all of whom were Democrats), he garnered large followings at his Saturday afternoon tamale events in parks in Latino neighborhoods. Sanchez received endorsements from the Hispanic Chamber of

Commerce and from Mel Martinez, secretary of the federal Department of Housing and Urban Development. Many Latinos in Houston told Sanchez that he was the first mayoral candidate to visit their communities, let alone converse with Latino voters in Spanish. Near the end of the campaign, polls showed Sanchez slightly ahead of Brown. To bolster his base and cast doubt on Sanchez, Brown solicited the support of Lavon Harris, sister of James Byrd Jr., who had been murdered in Jasper, Texas, by three White supremacists. Harris went on television and radio to speak out against Sanchez, portraying him as an opponent of the James Byrd Jr. Hate Crimes Act, which the Texas State Legislature had considered in 1999. Even though Sanchez, a city councilman at the time, had no official connection to the state legislation, Harris told voters that Sanchez was part of the effort to defeat the measure. Sanchez lost the support of moderate Whites and won virtually no African American votes. Although Sanchez received more votes of than any other mayoral challenger in Houston's history, he lost the election to Brown by a margin of 51.7 percent to 48.3 percent.

The Houston mayoral election offers an interesting contrast to Los Angeles in many ways. While both elections represented opportunities to elect the cities' first Latino mayors, the candidates and political environment were quite different. In Houston, the Latino candidate was a registered Republican and a Cuban American, while his opponent was a registered Democrat and an African American. Moreover, Houston's Latino population is predominantly Mexican American—of the city's 750,000 Latinos, 77 percent were of Mexican descent, 11 percent were of Central American descent, and less than 1 percent were of Cuban descent. Further, Houston's Latino population has historic ties to the Democratic Party, and exit polls from the 1999 election showed that Brown received 65 percent of the Latino vote (*Houston Chronicle* 1999). Thus, the 2001 campaign represents a significant test for the shared-ethnicity hypothesis. Would the heavily Mexican American and Democratic Latino electorate support Sanchez, a Cuban Republican? As in Los Angeles, Latinos comprise Houston's largest population group (37 percent of the total), followed by Whites (31 percent), Blacks (25 percent), and Asian Americans (5 percent). However, Houston's Latinos are younger and are less likely to be citizens than Latinos in Los Angeles. Thus, Whites represent the largest share of Houston's registered voters, and Latinos account for only about 14 percent. Latinos in Houston also lack a history of empowerment and mobilization. Hegstrom, who covers city politics for the *Houston Chronicle*, has noted that "unlike cities such as Chicago and Los Angeles, where Mexicans form organizations to push for their rights on both sides of the border, Houston-based immigrants remain remarkably disenfranchised" (Hegstrom 2003). This finding is consistent with scholarly research by Cano, who compares immigrant mobilization in Houston and Chicago and concludes that "Mexicans in Houston are very hidden" (2002). Indeed, a major analysis of registered voters in Houston during the 1990s found that Latinos are not politically active and continue to vote at very low rates (de la Garza, Haynes, and Ryu 2002).

Thus, Sanchez faced many obstacles in mobilizing the Latino community. To win, he would need to piece together a coalition including Latinos and conservative Whites, a strategy he implemented awkwardly but somewhat successfully. Sanchez, already a city councilman, campaigned heavily for Latino votes, advertised in Spanish, and frequently spoke to issues of immigrant rights. He won key endorsements from Latino civic groups, including the Latino Coalition and the Hispanic Business Roundtable, as well as the firefighters' union and other labor leaders. Politically, Houston is generally characterized by weak political parties and an absence of machine politics (Murray 2003), paradoxically making the mobilization of Latinos both more difficult (because the city has no formal institutions known to mobilize and energize Latino voters) and potentially easier (by helping the Republican Sanchez win some Democratic endorsements and create a mobilization campaign among Latino voters).

According to Houston-area Republican consultant Allen Blakemore, "Getting Hispanics to vote has been like herding cats. They are difficult to motivate, they have very poor participation rates, and they are anything but monolithic. They scatter all over the place" (Fleck 2001). Blakemore also noted that Sanchez's performance in the primary "may have been the most powerful exercise yet of Hispanic ballot influence in a citywide contest" and that in the runoff contest, Sanchez "will benefit from a growing conviction among Hispanics that they can elect one of their own as mayor" (Fleck 2001). In the end, Sanchez lost by ten thousand votes. The election highlighted new possibilities of Latino empowerment in Houston: exit polls indicated that Sanchez won a clear majority among Latinos and that Latinos voted at much higher rates than in the 1999 mayoral election.

Fernando Ferrer, Candidate for Mayor, New York City, 2001

Fernando Ferrer was born and grew up in a Puerto Rican neighborhood in the South Bronx. He was raised by his mother and grandmother, both of whom worked in the kitchen of the Waldorf-Astoria Hotel. He began shining shoes at age ten to earn extra money for the family, quickly learning the value of hard work and the importance of his family. After graduating from high school, Ferrer earned a scholarship to attend New York University and became an activist, trying to bring attention to the blight of the Bronx. He served as a city councilman for nineteen years before becoming the borough's president. He saw much social injustice, poverty, and discrimination in his Bronx neighborhood, and as a result he developed a strong commitment to fighting these problems and a focus on revitalizing the community. As a council member, he sponsored many resolutions that brought new services to the city, including affordable medical care, affordable housing, and programs requiring foreign-language translators in emergency rooms. Ferrer earned a reputation as an honest and hardworking politician and became a favorite in the Latino community. When he decided to run for mayor of New York City in 2001, he finished a surprising first in the Democratic primary; his opponent, Mark Green, then waged a negative campaign in the Democratic runoff, which was scheduled to be held on September 11 but was delayed because of the terrorist attacks that took place on that day. Many pundits felt that Green played on White New Yorkers' anxieties about the city's security and economic recovery. Green contended that Ferrer did not appreciate the magnitude of the impact of the attacks, depicting him as concerned only with ethnic minorities. As Ferrer promoted his message that there were "two New Yorks," with Latinos and African Americans left behind, Green responded by calling Ferrer divisive and unconcerned with the problems of the average New Yorker. Finally, Green attacked Ferrer's ties to Al Sharpton, who had endorsed Ferrer in the primary election. As the runoff campaign wore on, Black and Latino community leaders came out in strong support of Ferrer and publicly condemned Green's negative ads. In the end, however, the negative ads choked off Ferrer's support among moderate Whites by portraying him as too ethnic and too inexperienced to be mayor. But Green's primary strategy eroded his support among the Democratic base of Latino and Black voters, and many of them sat out the general election, in which Green lost to Republican Michael Bloomberg, a billionaire businessman.

Although New York City has the largest Latino population in the United States—more than 2 million—no Latino candidate had ever won the Democratic primary for mayor. Former congressman Herman Badillo ran for mayor in 1969 and again in 1973, when he reached a runoff before losing by a large margin to Abraham Beame, who became the city's first Jewish mayor. New York represents yet a third perspective on Latino politics, different from both Los Angeles and Houston. New York, still influenced by machine politics, is one of the few cities that use partisan mayoral primaries. In his career on the city council and as borough president of the Bronx, Ferrer had built strong support from the Latino and African American communities, and he looked to build on this Black-Brown coalition in his mayoral bid. His White and Jewish primary opponent, Mark Green, held the position of city public advocate and was a former colleague of Ralph Nader at Public Citizen. Ferrer, like Villaraigosa and Sanchez, attracted considerable media attention as a Latino mayoral candidate; in Ferrer's case, the attention was heightened by the fact that New York is the country's largest city. As in Los Angeles, New York's labor unions are heavily Latino, and they mobilized in support of Ferrer's candidacy. While Green campaigned for the Jewish and White vote, Ferrer held together a coalition of Puerto Rican, Dominican, Colombian, Mexican, and Black constituencies. While most Latinos in both Los Angeles and Houston are Mexican American, New York is quite diverse: 40 percent of its Latinos are of Puerto Rican origin, 23 percent are Dominican, 12 percent are South American, and 7 percent are Mexican. This diversity represents yet another challenge to the shared-ethnicity theory of Latino voting. Many analysts wondered about the extent to which non–Puerto Rican Latinos would support Ferrer.

During the contest, Green drew attention to Ferrer's ethnicity in a questionable if not overtly negative light. While Green may have dampened Ferrer's support among some Black, White, and Asian voters, these tactics only strengthened his support among Latinos, who saw the attack ads as visibly anti-Latino. Nevertheless, polls conducted on the eve of the election gave Ferrer a lead. Then came the terrorist attacks on the World Trade Center, which pushed the Democratic primary back to September 25. When the voting finally took place, Ferrer won 35 percent of the vote; Green was second with 31. The two men were set to face each other again in an October 12 runoff. Green stepped up his negative campaign and further consolidated his support among Jewish voters, who may have viewed the al-Qaeda attacks as anti-Jewish. As the primary runoff approached, the campaign became more focused on race and ethnicity, and Green ultimately defeated Ferrer, 51 to 49 percent. In the general election, however, Green could not consolidate the city's Democratic base, particularly among Latinos, and some observers questioned whether perceptions that he had conducted ethnic attacks against Ferrer might have soured Latino voters' view of Green (Perez-Rivas 2001). In 2000, Al Gore won more than 80 percent of the Latino vote in New York, and 2001 exit polls indicated that Ferrer received 84 percent of the Latino vote in the primary, yet Green received only 52 percent of New York's Latino votes, while Bloomberg took 48 percent (Pollock and Plaut 2002). Further, an analysis of majority-Latino precincts showed that turnout was far lower in the general election than in the primary.

Matt Gonzalez, Candidate for Mayor, San Francisco, 2003

Matt Gonzalez was born in the border town of McAllen, Texas. His mother was an immigrant from Mexico, his father a second-generation Mexican American. He received a scholarship to attend Columbia University in New York and then earned a law degree from Stanford University in California. Thus, he has had contact with the diverse populations in the three states with the largest Latino populations. His mayoral candidacy took place in San Francisco, a city traditionally known for its Chinatown, not for Latino empowerment, where he had become a successful public advocate after his graduation from Stanford. A self-described liberal progressive, Gonzalez took on such issues as homelessness, poverty, immigrant rights, racism, and environmental protection, quickly earning a reputation as a formidable attorney and public defender and becoming well acquainted with city and county government. In 1999, he ran for district attorney, finishing third and failing to make the runoff. However, he participated in televised debates, which markedly increased his visibility. In 2000, Gonzalez ran for the county Board of Supervisors (which is effectively the city council because San Francisco's city and county limits are contiguous) in the traditionally liberal Fifth District. Days after the primary election and just a few weeks before the runoff, he switched his party registration from Democrat to Green. He made the change as a consequence of the exclusion of Green Party Senate candidate Medea Benjamin from televised debates and of his frustration with the Democratic Party and its 2000 presidential candidate, Al Gore. Despite the city's liberal tradition, only 3 percent of San Francisco's voters are registered as Green Party members, and its progressive voters are known as strong supporters of the Democratic Party (DeLeon 2003). To the voters of San Francisco, Gonzalez's record and reputation were not affected by his party affiliation, and he easily won election. As a member of the board, Gonzalez promoted many progressive issues, including raising the minimum wage and building more affordable housing. His policies often conflicted with those of Mayor Willie Brown, but Gonzalez saw himself as protecting the underrepresented people of San Francisco. In 2003, the office of mayor was open following Brown's second and final term. Gonzalez and others hoped that a more progressive candidate would challenge moderate Democrat Gavin Newsom and bring new issues into the campaign, but no one emerged who had the cachet needed to energize the city. Just before the deadline for entering the race, Gonzalez learned that a private poll had found that he had the best name recognition and the highest favorable ratings among the progressive candidates. He ceased his efforts to recruit other candidates and agreed to run. During the general election, Gonzalez raised just $150,000 and relied heavily on the volunteers who showed up en masse at his rallies and events. In a crowded candidate field, Newsom failed to win a majority of the vote, and since Gonzalez finished second with 20 percent, a runoff was required. Gonzalez raised nearly $900,000 for the runoff, compared to almost $10 million for Newsom. Gonzalez nevertheless ran a tough campaign, and preelection polls showed Gonzalez with a two-point advantage. Voter turnout would determine San Francisco's next mayor.

The Green Party's candidate in the California's 2002 gubernatorial contest and in the following year's special gubernatorial recall election, Peter Camejo, won over some new Latino voters who were not enthusiastic about Democrat Gray Davis. However, fewer than 10 percent San Francisco's Latinos were members of the Green Party; 70 percent were registered Democrats.

In the nonpartisan primary election, Gonzalez faced four other Democrats (Newsom, a member of the Board of Supervisors; Angela Alioto, an attorney and former supervisor; Susan Leal, city treasurer; and Tom Ammiano, a member of the Board of Supervisors, former mayoral candidate, and gay-rights activist) and one Republican (chief of police Tony Ribera). While the Democratic candidates fought over moderate voters and assumed that those on the left would follow along, Gonzalez made a strong, grassroots-based run for votes among leftists, immigrants, and Latinos. While San Francisco is a majority-minority city in which Whites comprise only 44 percent of the residents, it differs from Los Angeles, Houston, and New York in that Asian Americans (31 percent of the population) are the largest minority group, followed by Latinos (15 percent) and Blacks (8 percent). Thus, a Gonzalez victory would require not only strong support among Latino voters but also a broad coalition of other groups. In addition, the district that Gonzalez represented on the county board was not heavily Latino but rather was the most progressive district, populated mostly by liberal Whites. His mayoral campaign thus emphasized such issues as increasing the minimum wage, affordable housing, environmental awareness, and immigrant rights, all of which resonated with many young and Latino voters. Further, Gonzalez had previously resided in the Latino Mission District for ten years, and he was well known and respected for his work on behalf of poor and immigrant communities. While many labor union leaders endorsed Newsom, Gonzalez was more popular among the rank and file. Gonzalez won a majority of Latino voters in the primary and did well with labor households, voters under age thirty-five, and gay and lesbian voters.

During the runoff, Gonzalez's support among Latino voters grew. *San Francisco Chronicle* stories cited an endless trail of "Gonzalez para Alcalde"

(Gonzalez for Mayor) posters in the heavily Latino neighborhoods of the Mission District (Hendricks 2003). Although Gonzalez had had a positive relationship with the Black community as public defender and as president of the Board of Supervisors, Brown, a former speaker of the California Assembly as well as San Francisco's outgoing mayor and an icon in the Black community, campaigned against Gonzalez. Like his Latino predecessors as mayoral candidates in Los Angeles, Houston, and New York, Gonzalez lost a very close election; however, his candidacy similarly demonstrated the appeal of an ethnic candidate. Despite his membership in a minor political party, Gonzalez captured 47 percent of the vote and is estimated to have won more than 80 percent of the Latino vote in the runoff. Moreover, voters under age thirty and Latinos turned out to vote at record levels. Indeed, many watchers of San Francisco politics believe that Gonzalez's strong campaign on the left pushed Newsom to adopt liberal policies as mayor, including issuing marriage licenses to same-sex couples (Redmond 2003). The Gonzalez candidacy offers the opportunity to determine the extent to which co-ethnic candidates, despite their political parties, mobilize and attract Latino voters.

Donald Mares, Candidate for Mayor, Denver, 2003

Donald Mares was born and raised in Denver. His family ancestry is traced to Mexico, but the Mares family, like many Latino families in Colorado, has lived in the United States for many generations. Mares grew up working in his family's restaurant in heavily Latino northwestern Denver, where he learned the importance of hard work, respect, and community involvement. After graduating from a Catholic high school, Mares earned a bachelor's degree at Stanford University and a law degree at the University of Pennsylvania. Mares returned to Denver, where he specialized in labor and employment law, and launched his political career, winning election to the state legislature in 1988 and to the state senate in 1991. Four years later, Mares was elected as the city's auditor, the first Hispanic to hold that post. He won reelection—the first auditor to do so in twenty-four years—and then decided to run for mayor. Term limits meant that the incumbent could not run again, and no front-runner was apparent. Two top Colorado Democrats agreed to help run Mares's campaign, and he felt that he had a good chance of winning. Mares's bid lacked some of the buzz that accompanied the other Latino candidacies discussed here because Denver had already elected a Latino mayor, Federico Peña, who won the post with strong support from Latino voters as well as African Americans and served from 1983 to 1991 (Hero 1992). Mares knew that African Americans and White liberals would form an important part of any winning coalition. During the general election, businessman John Hickenlooper, a Democrat who ran a probusiness, prodevelopment campaign, emerged as the man to beat. While Mares fared well with Latinos, Penfield Tate, an African American state senator, attracted a majority of the Black vote, and Ari Zavaras, the lone Republican challenger, won most of the conservative vote. Heading into the runoff, Mares hoped to gain Tate's endorsement and do well with Black voters. Tate and Mares had run very similar campaigns, emphasizing quality schools and the need for more jobs. After many meetings with Black leaders and talking to community groups, however, the Mares campaign was confounded when Tate endorsed Hickenlooper just before the runoff. The problem appeared to be rooted in the Black-Latino power dynamic. While Denver's Latino population had been growing rapidly, the African American population had stagnated. Some Black leaders might have thought that a Latino mayor would mean more resources for the Hispanic community and less for the Black community. Hickenlooper easily won the Black and White vote and defeated Mares by a two-to-one margin, although he maintained his support in the Latino community.

Mares's 2003 mayoral campaign took place as Latino voters were garnering national attention as a growing political force. Colorado attorney general Ken Salazar was considering a run for the U.S. Senate, and his brother, John, was seeking a congressional seat in the western part of the state. Colorado's Latino politics had changed substantially from Peña's time, when Latinos were a clear minority and held little political power. Despite his previous electoral success, Mares was seen as a weaker candidate than Villaraigosa, Sanchez, Ferrer, and Gonzalez. Polls showed Hickenlooper with a clear lead in the primary, and it was possible that he might win an outright victory there by capturing 51 percent of the vote. Thus, the Mares campaign had difficulty getting traction with both Latino and non-Latino voters.

Mares's showing in the primary, therefore, was impressive, as he took 22 percent of the vote and held Hickenlooper to 43 percent and thus forced a runoff. Mares attracted 51 percent of the Latino vote, while Zavaras, who is of Greek descent, won 16 percent and Hickenlooper took 14 percent. As in Houston and Los Angeles, where Black-Brown politics entered the equation, Mares would need strong support from African Americans to have a chance at winning. Peña, for example, had taken 86 percent of the Black vote in his 1983 victory (Muñoz and Henry 1990). Tate won 77 percent of the black vote in the primary, and the decision by him and other Black leaders to endorse Hickenlooper hurt Mares. As he was losing ground, the question became whether Mares could retain a majority of Latino voters or whether they would vote for Hickenlooper, given that both men were registered Democrats. Mares garnered 70 percent of the Latino vote in the runoff, although he lost by more than 30 points overall. In addition, voter turnout was much lower than in the 1983 election, perhaps because Hickenlooper's large lead in preelection polls curtailed interest in the contest.

FINDINGS FROM THE INTERVIEWS

Common Themes

Although all five of these candidates are Latino, their backgrounds (Mexican, Puerto Rican, and Cuban) and party affiliations (Democratic, Republican, and Green) differ. Moreover, they ran in varying electoral circumstances against varying opponents—Black and White, Christian and Jewish, incumbents and political newcomers. Despite such contrasts, all five mayoral campaigns shared some common themes with regard to ethnicity, thereby providing practical evidence of ethnic politics.

Table 3.1 provides a brief summary of the ethnic campaign strategies on which all of these candidates relied. Foremost, all five candidates noted that previous mayors had not attempted to incorporate the Latino electorate in each city. Even in Denver, which had elected a Latino mayor in 1983, Mares stated that Latino voters had become less and less visible over the ensuing twenty years. Thus, all of these candidates expressed their concern that Latino voters needed to be contacted, mobilized, and energized. For Latino candidacies to gain momentum, Latino constituencies needed to be on board—and they were.

TABLE 3.1.   **Summary of Ethnic Campaign Strategies**

Latino campaign manager	✓
Latino campaign consultant	✓
Latino vote strategy	✓
Canvassed in Spanish	✓
Spanish-based events	✓
Bilingual mailers	✓
Spanish TV ads	✓
Spanish radio ads	✓
Latino fund-raisers	✓
Discussed family immigrant story	✓
Latino endorsements	✓

All of the candidates also stated that Latino experts, Latino analysts, and Latino volunteers constituted important parts of the campaigns and were specifically targeted to become staff members in almost any capacity. All five of the candidates had paid campaign managers who were of Hispanic origin and who oversaw part of the citywide campaign. In addition, each campaign implemented an outreach strategy targeted at mobilizing the Latino community. In most cases, this strategy started simply, with hosted "get to know the candidate" events in heavily Latino communities that allowed the candidates to speak Spanish and interact with voters. Many Latino voters reported that they had never before interacted with political candidates and that they were proud to have Latinos simply running for mayor. These events and other campaign appearances at Latino gatherings enabled candidates to recruit additional volunteers. All five candidates stated that conducting extensive bilingual canvassing in Latino neighborhoods was one of their goals.

All of the Latino candidates also did not initiate but were subjected to ethnic-based attack ads. The interviewees discussed at length their opponents' decisions to draw attention to ethnicity and believed that they were portrayed as criminals, drug dealers, racists, uneducated, and inexperienced because they were Latino. In Houston and San Francisco, African American leaders campaigned against the Latino candidates, characterizing them as too concerned with Latino issues at the expense of Blacks. By labeling Latino candidates as "Mexican" or "Latin" in television, radio, and especially mail advertising, the opposition ensured that ethnicity was a prominent campaign issue, leading to the deterioration of White and Black support for the Latino candidates and hypermobilizing the Latino electorate. According to all of the candidates, their visibility and support among Latinos grew sharply in the wake of the attack ads. At the same time, voters of other ethnicities or races were driven away. Sanchez reported that when one of his campaign staffers made a get-out-the-vote-call to a man living in a conservative White Houston neighborhood, the voter responded, "So my only choices are between a Mexican and a Black? No thanks!" and hung up the phone. In San Francisco, progressive Blacks and Whites who had previously supported Gonzalez told precinct canvassers that he was too concerned with "Mexican" issues, even though Gonzalez's policy preferences had not changed. The Villaraigosa campaign lost significant momentum with White voters in Los Angeles after the Hahn commercials associated Villaraigosa with drug dealers and the Mexican mafia. In the end, all five Latino candidates lost their elections, in large part as a consequence of a lack of crossover voting by Whites and Blacks.

From a strategic standpoint, Latino candidates hope to connect with and galvanize the Latino electorate while presenting themselves as mainstream candidates acceptable to non-Latino voters. In practice, this task can be very difficult. All of the candidates and campaign managers interviewed stressed the importance of avoiding opposition and media portrayals of the candidacies as merely ethnic. At the same time, the interviewees noted the need to register and mobilize Latino voters because traditional campaigns have tended to ignore heavily Latino and heavily immigrant neighborhoods.

The Four Truths of an Ethnic Campaign

The interviews with Latino mayoral candidates and their campaign staff revealed many insights into campaign dynamics and the difficulties of running successful campaigns in some of the largest U.S. cities. Four common themes of Latino campaigns surfaced: the candidates (1) campaigned aggressively in Latino neighborhoods; (2) drew praise from average Latino voters; (3) faced ethnic attacks that rallied Latino voters; and (4) utilized a unique campaign approach I call *nuestra comunidad*. These four components provide the bases of an ethnic-candidate approach to U.S. politics that applies to almost any other viable campaign waged by a Latino.

Outreach to Latino Voters

Prior to 2000, few campaigns attempted to mobilize the Latino electorate for the simple reason that political operatives assumed that Latino barrios had no voters. According to de la Garza, Menchaca, and DeSipio (1994), traditional campaigns tended to skip heavily Latino neighborhoods because voter turnout was low there and campaigns assumed that most residents were not U.S. citizens and therefore were not eligible to vote. The result was a vicious circle in which the lack of personal outreach, canvassing, and engagement led to low turnout among the Latino community, and low turnout provided a rationale for the lack of attention to the Latino electorate. In 2000, however, political campaigns began to change the way they thought about Latino voters. Republican presidential candidate George W. Bush made an aggressive push for the Latino vote, challenging Democrat Al Gore for the presumably Democratic Latino electorate. Even then, however, Latino outreach was largely limited to an air campaign, with both Bush and Gore running commercials on Spanish-language TV and radio. Neither candidate did much in terms of canvassing Latino neighborhoods and engaging the Latino community. Although the number of

Latino voters was clearly growing, campaign consultants still remained skeptical about spending time and energy mobilizing the Latino community.

Latino candidates had a different perspective. In Houston, many experts of both parties advised Sanchez, a Republican, to steer clear of certain "Mexican" neighborhoods such as the Second Ward because "there were hardly any votes there, and they were all Democrat," so "knocking on doors" there would be "a complete waste of time." Sanchez was nevertheless "determined to take my message to the Hispanic neighborhoods because I knew they were interested in building a better Houston. It just happened that nobody had ever asked for their help." Sanchez viewed residents of such areas as potential new voters and allies. According to one of Sanchez's top consultants, "There were significant divisions within the party. Many Republican strategists wanted us to focus heavily on the country club vote and skip the [Airline neighborhood] market, but Orlando was committed to doing both, and he ran very well in Mexican precincts." Sanchez greeted Latino voters at street fairs and open-air markets, before and after church, and between soccer games at local parks. According to Sanchez, many of the Latinos with whom he spoke had never seen a mayoral candidate in their neighborhoods. A Republican campaign adviser added, "Orlando Sanchez has proven that Hispanics can turn out in record numbers and vote for a Republican. So, in that sense, his campaign has already thrown a wrench in the Democratic machine."

Even in New York and Los Angeles, two cities with large Latino populations, candidates were advised to avoid "overdoing it" in Latino neighborhoods. Politicos in both cities understood that Villaraigosa and Ferrer would campaign for Latino votes, but some advisers believed that a few quick photo ops in heavily Latino neighborhoods would suffice. While outsiders frequently portrayed the Latino candidates as needing to choose between "ethnic" and "mainstream" strategies, the candidates disagreed. Ferrer dismissed this claim: "Of course it is possible for politicians who hail from one ethnic group to appeal to their base and appeal to other groups of people. As a practical matter, not only to win but to govern, you have to achieve the widest and deepest and most diverse coalition you have to get support." Ferrer maintained a strong presence in New York's Puerto Rican, Dominican, Colombian, and Mexican neighborhoods, while his opponent, Green, seemed to concede the ethnic vote, hardly campaigning at all in Latino parts of town. In Los Angeles, Villaraigosa echoed, "Before my campaign, there was a sense among campaign professionals that knocking on doors on the East Side was a waste of time. However, we showed that Latinos are politically engaged and will vote at high rates. Now everyone in

L.A. talks about campaigning in Latino neighborhoods." Similarly, in San Francisco, Gonzalez's campaign drew "hundreds of young Latinos who had never been politically active before, who the other campaign was ignoring. But we reached out, and their support was just amazing."

A Sense of Pride

Such extensive outreach efforts brought the five candidates into contact with thousands of Latino voters from all walks of life. These men and women used such words as *proud, excited, relieved,* and *thankful* to describe their feelings regarding the Latino politicians' candidacies. Latino voters often told the candidates, "Thank you for running and representing our community." An elderly Denver woman said to Mares, "I haven't seen that other guy come one time to our community. Thank you for talking about our issues." In contrast to typical candidates, whom voters bad-mouth, shun, or laugh at, these candidates had very positive and welcoming experiences while stumping in Latino neighborhoods.

Older people frequently expressed their pride at finally seeing fellow Latinos run for mayor, while younger voters felt proud to have an example to follow, concrete evidence that new opportunities existed for Latinos. According to Ferrer's campaign consultant, "When we hosted events in the Bronx, in the Puerto Rican neighborhoods, thousands of people would show up. It was unbelievable for a local election. They were yelling, 'We love you, Freddy! You can do it!' As the campaign went on, our support grew even stronger among Latinos." The sense of pride may have resonated out of the strong support for the idea of the American Dream. For example, a 2007 survey conducted by the Center for the Study of Los Angeles found that 75 percent of Latinos felt that they would eventually achieve the American Dream, the highest percentage among any racial or ethnic group. Many Latino voters have lower levels of income, education, and homeownership, but they may nevertheless view co-ethnic candidates as a true success story, representing all of the Latino community.

When the Race Card Is Brown

While members of the Latino community loved the candidates, their political opponents took a different view. In fact, in most cases, these strong campaigns represented a real challenge to the political establishment and an obvious threat to opponents in a zero-sum contest where only one person can be elected mayor. In all five cases, therefore, the candidates and their campaign consultants endured attacks featuring subtle as well as overt racial messages. A Gonzalez adviser recalled that "as we went up in the polls, the attacks got more negative and more ethnic. They wanted to remind voters that we had a Mexican candidate. In the Black neighborhoods, they distributed misinformation about Matt, that he didn't support civil rights. He worked all his life as a lawyer, as a public defender, to defend civil rights. It was a smear campaign." In addition, former mayor Brown's vigorous anti-Gonzalez campaign in the Black community used many references to race and ethnicity. Whereas Gonzalez characterized his county board votes against Brown's appointments as reflecting the fact that "they weren't progressive enough," Brown "went around saying that I had voted against [the appointees] because they were Black."

Race and ethnicity found its way into the campaigns in Los Angeles, New York, and Denver as well. In Los Angeles, Villaraigosa called the cocaine commercial "a low blow" that was meant to "somehow depict me as a supporter of gangs, drugs, and crime." Although Villaraigosa would not say so, campaign consultants believed that the ad sought to portray him as "as Mexican as possible." Said one, "The ad has him tied to a Mexican American drug dealer, with images of drug use, images of Antonio, and then the tag line was 'Los Angeles can't trust Antonio Villaraigosa' when what they were really trying to say is 'Los Angeles can't trust a Mexican as mayor.' It was despicable." In Denver, Mares faced the subtle yet constant murmur that the city needed a White mayor after Peña's tenure and that of his successor, Wellington Webb, an African American who served from 1991 to 2003. Mares pushed a campaign of diversity in hiring and appointment to reflect Denver's population, noting that as mayor, "You represent a diverse community, and you need to be reflective of the richness of that community" and arguing that Hickenlooper had done a poor job of hiring and promoting minorities in the businesses he owned. However, White voters did not seem to want reminders about diversity after twenty years of non-White mayors. Hickenlooper cooperated, appealing for a "new face for Denver," although he insisted that such statements referred to new economic development opportunities rather than the color of his skin. One Mares campaign adviser said, "I believe there was a strong undercurrent [among Whites] that the minorities had their turn, so now it's our turn." Likewise, a union leader who assisted with Mares's get-out-the-vote campaign stated, "We have seen over and over again people talking about wanting a White mayor." A longtime Denver political observer not tied to either campaign agreed: "It seems somewhat interesting that White folks, even if they're liberal Democrats, are more likely to support a White candidate for mayor."

In New York, the response to terrorism became a central issue in the wake

of the September 11 attacks. Green repeatedly attacked Ferrer as soft on terrorism and said that his plan to rebuild New York was clouded by patronage and
ethnicity. Green insinuated that Ferrer was trying to get business deals for
Puerto Ricans in the Bronx rather than focusing on rebuilding Lower Manhat-
tan and even suggested that new terrorist attacks would result from a Ferrer
victory. His final campaign commercial, largely about terrorism, described Ferrer as "borderline irresponsible" and closed with images of the burning World
Trade Center and the words "Can New York afford to take a chance?"

Green's supporters went a step further, specifically linking Ferrer to "local
terrorists." One mailer sent to millions of households bore the headline "An
Open Letter to the Voters of the City of New York" and linked the perpetrators
of the September 11 tragedy to the election:

> One of the candidates is actively supported by these local terrorists . . . seeking
> to violently destroy the very fabric upon which this city is founded. . . . These lo-
> cal terrorists possess the same demented and perverted values as those who at-
> tacked the World Trade Center. . . . We must all work together to ensure the de-
> feat of these local terrorists and the defeat of any politician they support. . . .
> Vote for Mark Green for Mayor.

Ferrer described the attack ads as "ugly" and "divisive." He continued, "For
someone who really does portray himself as a great unifier to do that in this
moment in the life of this city is so cynical, so awful, so ugly, so divisive that it
just turns my stomach." Campaign consultants concurred, calling Green's campaign "the ugliest in the history of New York" and labeling the ads "reprehensi-
ble" and "shameful."

Race took the most prominent role in the Houston election. At one point,
Sanchez surged ahead in the polls, causing the election to become really ugly.
While on the city council, Sanchez had voted against a nonbinding "statement
to the legislature" regarding a hate crimes measure it was considering because
the matter "was not a city council issue." Brown raised the subject to paint
Sanchez as a racist. Although Sanchez had favored the bill itself and had "called
legislators [he] knew and lobbied them to support the bill," he faced an on-
slaught of ads contending that he had opposed the hate crime legislation, opposed civil rights reforms, and was anti-Black. Harris, whose brother had been
murdered by White supremacists, recorded a message in support of Brown in
which she said,

Some of Mr. Sanchez's supporters are sending out fliers calling Mr. Brown racist names. Mr. Sanchez refused to condemn this hate material. . . . The election for mayor is important to me because Mr. Sanchez helped lead the fight against the James Byrd Jr. Hate Crimes Law. Please make sure to vote for Mayor Brown, because if hate wins, Houston loses.

According to one of Sanchez's advisers, "The Democrats couldn't really run on Lee Brown's record, so they had to just run against Orlando personally and, yes, racially." Sanchez described Harris's ads as "devastating, . . . hurtful, [and] untrue. As an immigrant, I heard my share of racial slurs growing up. There is no place for calling me a racist. It is beyond decency, yet that is what they did."

Brown further argued that Sanchez's vigorous campaign for Latino votes was itself a racially divisive tactic and accused Sanchez of "consciously targeting a certain ethnic group that speaks a certain language and emphasizing a last name that definitely appealed to many," suggesting that this tactic was somehow equivalent to the Byrd attack ads. According to Sanchez, Brown saw Latinos and Blacks as competing interest groups that could not come together in any sort of coalition: "They see the pie as finite and limited. If a Hispanic gets in, they see a diminution of services [for Blacks]. But it really isn't that way at all."

In all five of these mayoral campaigns, Latino candidates' opponents attempted to play on White voters' fears that a Latino mayor would be dangerous for the city. Further, in four of the five cases, attack ads sought to divide Blacks and Latinos, who had proven a valuable coalition in previous elections. In New York, where Blacks and Latinos formed a voting bloc, Ferrer's ties to Black leaders were used against him, presumably to worry White voters: "Freddy Ferrer is the same as Al Sharpton. Electing Ferrer is letting Sharpton run the city." In every case, the opponent who injected racial/ethnic attacks into the campaign was a Democrat. In every case, the Latino candidates stated that their support within the Latino community strengthened as the perception of ethnic attacks increased. Sanchez's take on Houston was typical: "Latino voters viewed the attacks as baseless and divisive and as attacks on all Latinos, not just my campaign."

Nuestra Comunidad

Whether as a result of the racialized campaign environment or persistent outreach to the Latino electorate, Latino candidates quickly cultivated a strong sense of shared community and linked fate with Latino voters. In particular, candidates connected as part of the Latino community. Candidates of all backgrounds have increasingly brought a populist message to the campaign trail, using phrases such as "This is your campaign," "We can do this together," "This is our city," and perhaps most famously, "Yes we can." However, when minority candidates addressing minority audiences use collective pronouns such as *we* and *our*, a deeper connection results. For Latino candidates and Latino voters, I call this the notion of *nuestra comunidad* (our community).

The idea of *nuestra comunidad* makes the connection between Latino candidate and Latino voters immediately apparent. First, candidates are highlighting their shared ethnicity, often addressing Latino crowds by moving back and forth between English and Spanish, a common practice among second- and third-generation Latino voters. Second, candidates are making a claim on a shared symbolic ethnic space, which is also often a shared geographic space (a particular part of the city). Candidates demonstrate that they are either from *la comunidad* (born and raised there, went to school there, and so forth) or part of *la comunidad* (having served on a community board or having worked as community organizer) in a way that non-Latino candidates cannot. Third, *nuestra comunidad* also implies a sense of shared issue agenda. While all the candidates I interviewed emphasized that Latino voters share the same goals as all voters—better neighborhoods, less crime, better schools, access to better jobs, and the like—evoking *nuestra comunidad* during stump speeches creates an underlying sense of solidarity on the issues. Latino candidates have the opportunity to make a stronger personal and ethnic connection with Latino audiences through *nuestra* politics. In contrast, even the best-intentioned Anglo or Black candidates will remain outsiders by speaking about "the Latino" community or "your" community.

Latino candidates and their campaign staff had an inherent commitment to the politics of *nuestra comunidad* even when campaigns made no special efforts to invoke it. According to one Mares adviser, "We didn't need a distinctive Hispanic strategy. That was Don's neighborhood. He grew up there. He knew the issues and the people." In New York, Ferrer ran numerous Spanish-language commercials emphasizing that the candidate "is one of us" and highlighting his upbringing in a Latino neighborhood, his service to Puerto Rican community organizations, and his twenty-three years of representing the Bronx in the city's government. In addition, Ferrer highlighted his outrage at perceived popular-culture slurs against segments of the Latino community earlier in the year and thus demonstrated his panethnic consciousness:

I have been, not merely as borough president of the Bronx but as a Puerto Rican, singularly responsive to these issues. Whether it was *Seinfeld's* very unfunny jokes . . . that denigrated an entire community and an institution called the Puerto Rican Day Parade or whether it was [David] Letterman telling some more unfunny jokes about a community that is not mine in particular . . . all Latinos are related. And in fact, a slur against a Colombian community had to be responded personally by every leader of this city.

Ferrer also illustrated his commitment to represent all Latinos with his position on the issue of immigration. Puerto Ricans are U.S. citizens by birth and face no legal obstacles in moving to the mainland. Nevertheless, Ferrer suggested that immigration and citizenship had personal significance for him and that he would fight for immigrant rights:

The mayor has to go beyond slogans that he likes immigrants, that New York City is the city of immigrants, that immigrant families are wonderful and get to real delivery. . . . The mayor has to be a champion with the congressional delegation and in the United States Congress to call not merely for the basics, but the mayor has to call for finally amnesty in this country—give people the opportunity, give immigrant families, give all of our families the opportunity to reunite and to live legally and to exist legally in this country.

Ferrer demonstrates the *nuestra comunidad* approach by criticizing non-Latinos for using immigration taglines that lack substance and by using the phrase *our families,* making it clear that he is from a Latino immigrant family despite the technicality of his U.S. citizenship by birth. When Ferrer made such public statements in Mexican and Colombian neighborhoods, he further reinforced the bonds of ethnic solidarity and community.

In Denver, the race for the Latino vote heated up about two weeks before the final election. Mares referred to northwestern Denver, where he was raised, as "my stomping grounds" and repeated, "That is my community. That is my neighborhood." When campaigning among members of the Chicano community, Mares said, he could be himself, and he encountered many old friends. In contrast, when Hickenlooper first campaigned in northwestern Denver just one week before the election, he relied on every ethnic symbol possible. According to the *Denver Post,* "He arrived in a lowrider as a mariachi band serenaded in the background. Boasting small-business expertise and a long-held love for the area, mayoral hopeful John Hickenlooper opened a north Denver office Monday at a Mexican restaurant in hopes of convincing residents of the predominantly Latino neighborhood to vote for him in next week's mayoral runoff." One Mares adviser described Hickenlooper's Latino outreach as "100 percent fake." Said Mares, "My mother and father had a restaurant across the street [from Hickenlooper's new office] and had it there before John even thought of where Colorado was."

The Latino candidates in Los Angeles and San Francisco tapped into the California Chicano community's vibrant history of community organizing. The state's Latinos already had a strong sense of community as a result of Republican governor Pete Wilson's support for anti-immigration policies. Specifically, Propositions 187, 209, and 227 politicized the Latino community and created a strong ethnic awareness (Segura, Falcon, and Pachon 1997; Pantoja, Ramírez, and Segura 2001). Villaraigosa and Gonzalez built on this existing sense of Latino political community by demonstrating their past commitment to Latino issues. Villaraigosa had "a definite comfort level campaigning on the [Latino] East Side. These were people, businesses, community centers that I had known for over thirty years and that had helped me get to where I am today. . . . Whenever I campaigned in Boyle Heights or Mount Washington, I would run into somebody from my old neighborhood. I was proud to represent the Latino community in Los Angeles, but of course, I was running for mayor to represent all of Los Angeles." During campaign events in heavily Latino neighborhoods, people in the crowd would routinely yell, "¡Viva Antonio!" and he would respond, "Vamos a ganar juntos" (We are going to win together) or "Ésta es su elección" (This is your election). Although Gonzalez had grown up in Texas rather than California, he was still plugged into San Francisco's Latino community. During his time as a public defender, he frequented Mission District cafes and *panederias* and provided free legal advice and assistance to immigrant families. His familiarity and popularity gave him a clear advantage over his Anglo opponent in the Latino neighborhoods. Speaking before Latino or immigrant audiences, Gonzalez frequently referenced his home in the Mission District, his immigrant mother, and his upbringing in a town along the Texas-Mexico border. He often opened with "Yo conozco a las familias inmigrantes" (I know immigrant families) and talked about his parents, the scholarship he received to attend Columbia University, and his move to California, establishing an immediate connection to voters. According to Gonzalez, "It was natural to relate to Latino voters because I live here and these are my issues." Echoed Gonzalez's campaign manager, "We didn't need to make any special effort. Matt was a part of the Mission District. It was his community, and the voters knew that." Another Gonzalez consultant said that "even though Matt had rejected the Democratic Party, the Latino community in San Francisco still embraced Matt because they knew he would stand up for their issues."

All of the candidates evidenced a very strong commitment to the Latino community and were aware of the issues that were important to its members, enabling the establishment of real and meaningful connections between candidates and voters. By evoking the concept of *nuestra comunidad,* the Latino candidates provided a clear ethnic cue for voters in *la comunidad.*

This chapter has established a framework for the individual-level analyses that follow. To sum up, I found that Latino candidates for mayor in five of America's largest cities made strong connections with Latino voters. The candidates themselves took extra steps to conduct outreach in Latino communities, hire Latino staff, advertise bilingually, and talk about issues important to the Latino community. While traditional campaigns often ignore heavily Latino neighborhoods, these candidates and their campaigns viewed Latino voters as an integral part of their base and attempted to increase the engagement and recruitment of the Latino electorate.

No two campaigns reviewed in this chapter were alike; each had a very unique context and political environment, with Latino candidates of different national origins, ideologies, and partisanship. The cities studied are diverse as well, covering populations on the West Coast, the East Coast, the Mountain West, and the Southwest. Yet across the diversity of candidates and geographies, an overwhelming sense of Latino mobilization came through from the discussions with the candidates and their advisers. Although each had a different campaign style and substance, all five Latino mayoral candidates represent a clear instance of ethnic cues in American politics. I now turn to the experiences of Latino voters who are presented with co-ethnic candidates.

Does Ethnic Identification Trump Party Identification? Evaluating Latino Vote Choice in a Hypothetical Setting

Latino voting preference is a relatively understudied topic among scholars of political behavior and Latino politics alike. With few Latino candidates running for office in the 1970s and 1980s, early scholars of Latino politics devoted little attention to the impact that co-ethnic candidates might have on Latino vote choice. Instead, early studies tended to focus on either participation (i.e., turnout) or party affiliation but not on vote choice (see Stokes-Brown 2006). The research on Latino candidates was more descriptive in nature, focusing on major figures such as Henry Gonzalez and Corky Gonzalez as case studies, not empirical analyses of Latino voters. What we know about Latino candidate preference is generally limited to surveys conducted by the media or policy centers and based on straightforward assessments of reported vote choice in congressional or presidential elections. In recent years, survey data from the Tomás Rivera Policy Institute, the Pew Hispanic Center, and the Willie C. Velasquez Institute document the rates at which Latinos have voted Democratic or Republican in congressional races or voted for George W. Bush or John F. Kerry in the 2004 presidential election. Thus, our understanding of Latino vote choice remains driven by partisan-attachment models, most likely examining a contest between an Anglo Democrat and an Anglo Republican (e.g., Kerry versus Bush, Gore versus Bush, Clinton versus Dole).

Before turning to actual election results in chapters 5 and 6, I examine stated candidate preference in hypothetical elections with Latino and non-Latino options on the ballot, taking up the question of whether shared ethnicity affects Latino voting behavior. Specifically, does the presence of a Latino candidate mobilize the Latino electorate, resulting in support for the co-ethnic candidate that is stronger than partisanship or issue preference alone would have predicted?

Since 2000, Latino candidates have gained national attention in both successful and unsuccessful bids for public office. In the fall of 2002, two Mexican American candidates, Tony Sanchez and Dan Morales, squared off in the Texas Democratic gubernatorial primary, and Sanchez went on to face Rick Perry in the general election for governor. In New Mexico in 2002, both the Democratic and Republican candidates for governor were Latino; Democrat Bill Richardson's victory made him the country's only Latino governor. During the contentious 2003 California recall election, Cruz Bustamante was the only major Democratic candidate to contest the governor's seat. The 2004 national elections sent two Latinos, Ken Salazar (D-Colorado) and Mel Martinez (R-Florida), to the U.S. Senate, while Utah residents elected two Latinos to the state assembly, bringing the number of states with Latinos in their legislatures to thirty-six. And in 2008, Rafael Anchia ran for U.S. Senate in Texas, bringing high-profile Latino candidates to the political scene in almost every state with a Latino population. Thirty years ago, Latino voters rarely saw Spanish surnames on the ballot; today, most Latinos entering the polling booth will see Spanish surnames on the ballot for offices ranging from the local school board to the U.S. Congress. Given the changes in the composition of viable candidates for all levels of office, reevaluating how voters make political decisions makes sense. Does a feeling of shared ethnicity with a Latino candidate provide a cue to Latino voters?

In their analyses of existing research on Chicano and Latino politics, Ambrecht and Pachon (1974) and de la Garza and Garcia (1985) have noted that previous studies have downplayed the role of shared ethnicity. A decade later, DeSipio's analysis (1996a) of Latino political behavior in the early 1990s reaffirmed the socioeconomic and resource-based model. Although DeSipio argues that shared ethnicity plays an instrumental role around a series of issue concerns shared in the Latino community, his findings (based on data from the 1989 Latino National Political Survey) do not support a significant association between shared ethnicity and political behavior. This chapter presents two improvements in modeling Latino vote choice: (1) inserting a Latino candidate as one of the options; and (2) controlling for an individual's level of ethnic identification. I anticipate that in contrast to previous research, shared ethnicity will significantly affect Latino voting preference and that this effect will hold after controlling for standard predictors of political participation as well as election-specific issues.[1]

But the effect of ethnic attachment on political behavior is not the same for all Latino voters. The strength of ethnic identification varies among Latinos, making it necessary to include a measure of the degree of ethnic identification. As chapter 2 shows, data from the 2006 Latino National Survey (Fraga and Guerra 2006) suggest a high but varied degree of ethnic identity. Overall, 65 percent of Latino voters stated that their ethnic identification was very strong, 25 percent stated that it was somewhat strong, and 10 percent stated that it was not very strong. How does this variation in degree of ethnic attachment shape vote choice? In this chapter, I argue that for Latinos with high levels of ethnic attachment, the presence of a candidate with a Spanish surname provides a political boost for otherwise tuned-out voters (see, e.g., J. A. Garcia and Arce 1988; Hero et al. 2000). Specifically, co-ethnic candidates may increase voters' levels of political awareness and interest in the election, increase the likelihood that they will be contacted and asked to vote, generate a sense of psychological engagement with the political system, and strengthen feelings of shared group consciousness (see, e.g., Uhlaner 1989a, 1989b; Leighley 2001). The net result should be more Latino votes for the Latino candidate. I argue not that all Latinos will always prefer the co-ethnic candidate but only that being Latino will earn a candidate more votes than standard models of Latino vote choice might ordinarily predict. Specifically, I propose a direct test of partisanship versus ethnicity in which Latino voters are asked to choose between a candidate who is from the same party and one who is from an opposing party but who is of the same ethnicity.

Research on ethnicity and candidate preference generally has concluded that Latino voters do not adhere to ethnic politics. Cain and Kiewiet (1984), Graves and Lee (2000), Michelson (2005), and Abrajano, Alvarez, and Nagler (2005) demonstrate that partisanship, not ethnicity, is the deciding factor in Latino vote choice. Stokes-Brown (2006), however, finds that Latinos' racial identity influences their vote choice for a Latino candidate.[2] This chapter concurs.

ETHNIC IDENTIFICATION AND LATINO VOTING

Chapter 2 outlined the factors contributing to Latinos' shared ethnic experience and why they might be expected to act on it. Chapter 3 demonstrated that Latino candidates increase the degree of outreach and mobilization to Latino voters. Given the decline of party control over campaigns and the rise of candidate-centered elections (Wattenberg 1994), a growing emphasis on candidate qualities rather than issues (Popkin 1991), and the reliance on ethnic-based outreach and mobilization by candidates of both major parties (Segal 2003), it may not be surprising that ethnic identification is now salient to Latino vote choice.

This research builds on the theories advanced by Miller et al. (1981), Uhlaner (1989a), Leighley (2001), and Bobo and Gilliam (1990), among others. Miller et al. note that group identity is a necessary precondition for group-based collective action and that those who have a high group identity are the most likely to fall into line and demonstrate politicized group consciousness. Uhlaner refines a theory of group relations to demonstrate that political participation is rational, despite high costs, because in-group members receive additional benefits from a sense of shared group consciousness. She argues that groups with more unified support for a candidate or issue have a stronger sense of group identity, which they can use as a bargaining chip to collect additional in-group benefits. Leighley proposes a new model for examining Latino and Black political participation that takes into account shared group consciousness, minority empowerment, and geographic racial context to improve on traditional socioeconomic models. In particular, she argues that ethnic candidates direct more resources to mobilizing ethnic communities and deserve more attention in understanding Latino voting behavior. According to Bobo and Gilliam, minority elected officials empower minority communities, resulting in higher levels of voting and bloc voting. In particular, Black mayors empower Black voters through feelings of shared group consciousness and in-group benefits. Bobo and Gilliam also provide a framework that envisions minority candidates and officeholders as instrumental in explaining minority participation. I expand this hypothesis to Latino voters and Latino candidates. However, instead of focusing only on mayoralties as evidence of minority empowerment (as do Bobo and Gilliam), we should expand this notion to other levels of elected office such as congressional and state legislative districts. Finally, from a practical perspective, Sosa, a media consultant and presidential campaign adviser, notes that in his experience conducting focus groups and targeting Latino voters, positive ethnic identification with the candidate is an important factor. Specifically, he argues, "Issues also work, but only *after* Hispanic voters like and trust the candidate" (2004). When the candidate is a fellow Hispanic, Sosa notes, it is very easy to earn the trust and affection of Hispanic voters.

I include two new data sets and propose an alternative mechanism for measuring shared ethnicity that may account for its lack of relevance in previous research. Earlier attempts to include ethnicity in a model of Latino political behavior considered it an all-or-nothing issue in which all Latinos have the same level of ethnic identification. Instead, I propose a scale, similar to the measure of party identification, that places Latinos on a spectrum from low to high levels of ethnic identification. This scale includes both direct and indirect measures of ethnic identification. More accurate assessments of the degree of shared ethnicity demonstrate that Latinos with higher levels of ethnic identification use ethnicity in their political decision making. Surveys do not always include multiple items concerning ethnic identification, however, and proxy measures are hard to come by with aggregate-level election data. While scholars must make do with the tools at their disposal, they should also push for the inclusion of additional items related to ethnic identity in data sets and models exploring Latino political behavior.

The data employed here come from two unique surveys of Latino registered voters. The first is a 2000 survey regarding vote choice among hypothetical candidates (one Latino, one non-Latino) conducted by the Latino Issues Forum (LIF), a San Francisco–based nonpartisan and nonprofit organization that studies policy issues important to the Latino community. The second is a 2002 Tomás Rivera Policy Institute (TRPI) survey that explores crossover voting tendencies among Latinos in California and New York. I argue that after controlling for partisanship and issue preference, ethnic identification will lead Latino voters to support ethnic candidates even across ideological or party lines.

WHY ETHNIC IDENTITY MATTERS TO VOTE CHOICE

During the 1990s, the Latino electorate grew faster than any other segment of American voters. With numbers that increased from 3.7 million in 1988 to 5.9 million in 2000, Latino voters received attention from both the national media and the Democratic and Republican Parties in the 2000 presidential election. While Latinos have generally favored Democratic candidates, scholars and pundits have characterized the Latino electorate as heterogeneous and fluid (Pachon 1999). Earlier efforts to test the connection between Latinos' ethnicity and vote choice have found partisanship to be an intervening variable of greater weight, leading scholars to conclude that ethnicity has only an indirect effect (Cain and Kiewiet 1984; Graves and Lee 2000). That is, ethnicity predicts party identification, which predicts vote choice, but no direct tie between ethnicity and candidate preference exists. More recently, an experimental study by DeFrancesco Soto (2006, 2007) has suggested that ethnicity may trump partisanship. Using a controlled experiment, DeFrancesco Soto exposed Latino subjects to two treatments related to partisanship and ethnicity. In one, a non-Latino Democrat was pitted against a Latino Republican; in the second, a Latino

Democrat was pitted against a non-Latino Republican. A short platform was read for each candidate. When the Latino Republican was used, Latinos were significantly more likely than members of the control group to rate the Republican candidate favorably. Although DeFrancesco Soto's experimental data do not prove that ethnicity predicts vote choice, her findings for candidate evaluations suggest that shared ethnicity is relevant even when the Latino candidate is from the opposing party. DeFrancesco Soto's findings are important because they turn conventional wisdom on its head and open the door for considering ethnic identity alongside partisanship as relevant predictors of Latino candidate preferences. Building on her work and recognizing Latino voters' areas of difference on policy issues, I argue that ethnic identity unites Latinos, both explicitly and implicitly, and plays a central role in understanding voting behavior.

Three trends over the past couple of decades have made ethnicity a central component of Latino politics. First, the Latino community has witnessed an increase in ethnic-based discrimination, increasing the likelihood that ethnicity will have a distinct impact on Latinos' political behavior. Anti-immigrant ballot measures, the rollback of affirmative action, and attacks on bilingual education have alienated and angered Latino voters in many states (Segura, Falcon, and Pachon 1997; Pachon 1998, 1999; Pantoja, Ramírez, and Segura 2001; Ramírez 2007). Furthermore, public opinion data suggest that Latinos increasingly feel themselves to be targets of ethnic discrimination.[3] Raids by Immigration and Customs Enforcement officials in 2007 and 2008 targeted suspected illegal immigrants at their places of work, at public hospitals, at community centers, and at their children's schools. In some cases, legal immigrants and naturalized citizens were detained and questioned, while in other cases U.S.-born children were separated from their immigrant parents, sending shock waves throughout the Latino community and heightening perceptions of discrimination. Second, the number of viable Latino candidates for public office has increased dramatically (Pachon and DeSipio 1992; Hero et al. 2000; National Association of Latino Elected and Appointed Officials 2008), creating the opportunity for ethnic identity to emerge in the political sphere. Had the number of co-ethnic candidates stagnated or declined, the occasional or rare Latino candidate would be unlikely to mobilize or energize the Latino community in the same way. Third, rapid growth in Latinos' rates of naturalization, registration, and voter turnout has given legitimacy to the size and significance of the Latino electorate (Sierra et al. 2000). The convergence of these three trends has produced an environment in which ethnic identity may remain a principal component for Latino voters.

Because the survey data presented here are based on experimental design and are not from a national sample, actual election results from across the country were gathered and examined and are presented in chapter 5. In addition to the empirical cases reviewed there, some additional real-world evidence of ethnic voting comes from recent mayoral elections in Miami and Colorado Springs, where Latino candidates won office in nonpartisan elections, supporting the hypothetical survey data.

In Colorado Springs, Lionel Rivera, a registered Republican, received about 70 percent of the vote from the Latino community, which had voted heavily in favor of Democrat Al Gore in 2000. In 2004, the same heavily Latino precincts that supported Rivera and Gore backed Ken Salazar, the Democratic candidate for U.S. Senate, at rates far exceeding those for Democrat John Kerry's presidential bid (Juenke-Gonzalez and Sampaio 2008). In Miami, second-generation Cuban American Manny Diaz, a Democrat, emphasized his strong ties to the Cuban community and won more than 70 percent of the Latino vote although most of the community's voters are Republicans and had previously favored President George W. Bush and Mayor Joe Carollo. Like the evidence presented in chapter 5, these elections support the idea that ethnic identity plays a primary role in candidate preference. Most models of Latino voting do not include ethnic identity as a crucial variable.

Chapter 2 laid out a general framework for ethnic voting among Latinos. While Latino voters' preference for Latino candidates, all else being equal, may seem straightforward, we now turn to the electoral circumstance when all else is not equal. Will ethnic attachment be a significant predictor of vote choice when the partisan tables have been turned? Will Latino Democrats or liberals vote for Latino Republicans or conservatives, or will party and ideology trump ethnicity? The scholarly research offers almost no data on these questions because few empirical studies of Latino crossover voting have been conducted. Michelson has found that Latino voters in California's Central Valley voted for the White Democratic incumbent in a U.S. House election against a Latino Republican challenger, concluding that "despite the saliency of ethnicity, partisanship remains a more powerful predictor of vote choice for California Latinos" (2005, 22).

Research on the general topic of crossover voting can be divided into two categories: (1) theory and research aimed at explaining the practice of ticket splitting and general issues of crossover voting (Cohen, Kousser, and Sides 1999); and (2) theory and research aimed at explaining racial crossover voting among Black and White voters, typically in the presence of a Black candidate.

As Bullock notes, "Voting for a candidate of one's own race may be a product of racism, or it may be the result of reliance on a simple, readily available cue" (1984, 240). In the South, many Whites began voting Republican when Black Democrats appeared on the ballot.

The case for ethnic voting rests on some basic premises. First, creating a zero-sum contest between ethnicity and partisanship is wrong. Instead, the variables work in concert with each other, with ethnicity equaling partisanship in importance in vote-choice models. That is, we should not set the bar so high that a Latino Republican would need to win 90 percent of the Latino vote for ethnicity to be considered relevant. Instead, we should establish a benchmark of partisan-driven voting in an election with no Latino candidates and then compare outcomes for Latino candidate elections to this base. Thus, if the Mexican American Republican in Michelson's (2005) analysis received an estimated 40 percent of the Latino vote while the prior Anglo Republican candidate received just 20 percent, we have found evidence in favor of ethnic voting. Had the Latino Republican received 60 percent of the vote, the findings would have been clearer, but the underlying question should not change: Does an ethnic candidate attract considerable crossover votes that a nonethnic candidate does not? Juenke-Gonzalez and Sampaio (2008), for example, argue that ethnicity played little role in the 2004 Colorado Senate election; however, their findings suggest that Salazar outpolled Kerry by as much as 10 points among Latinos. Finally, we should not assume that every Spanish-surnamed candidate will win over Latino voters. Like Anglo or Black voters, Latinos will not vote for a bad candidate who runs a poor campaign. Instead, we would expect potential crossover candidates to have some political experience, to be politically moderate, and to emphasize their policy congruence with the Latino community (e.g., Republicans would emphasize their views on abortion or gay marriage, while Democrats would emphasize their views on public education funding or immigrant rights).

MEASURING LATINO ETHNIC IDENTITY

Chapter 2 outlined the components of shared ethnic identity among Latinos. Overlapping ethnic and cultural bonds unite Latinos of different national origins, providing the basis for the emergence of a shared ethnic identity. However, we should not assume that ethnic identification is equally strong among all Latinos. In fact, this chapter provides a range of ethnic identities for Latinos and examines the question of whether those with high degrees of ethnic attachment are more likely to vote along ethnic lines. With this in mind, it is possible to identify the roots of a shared ethnic experience among Latinos.

No consensus exists on how best to measure shared ethnic identity. As discussed in chapter 2, studies of Black political behavior often rely on Dawson's notion of "linked fate" (1994), which often serves as a strong predictor of political behavior, but the situation for Latinos is more complicated. Thus, instead of employing an explicit linked-fate measure to tap into shared ethnicity, I rely on the idea of commonality—that is, how much Latinos have in common with one another—a measure that Sanchez (2006) and Masuoka (2006) use in their studies on Latino group consciousness. If Latinos follow a trajectory similar to that of African Americans, Latinos who feel a stronger sense of commonality (shared ethnicity) can demonstrate their feelings by voting for co-ethnic candidates.

The shared commonality measure is not available in every data set, although its use among Latino politics scholars is growing. The TRPI survey uses this precise question, but the LIF survey does not. However, both surveys contain a number of questions regarding the importance of ethnic attachment in the political arena that we can use to create a scale of ethnic identity or ethnic attachment.

Coupled with a high sense of shared ethnic identity or commonality, notions of political underrepresentation rather than issue alignment may drive Latino voters to follow ethnic cues. I agree with DeSipio's (1996a) argument that for ethnicity to become a salient mobilizing force, a link beyond just culture must exist to unite Latinos politically. While he points to a distinct perspective on policy issues, the presence of a viable Latino candidate can be another such condition. Latinos have not won elected office in proportion to their numerical strength in this country, and a sense of underrepresentation may well increase Latino voters' excitement about the possibility of electing Latino candidates regardless of their party affiliation.

The concept of underrepresentation is closely related to a second component of ethnic attachment, perceived amount of influence. Miller et al. (1981) include underrepresentation as an important factor in group consciousness: the group must not only have an identity but feel that it has too little power in society. To the extent that such questions are available, scholars should incorporate perceived influence into measures of ethnic attachment.

Finally, I expect that ethnic issues and symbols to play a role in shaping Latino ethnic attachment in the political or electoral arena. Do Latinos list race relations or immigration as top concerns? Does an endorsement from a Latino organization add value to a candidate? Is it important that a candidate conducts a bilingual campaign? All of these aspects contribute to a politicized ethnic identity among Latinos that should correlate to voting for a Latino candidate, even across partisan or ideological lines.

Given that ethnicity plays a role in elections, competing theories of candidate preference have arisen. What is the influence of issues or partisanship relative to the influence of ethnic identity? We can test the following hypotheses:

H1: *Controlling for party identification and issue preference, Latino voters' levels of ethnic identity will increase the likelihood that they will support Latino candidates.*

H2: *Controlling for party identification and level of ethnic identity, issue congruence will increase the probability of supporting candidates with whom Latino voters agree on the issues.*

H3: *Controlling for level of ethnic identity and issue preference, party identification will predict candidate preference among Latinos (Democrats vote Democratic; Republicans vote Republican).*

DATA AND METHODOLOGY

Using registered voters as the unit of analysis, I test whether Latino identity is an important predictor of vote choice. Survey data collected in California by the LIF in 2000[4] and in New York and California by the TRPI in 2002 permit the examination of whether Latino voters with strong ethnic identities prefer co-ethnic candidates or whether issue position and partisanship dictate candidate preference.

Specifically, the LIF survey offered respondents the chance to vote in a hypothetical election between candidates named *Smith* and *Hernandez*. Respondents were informed of each candidate's stance on the issues, with Smith portrayed as a traditional Democrat and Hernandez as a traditional Republican, although no party labels were given.[5] The absence of party labels corresponds to nonpartisan local elections, which are typical of most states. In addition, offering issue positions for each candidate provides an optimal environment for testing the classic Downsian model that voters prefer the candidate who is spatially closest to their preferences (Downs 1957).

The TRPI survey asked partisan identifiers how they would vote in an election that pitted a non-Latino partisan versus a Latino nonpartisan to assess the probability of crossover voting when Latino candidates are present. While no information about the candidates was given, more than a quarter of all respondents picked the Latino nonpartisan over a non-Latino party member.

The LIF survey was conducted in February 2000, prior to California's presidential primary (held on March 2), and included interviews with 750 registered Latino voters (Arteaga 2000). The TRPI survey was conducted in October 2002, prior to the November midterm elections. Although Latino voters have recently been the subject of many surveys, these data are unique because registered voters were asked to decide in a hypothetical election between Latino and non-Latino candidates.

Rather than giving party cues, the LIF survey described each candidate's platform, allowing voters to decide based on the issues. Given that most California Latinos are registered with the Democratic Party (Cain, Kiewiet, and Uhlaner 1991; de la Garza et al. 1992; Uhlaner and Garcia 2005) and that California's Republican Party has a serious image problem with Latinos (Michelson 2005), the LIF survey offered the challenge of a candidate with a Latino surname and a Republican-oriented platform versus a candidate with an Anglo surname and a Democratic-oriented platform. This method provided an optimal environment in which to test whether issues and partisanship or ethnic identity influenced Latino candidate preference. The anti-immigrant, anti-Latino ballot measures in California, endorsed by the Republican Party, drove Latino voters away from the GOP and into the waiting arms of the Democrats (Barreto and Woods 2005). Furthermore, because the issue platforms of each candidate were provided, the study meets Downs's (1957) hypothetical example of perfect information. If Downs's thesis is correct, voters will align themselves with the candidate with whom they share common issue positions, regardless of race or ethnicity.

The TRPI survey asked all registered voters about their party affiliations; independents were asked about the party to which they felt closer. The follow-up question got to the heart of the debate on partisanship versus ethnicity. Democrats were asked, "In an election between a non-Latino Democrat and a Latino Republican, which candidate would you prefer?" Republicans, conversely, were asked, "In an election between a non-Latino Republican and a Latino Democrat, which candidate would you prefer?" While the LIF survey deliberately does not cue partisanship, the TRPI survey does so; together, therefore, the data provide a complete portrait of Latino vote choice and the role of ethnic candidates.

Ordered-probit and probit-regression techniques are employed to accurately predict the trichotomous and dichotomous dependent variables. Post-estimation analysis assesses the predicted probability of a vote for the co-ethnic candidate given changes in the key independent variables (Long 1997; Long and Freese 2001).

Dependent Variables

The LIF survey asked respondents to pick which of two statements about candidates for public office came closer to their views.

> A. Smith says state and local governments can do a great deal to improve the quality of life for Latinos in California. Smith believes in HMO reforms, improving public education, and providing more affordable housing.
>
> B. Hernandez says state and local governments have too much power to regulate individuals and community life for Latinos in California. Hernandez believes in traditional family values, reducing taxes and increasing job opportunities, and reducing crime.

The question had five possible answers: Smith, Hernandez, Neither, Both, and Don't Know.[6] The answers were sorted in two ways, yielding the two dependent variables analyzed here. First, voters who said Neither, Both, or Don't Know were grouped together as "undecided" (about 28 percent of the sample). Second, voters who did not state a preference for either Smith or Hernandez were dropped, and only those with a clear preference for one of the candidates were analyzed.

Because a large number of respondents—more than a quarter—fall into the "undecided" category, I kept them in the analysis. Prior to an election, some segment of the electorate remains torn between two candidates. Thus, these respondents represent a real portion of the electorate.[7] However, because they have not articulated a clear preference, they may blur the results. Since we are interested in candidate preference, and voters ultimately must choose between the two options or abstain, the second dependent variable includes only those who indicated a preference for Smith (0) or Hernandez (1). The two models produce the same results with regard to the key independent variables of policy preferences and ethnic attachment.

The TRPI data yield very similar dependent variables, with respondents asked to choose between a Latino nonpartisan and a non-Latino co-partisan.[8] Republicans were asked whom they would prefer in an election between a Latino Democrat and a non-Latino Republican, while Democrats were asked the inverse. As with the LIF survey, many voters responded that they were unsure, and two similar variables were created, with a trichotomous measure that includes undecided voters at the midpoint and a dichotomous variable that examines only voters with stated preferences.

WHEN ETHNICITY TRUMPS PARTISANSHIP

The findings include three general themes. First, policy preferences matter in determining candidate preferences. Second, ethnic identity is an important determinant of vote choice among Latinos. And third, Latino voters possess a latent predisposition for co-ethnic candidates that cannot be explained by self-reported ethnic identity or policy preferences. Before exploring the first two themes in the multivariate regression analysis, I briefly review the survey results with respect to the underlying preference for the Latino candidate.

Generally, the TRPI showed modest support for crossover voting (table 4.1). Overall, 26 percent of respondents indicated that they would vote for a Latino of the opposing party rather than a non-Latino party member. Given that no information was provided about the potential candidates, this estimate seems high and lends support for the hypothesis that Latino candidates can attract Latino votes, independent of partisanship. The TRPI survey also asked respondents how they planned to vote in their upcoming congressional elections. By matching voters' party identification to their stated vote preference in the congressional election, we can examine the Latino candidate's effect on changing vote preference. As the table shows, the presence of a Latino candidate not only immediately commands crossover appeal but also creates more uncertainty in the electorate, suggesting that still other voters might opt for the Latino candidate if more information were provided. Although partisanship is considered far and away the best predictor of vote choice (see, e.g., Petrocik 1989), only 40 percent of Latinos chose the candidate of their own party over the Latino of the other party. For Latinos, the presence of a co-ethnic candidate

TABLE 4.1. **Impact of Latino Candidate on Crossover Voting**

	Partisan	Undecided	Crossover
Vote for Congress	84	8	8
Vote when Latino candidate of *opposite party* is listed	40	34	26
Difference	−44	26	18
Percentage difference	−52%	325%	225%

Source: Tomás Rivera Policy Institute survey of Latino voters in California and New York, 2002.

may turn fifty years of political science conventional wisdom on its head (e.g., *The American Voter* [1960]). Further, no immediate party difference was recognizable, with both Democrats and Republicans willing to cross over at the same rate (26 percent).

These results are consistent with those of the LIF survey, where Latino voters preferred Hernandez over Smith by a two-to-one margin (see table 4.2). Democrats and Republicans alike preferred the more conservative Latino over the more liberal non-Latino. Table 4.2 provides a number of detailed breakdowns of vote choice by issue position and partisanship. In addition to these characteristics, the survey directly asked Latinos if they would vote for various ethnic and partisan candidates. Even respondents who said that they would vote for a White Democrat in an election preferred Hernandez over Smith (50 to 25 percent), and respondents who said that they would not vote for a Latino Republican also preferred Hernandez over Smith (52 to 25 percent), thus contradicting their stated views.

While these results are informative and interesting, they do not fully test the mobilizing influence of Latino candidates. For this analysis, multivariate probit regression was employed to derive two sets of estimates (see tables 4.3 and 4.4). While the variables in the models remain constant, two versions of the dependent variable are tested. First, where it takes on a trichotomous distribution, ordered probit estimates are presented; second, when the undecided voters are removed and the dependent variable is dichotomous, standard probit measures are presented. In addition, for both models, postestimation analysis is used to present the changes in predicted probability.

Table 4.3 reports the full results for the ordered-probit and probit models predicting vote choice for Hernandez. The results confirm both the issue-posi-

TABLE 4.2. Issue Preference and Candidate Preference

| | Candidate Preference | | | |
Issue Variables	Smith	Undecided	Hernandez	n
Overall sample	25	28	48	750
Reduce crime	25	28	47	678
Family values	22	28	50	638
Public education	26	28	47	687
Affordable housing	25	29	46	516
Democratic voter	28	23	48	333
Republican voter	27	22	52	155

Source: Latino Issues Forum survey of Latino voters in California, 2000.

TABLE 4.3. Determinants of Vote for Latino Candidate (Hernandez)

Independent Variables	O-Probit	Pr. Chg.	Probit	Pr. Chg.
Smith issues	−.1612**	−.3022	−.2027**	−.2797
	(.0680)		(.0989)	
Hernandez issues	.1797**	.2635	.2734***	.4153
	(.0765)		(.1008)	
Democratic voter	−.0472	−.0188	−.1695	−.0616
	(.1199)		(.1714)	
Republican voter	−.0183	−.0073	−.1648	−.0608
	(.1410)		(.1873)	
Strong Democrat	−.0240	−.0096	−.0716	−.0260
	(.1191)		(.1593)	
Ethnic mobilization	.0508**	.1980	.0738**	.2769
	(.0242)		(.0339)	
Ethnic attachment	.0418*	.2598	.0621**	.3635
	(.0220)		(.0311)	
Will vote for	−.0942	−.1495	−.1163	−.1635
White Democrat	(.0576)		(.0727)	
Won't vote for	−.0313	−.0499	−.0445	−.0644
Latino Republican	(.0487)		(.0643)	
Low sophistication	.1125	.0448	.1567	.0561
	(.1094)		(.1470)	
Female	−.0104	−.0041	−.0337	−.0122
	(.0986)		(.1347)	
Mexican origin	.1422	.0565	.1651	.0611
	(.1123)		(.1638)	
Foreign born	.1453	.0579	.2224	.0791
	(.1170)		(.1562)	
Speak Spanish	−.0490	−.0389	−.0708	−.0517
	(.0700)		(.0916)	
Age	.0171	.0679	.0382	.1361
	(.0175)		(.0245)	
Education proxy	−.0484	−.0769	−.0578	−.0845
	(.0331)		(.0435)	
Income $20,000–$39,999	.2280	.0908	.3253*	.1136
	(.1598)		(.1970)	
Income $40,000–$69,999	−.0775	−.0308	−.0699	−.0256
	(.1633)		(.2043)	
Income over $70,000	.2484	.0987	.3405	.1153
	(.2119)		(.2602)	
Income not reported	.0243	.0097	.1877	.0663
	(.1478)		(.2072)	
Los Angeles County	−.0878	−.0349	−.1038	−.0379
	(.1043)		(.1403)	
Constant / Cut1	.3612		−1.541	
	(.7129)		(1.008)	
Cut2	1.116			
	(.7114)			
N	587		429	

Note: Standard errors in parentheses.

Pr. Chg. columns report changes in predicted probability for the dependent variable when the independent variable is moved from its minimum to its maximum value.

*p < .05   **p < .01   ***p < .001

tion and the ethnic-attachment hypotheses, suggesting that Latino voters may require a more complicated (nuanced) theory that incorporates both hypotheses. As the issue-preference hypothesis speculates, those respondents who have the same stance on the issues as a candidate are likely to prefer that candidate. In this example, the variable *Smith Issues* has a significant and negative relationship with a vote for Hernandez, while *Hernandez Issues* is significant and positive, as expected.[9] The findings provide no support for the partisanship theory: neither the *Democratic Voter* nor *Republican Voter* variables has a significant effect on vote choice. Although California's Latino voters evidenced a strong attachment to the Democratic Party during the 1990s, this attachment does not influence vote choice for Smith, the more liberal candidate, although immigration-related themes were not emphasized for either candidate. Even the variable *Strong Democrat* (based on the intensity of Democratic partisanship) was not a negative predictor of voting for Hernandez, as we might expect. This result fits nicely with Wattenberg's (1987, 1994) findings that campaigns are becoming candidate-centered and that political parties are losing their stronghold on voter decisions.

Further, when a co-ethnic candidate is present, the candidate focus of the campaign may be augmented for Latino voters. Studies of the 2001 Los Angeles mayoral campaign, a nonpartisan election, revealed that Latino voters were eager to elect a Latino mayor, and exit polls found that Latino voters overwhelmingly supported the Latino candidate (Sonenshein and Pinkus 2002; Sonenshein 2003). Indeed, table 4.3 seems to confirm the ethnic-attachment hypothesis. Both *Ethnic Mobilization* and *Ethnic Attachment* demonstrate a significant and positive effect on voting for the Latino candidate.[10] This result indicates that Latinos who identify with ethnic themes in mobilization and candidate characteristics are more likely to vote for a co-ethnic candidate, even after we control for partisanship and issue preference. This finding is consistent with the idea of group consciousness because it suggests that those voters who view ethnicity as an important mobilizing force are likely to prefer co-ethnic or co-racial candidates.[11] In addition, individual voter characteristics have no statistically significant effect in the multivariate analysis. Foreign-born, Spanish-speaking-household, and Mexican-origin respondents are no more likely to prefer Hernandez over Smith, all else being equal. Income, which is generally associated with voting Republican, also has no effect.

On their own, the probit coefficients reveal little further information about which variables are significant and their directional impact. Using postestimation analysis (Long 1997; Long and Freese 2001), we can more precisely determine each independent variable's specific contribution to vote choice. The "Pr. Chg." columns allow us to assess the magnitude of the effect of each independent variable.

Not only is shared ethnicity a statistically significant predictor of vote choice, it has roughly the same effect as issue preference in explaining Latino voting. Looking to the ordered-probit results, voters who rate *Hernandez Issues* "very important" are 26.4 percent more likely to prefer Hernandez than those who rate both issues "not important at all." Likewise, those who rate *Smith Issues* positively are 30.2 percent less likely to prefer Hernandez than those who do not value those issues. Both ethnicity variables also show considerable influence on vote choice. While Latinos who respond to ethnic-based mobilization are 19.8 percent more likely to prefer Hernandez over Smith, voters who react favorably to ethnic-based campaign characteristics and have high scores in *Ethnic Attachment* are 25.9 percent more likely to prefer the co-ethnic candidate. Taken further, if the changes in predicted probability of these two shared ethnicity variables are combined, voters who holds both viewpoints are more than 45 percent more likely to prefer Hernandez. Thus, ethnic identification is the key determinant of vote choice.

Table 4.4 shows the results from the TRPI survey for crossover voting. These results show many similarities to the LIF results, suggesting that the LIF findings are not an artifact of the data set alone. Further, the fact that the experiment included cues about the candidates' partisanship adds a new dimension to the results of the LIF survey, providing more confidence in the overall findings.

When the partisanship of the candidates is stated and issues are not, partisanship is a significant predictor of vote choice and issue congruence is not a significant predictor. Respondents who thought that the Democratic Party could best address their most important issue (*Democratic Issues*) were no more likely to side with a Democratic candidate, as was true for *Republican Issues*. However, Latinos who had stated a preference for voting Democrat in their congressional races (*Democratic Voter*) were significantly less likely to side with a Latino Republican in both the ordered-probit and probit models. Strong partisan identifiers were also less likely to prefer the co-ethnic crossover candidate. These results are straightforward and are not unexpected.

Even after we control for issues and partisanship, the findings offer strong support for ethnicity as an important predictor of vote choice. The *Shared Commonality* variable (how much respondents feel they have in common with other Latinos) demonstrated a positive and significant relationship with voting for the Latino crossover candidate.[12] In fact, ethnicity had a substantive impact

TABLE 4.4   Determinants of Cross-over Voting for Latino Candidate

Independent Variables	O-Probit	Pr. Chg.	Probit	Pr. Chg.
Democratic issues	−.0984	−.0308	.0431	.0164
	(.1087)		(.1588)	
GOP issues	−.0032	−.0010	−.0182	−.0069
	(.1471)		(.2184)	
Democratic voter	−.3552***	−.1158	−.6318**	−.2448
	(.1186)		(.2721)	
Republican voter	−.0160	−.0050	−.0805	−.0303
	(.1507)		(.2862)	
Strong partisan	−.1618**	−.1047	−.2274**	−.1754
	(.0652)		(.0984)	
Shared commonality	.0945*	.0861	.1943**	.2118
	(.0506)		(.0756)	
Ethnic attachment	.1374**	.1318	.2698***	.3038
	(.0688)		(.1005)	
Perceived discrimination	−.012	−.0113	−.0175	−.0199
	(.0453)		(.0652)	
Female	.0452	.0142	.0746	.0283
	(.0940)		(.1370)	
Mexican origin	.1156	.0364	.2133	.0811
	(.1375)		(.1905)	
Puerto Rican origin	.0049	.0015	−.0654	−.0247
	(.1402)		(.1957)	
Foreign born	.0246	.0077	.105	.0398
	(.1266)		(.1663)	
Third generation	−.1864	−.0557	−.2523	−.0924
	(.1479)		(.2240)	
Speak Spanish	.0047	.0030	.018	.0136
	(.0766)		(.1036)	
Age	.0018	.0387	.0005	.0126
	(.0033)		(.0047)	
Education	−.0773**	−.1187	−.1255**	−.2314
	(.0391)		(.0532)	
Income $25,000–$34,999	.1851	.0606	.1862	.0719
	(.1580)		(.1926)	
Income $35,000–$49,999	.1001	.0322	.0885	.0339
	(.1540)		(.2189)	
Income $50,000–$79,999	.148	.0481	.1501	.0579
	(.1522)		(.2328)	
Income over $80,000	.2791	.0944	.3243	.1271
	(.1769)		(.2860)	
Income not reported	.1295	.0481	.1385	.0534
	(.1382)		(.2044)	
California	−.0119	−.0037	−.1113	−.0422
	(.1455)		(.1882)	
Constant / Cut1	−.2995		−.3075	
	(.3627)		(.5410)	
Cut2	.6398			
	(.3631)			
N	627		414	

Note: Standard errors in parentheses.

Pr. Chg. columns report changes in predicted probability for the dependent variable when the independent variable is moved from its minimum to its maximum value.

*p < .05   **p < .01   ***p < .001

similar to that of strong party identification. Latinos who had high degrees of shared commonality were 8.6 percent more likely to prefer the Latino crossover candidate in the ordered-probit model and 21.2 percent more likely to do so in the probit model. In comparison, strong party identifiers were 10.5 percent less likely to vote against their party and pick the crossover Latino candidate in the ordered model and 17.5 percent less likely to do so in the bivariate model. Further consistency with the LIF data is found in the *Ethnic Attachment* variable (which combined three ethnic measures) and had a positive and significant relationship with vote choice.[13] *Ethnic Attachment* has the largest substantive effect of any variable in the model. We might expect that when partisanship is cued (as in the TRPI survey), ethnicity may play less of a role. However, both of the shared ethnicity variables predict crossover voting. When voters know both the partisanship and ethnicity of the candidates, ethnicity and ethnic identification can influence vote choice. Perceived discrimination, which Sanchez (2006) finds to be associated with Latino collective action and group consciousness, has no statistically significant effect on crossover voting.

Finally, the results indicate that education has an inverse relationship with crossover voting, a relationship that may also result from voters' level of political information. While the candidates' ethnicity may serve as an important information shortcut or heuristic device, the most educated and informed voters may make decisions based more on issue position, partisanship, and campaign promises.

In addition to the changes in predicted probability reported in tables 4.3 and 4.4, I also estimated the predicted probability of voting for the co-ethnic candidate for low ethnic identifiers relative to high ethnic identifiers. Holding all other values at their mean, I set the shared ethnicity variables to their lowest value and estimated the probability of vote choice outcomes and then set the shared ethnicity variables to their highest value and reestimated vote choice. For the LIF data (see figure 4.1), I adjust the values for ethnic mobilization and ethnic attachment at the same time, moving from low to high. For the TRPI data (see figure 4.2), I adjust the values for shared commonality and ethnic attachment in the same manner. Both comparisons show a pattern in which Latinos at the lowest level of shared ethnicity are more likely to vote for the co-partisan candidate than the co-ethnic candidate and those at the highest level of shared ethnicity are more likely to select the co-ethnic candidate than the co-partisan. These results provide strong evidence that ethnic loyalty can trump party loyalty.

While these results are based on hypothetical candidates in a survey, some

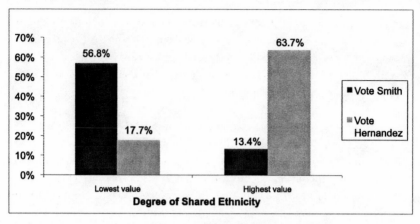

FIG. 4.1. Predicted probability of Hernandez vote

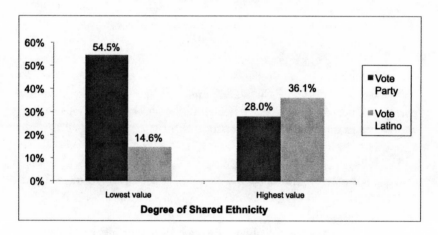

FIG. 4.2. Predicted probability of crossover voting

real evidence for support of Latino Republican candidates comes from the 2002 California State Assembly elections. Four Latino Republicans were reelected with strong support from Latino voters in their districts, while Republican Gary Mendoza, a statewide candidate for insurance commissioner, received the highest level of Latino support of any Republican candidate for statewide office and even outpolled the Anglo Democratic challenger in some heavily Latino precincts (Los Angeles County Registrar 2002). In central Florida, a Puerto Rican Republican was elected to the state legislature in a majority-Latino district that had previously voted Democratic. In addition, in nonpartisan contests, Latinos have shown strong support for Latino candidates despite differences in ideology or partisanship, as in the mayoral elections in Colorado Springs and Miami discussed earlier and in the mayoral elections in Houston and San Francisco discussed in chapter 5.

DISCUSSION

The results presented here show that traditional theories of candidate preference need to be augmented for Latino voters when a co-ethnic candidate is present. Issue position, partisanship, and candidate evaluation may not fully explain why Latinos vote as they do. Instead, we can refine our understanding of vote choice by including measures of ethnic attachment in the model. Specifically, I have found that Latinos with high degrees of ethnic attachment are more likely to prefer Latino candidates, absent party labels. Even when controlling for issue positions and party preference, ethnicity has a direct influence on vote choice. I obtain this finding in part because I use a more sophisticated measure of ethnicity. While previous research looked to a two-stage, indirect model after failing to find evidence of a direct influence, I have established that there is no need to pursue the indirect model. Rather than conceptualizing ethnicity as all-or-nothing, we need to include scales of ethnic identification that account for the relative importance of ethnicity to an individual. However, ethnicity may have both direct and indirect influence on vote choice—that is, ethnic attachment not only may directly affect Latino voters' choice of candidates but also may affect partisanship and policy preferences, which, in turn, affect vote choice.

With more Latinos running for office than ever before, a new paradigm is emerging that challenges traditional notions of political behavior. This research is important because it demonstrates that shared ethnic identity exists among Latinos and that ethnicity constitutes an important determinant of vote choice when a Latino candidate appears on the ballot.

The Impact of Latino Mayoral Candidates on Latino Voters: New Evidence from Five Mayoral Elections, 2001–2003

"As a result of research efforts on voting behavior of Chicanos, several patterns have been identified. The more consistent findings have been significantly lower rates of voter registration and turnout than Anglo and black voters." (J. A. Garcia and Arce 1988, 128)

In the two decades since this finding first emerged, scholarship on Latino politics and electoral behavior still finds that Latinos are less likely to participate in politics than are members of other racial and ethnic groups (see, e.g., Wolfinger and Rosenstone 1980; Calvo and Rosenstone 1989; Verba, Schlozman, and Brady 1995; Arvizu and Garcia 1996; Shaw, de la Garza, and Lee 2000). Latino participation rates remain low for some well-documented and generally well-known reasons that apply in a variety of contexts, including demographic factors (De-Sipio 1996a; Hero and Campbell 1996) and issues surrounding immigrant status and citizenship (J. A. Garcia and Arce 1988; Calvo and Rosenstone 1989; Uhlaner, Cain, and Kiewiet 1989). Indeed, several essays devoted to the Latino vote that appeared in the 2000 preelection volume of *PS: Political Science* conclude that the promise of Latino political participation remains largely unfulfilled (Affigne 2000; Hero, Garcia, Garcia, and Pachon 2000; Marquez and Jennings 2000; Montoya, Hardy-Fanta, and Garcia 2000; Schmidt, Barvosa-Carter, and Torres 2000; Sierra et al. 2000).

This chapter tests whether co-ethnic candidates affect Latino voter turnout and candidate preference across a variety of real election results. In light of the increases in the number of Latino voters and Latino candidates for office, it is important to ask whether Latino voters follow an ethnic-voting model that emphasizes shared ethnicity and ethnic candidates or a strictly Downsian cost-benefit-analysis model. More than forty years ago, Wolfinger noted that "the most powerful and visible sign of ethnic political relevance is a fellow-ethnic's name at the head of the ticket" (1965, 905). While some scholars provide strong theoretical support for this claim (Fraga 1988; Hero 1992), no comprehensive body of empirical evidence has been amassed demonstrating that shared ethnicity is salient for Latinos, and no coherent theory exists that accounts for the empowering role of co-ethnic candidates.[1]

For the most part, previous empirical studies understate or ignore the effect of electoral context and of the presence of competitive Latino candidates. Building on literature covering minority political behavior rooted in ethnic identity and shared group consciousness, I argue that under some circumstances, Latinos should be more likely to vote than non-Latinos and more likely to vote for co-ethnic candidates. In 2001 and 2003, Latino candidates contested mayoral elections in some of the largest U.S. cities—Los Angeles, Houston, New York, Denver, and San Francisco. While none of the five Latino hopefuls ultimately won election, their impact on Latino political behavior cannot be ignored. Given the right set of circumstances, Latino registered voters are likely to turn out at rates higher than those of non-Latinos and to support co-ethnic candidates.

Each of the five cities has a unique political and cultural environment, making the results of this study more broadly applicable. Further, these elections challenge the conventional wisdom that Latinos vote heavily Democrat, as the Latino candidates in these case studies represented the Democratic, Republican, and Green Parties and held a broad array of political ideologies. In no two cities were the Latino candidates or their non-Latino opponents politically identical. In addition, the candidates were of Mexican, Puerto Rican, and Cuban backgrounds. Some were immigrants themselves; others had immigrant parents or grandparents. Thus, these five cities provide an ideal setting in which to test whether shared ethnicity between Latino candidates and voters is a mobilizing factor. In these localities, Latino candidates and Latino voters generated political excitement and influenced elections, with the result that "Democrats and Republicans got a reminder . . . that Hispanic voters are a fast-growing and crucial swing vote tied more closely to ethnic than party loyalty. That dynamic of ethnic loyalty, which played out in very different ways in the three cities' mayoral races, could be important in many [future] races" (Lester 2001). While the data sets come from five discrete elections, the argument should not be seen as a description isolated to unique events. Rather, the findings in this chapter have implications for the future of multicultural urban America. Latinos are no longer concentrated in the Southwest. Latinos are now the largest minority population in twenty-three states, including Washington, Idaho, Nebraska, Kansas, Iowa, Vermont, and New Hampshire. As Latino citizenship, registration, and voter mobilization increase across the country, we should not be surprised to find similar results for Latino participation and candidate preference under similar circumstances.

Over the past twenty years, increasing numbers of Latinos have run for office in the United States, creating a political environment in which Latino voting rates have risen. As this trend continues, it will become more difficult to isolate studies of Latino politics from mainstream studies of voting and elections. This research thus sheds new light on long-standing and potentially outdated notions of minority participation. As the political landscape changes in the twenty-first century and Spanish-surnamed candidates become common in U.S. elections, pundits and scholars alike will need to revisit the question of Latino and minority participation.

ETHNIC POLITICS REVISITED

Despite the prevailing belief that Latinos are generally less likely to participate politically than non-Latinos, more recent works indicate that at least in some circumstances, Latinos are likely to turn out at rates at least comparable to those of other racial and ethnic groups (Kaufmann 2003; Barreto, Segura, and Woods 2004). These studies generally build on evidence that particular contexts may lead to increased Latino political interest and involvement (de la Garza, Menchaca, and DeSipio 1994; Diaz 1996; Wrinkle et al. 1996; Hritzuk and Park 2000; Pantoja and Woods 2000; Pantoja, Ramírez, and Segura 2001). Most of these analyses have found that changes in several measures of Latino participation result in part from the electoral environment but still conclude that Latinos are, on average, less likely to engage politically after taking demographic and naturalization factors into account.

Two elements play a major role in creating an electoral context in which Latinos will be more likely to participate: (1) a combination of issues and circumstances during the latter half of the 1990s, arguably part of a national anti-immigrant movement; and (2) the prominent and viable candidacy of a Latino contestant for mayor, a top-of-the-ticket post. Further, in all of the cities studied here except Denver, the election represented the first time a Latino candidate had launched a serious bid for the office.[2]

The Ethnic-Candidate Paradigm

This book emphasizes an ethnic-candidate paradigm of American politics established in the twentieth century (Dahl 1961; Wolfinger 1965; Parenti 1967) and advances the idea for Latinos in the twenty-first century. As the U.S. Latino population grows and more Latino candidates run for mayor, state offices, and the U.S. Congress, scholars and pundits will need a firm understanding of the dynamics at play within the Latino community as well as between the Latino and non-Latino communities. It is not enough to simply state that co-ethnic candidates matter. We need a sound understanding of why they matter so that we can identify cases and sort out results. Chapter 2 argued that two factors make co-ethnic candidates salient to Latino voters. First, by definition, people who self-identify as Latino are members of a common ethnic group, and for a variety of reasons, ethnicity is a salient political issue for Latino voters (for a full development of this argument, see Sanchez 2006). Second, campaigns increasingly emphasize candidate characteristics, and they increasingly matter to voters. The convergence of a growing Latino electorate and a campaign system that focuses on candidate traits provides the foundation for exploring the impact of shared ethnicity and co-ethnic candidates.

According to DeSipio, Latino voter participation may be influenced more by traditional socioeconomic and demographic predictors of political participation than by ethnicity. He argues that "ethnicity will come to play less of a role in their political decision-making than will other societal divisions" (1996a, 8). While ethnicity is likely to have "no distinct impact" in this model, it could emerge under "unique circumstances" or in response to "ethnic-based discrimination," scenarios that DeSipio describes as "unlikely" (9). While DeSipio is correct in establishing these criteria as necessary for the development of ethnicity as a central component of the politicization of Latinos, I think he underestimates the possibility of its occurrence. The ethnically charged context found in California, Texas, New York, and Colorado during the 1990s, immediately preceding the 2001 and 2003 mayoral elections studied here, offers such an example. While some states experienced greater discrimination and protest related to Latino issues than did other states, many examples abound in each of these four localities, perhaps as a consequence of a national anti-immigration trend (Nelson 1994; Fry 2001). Indeed, such contexts exist in states as diverse as Arizona and Iowa, both of which witnessed the rise of anti-immigrant groups in response to the growing Latino and immigrant populations. As viable Latino candidates emerge elsewhere, it is reasonable to suspect that the political environment may foster similar periods of ethnic politics.

Beginning with the anti-immigrant and arguably anti-Latino 1994 Proposition 187 initiative and extending through the 1996 antibilingual-education (Proposition 209) and 1998 anti-affirmative-action (Proposition 227) initiatives, Latino politics in California has recently been a response to perceived attacks. Proposition 187 proposed banning illegal immigrants from receiving public social services, nonemergency health care, and public education. The initiative was couched in anti-Latino rhetoric (one GOP state senator suggested that all Latinos would be required to carry identification cards), and Latinos quickly mobilized in near-unanimous opposition. While this mobilization did not translate into massive numbers of Latino votes in that year, subsequent election cycles showed the measure's effects.

Just two years later, California's voters passed Proposition 209, which repealed most affirmative action programs in the areas of public contracting, jobs, and education. As with Proposition 187, Latinos were nearly unanimous in their opposition to the anti-affirmative-action measure. Exit polls found that three of four Latinos turned out against Proposition 209 (*Statewide Survey* 1996). In the 1998 primary election, Latinos were again the perceived targets of a conservative initiative—this time Proposition 227, which sought to end bilingual education. Opposition to the initiative came from many different quarters, as many in the Latino community worked to couch the end of bilingual education as the third in a trilogy of wedge issues that attempted to demonize Latinos and to mobilize conservative Anglo voters ("Race, Ethnicity" 1998).

While the examples from California are typically the best known, ethnically charged environments also existed in Colorado, Texas, and New York. First, immigrant-based protest movements arose in all three states in response to the 1996 Welfare Reform Act, which prevented many immigrants from receiving state and federal benefits. In addition, local issues drew attention to the Latino community as the Other.

In Colorado, more than twenty years of court-ordered busing came to an end in 1995, resulting in the rise of segregation in the Denver school system. Latino community leaders publicized the issue but could not change the busing policy. As a result, activists argued, Latino children were experiencing discrimination. In 1998, Buckeye Elementary School was the target of a federal investigation of claims of discrimination against Latino students. The federal Office of Civil Rights filed suit against the school, and Denver's Latino community became active in the case. In 2001, the Isle de Capri casino, near Denver, was found to be in violation of civil rights when it ordered workers not to speak Spanish while on the job. The case received front-page headlines, and the casino lost a $1.5 million settlement.

In Texas, tensions mounted over two issues, immigration and claims of police brutality. Many Texas immigrants-rights organizations took a negative view of the Clinton administration's crackdown on illegal immigration during the mid-1990s. The Immigration and Naturalization Service became an easy target for activists, and numerous protests and rallies were held in South Texas and in cities with large immigrant populations, such as Houston. At the same time, the Houston police department came under scrutiny for its actions in heavily Latino neighborhoods. In part, the investigation resulted from a collaborative effort in which the department and the Immigration and Naturalization Service conducted "street sweeps" to find and deport undocumented immigrant "criminals." Increased tensions arose between Houston's Latino population and the police department, and in 1998 a suspect in a drug case, Pedro Oregon, was shot nine times in the back by six Houston police officers. The officers were eventually fired, but months of vigils, rallies, and protests took place in the Latino community. Speakers at Houston political rallies often cited such events as evidence of the need for more Latino representation.

New York City, known for its rich immigrant history, also witnessed an increase in racial and ethnic tensions during the 1990s. In 1999, billboard advertisements went up in Queens and Brooklyn that blamed immigrants for a host of the city's social ills. A group, New Immigrant Community Empowerment, responded by erecting pro-immigrant billboards and beginning a large-scale campaign to register immigrants to vote.

Given elite and media attention to these issues, Latinos are more likely to side with other Latinos—even if they have nothing more in common than their Hispanic origins—on matters of political significance. Latinos have been targeted without regard to age, generational status, citizenship, language skills, or national origin. Consequently, these issues and the political climate they engendered made Latinos more cohesive as a political force and more likely to weigh in on political issues directly affecting them. This description of events ties in nicely with the notion of ethnic identification or shared group consciousness, which has recently enjoyed something of a rebirth. For a time, many scholars echoed Dahl's sentiment that the "strength of ethnic ties as a factor in local politics surely must recede" (1961, 62). However, research in subsequent decades has demonstrated the importance of group identification in understanding minority political behavior. While the weight of this research has focused on the experience of African Americans, scholars have more recently taken up the question of how Latino group identity may affect political engagement. The 1990s political contexts of all of these states have assured that Latino identity will remain a significant political factor for some time.

The concept of group consciousness is rooted in attempts to resolve the question of relatively high Black political participation in the face of limited political resources (Olsen 1970; Verba and Nie 1972; Miller et al. 1981). The idea was that members of minority groups who shared an identity would be more likely to participate if they saw their group as politically disadvantaged. This theory nicely fits the position of Latinos in the 1990s and early twenty-first century.

Early work in this area focused on African Americans and found that strength of identification with the politically disadvantaged group served as a strong predictor of participation (Olsen 1970; Verba and Nie 1972). Still, these analyses and others find that minority participation as a whole lags behind that of whites (Verba, Schlozman, and Brady 1995). Together, group identification and a politicized context should produce more active participation among group members. While this scholarship does not directly address Latinos, its findings underscore the expectation for Latino voter turnout in 2001.

In a relatively early attempt to apply similar questions to Latino populations, F. C. Garcia, Garcia, and de la Garza begin with the premise that "ethnicity may provide a structuring basis for [Latino] values, opinions and attitudes" (1991, 22). This research indicated that at least in the late 1980s, a shared identity might be limited among Latino subgroups. Other works reached the same general conclusion, as these and other authors agreed that other factors, including immigration, citizenship, generational status, and English proficiency, likely confound the development of a Latino group identity. At minimum, the development of a pan-Latino identity is certainly hindered by the distinct national origins and cultures of the groups who fall under the term *Latino*. However, as Sanchez (2006) and Masuoka (2006) point out, a Latino identity has emerged, largely as a result of the context present in the late 1990s.

In recent work, Leighley (2001) has extended the shared-group-context argument to the Latino electorate, identifying three contextual influences that reduce the costs and increase the benefits of Latino voting: elite mobilization, relational goods, and racial/ethnic context, the latter two of which are directly applicable in this framework. The relational-goods theory, developed by Uhlaner (1989b), argues that various incentives exist only for in-group members and that they depend on the interaction or participation of group members. Some of the incentives that increase the benefits include social approval, identity formation and maintenance, a desire to experience one's history, friendship, recognition and acceptance, and solidarity (Leighley 2001, 17–18). In particular, Uhlaner suggests that groups with more unified support for a candidate have a stronger sense of identity and will experience higher levels of turnout, as will groups that are more geographically concentrated. In these five cities, where Latinos appeared to rally around the Latino candidates' campaigns and were more or less geographically concentrated in pockets, we should expect the relational goods to produce elevated voter turnout among the in-group, Latinos. Second, Leighley adds the importance of racial/ethnic environmental variables to account for a shared sense of group identity and eagerness to participate. The immediate social context of an individual is significant because it increases the chances of ethnic mobilization, and as group size increases, so too do the chances of electoral success. Most studies of participation have focused too heavily on individual-level measures, such as demographic characteristics, that perform poorly for minority groups. According to Leighley, "Our theories of participation assumed to be generalizable across racial and ethnic groups are tested primarily on Anglos and typically ignore the contextual characteristics emphasized in theories of minority participation, while theories of group mobilization are rarely tested empirically in a systematic fashion across racial and ethnic groups" (2001, 6).

After a lengthy review of many investigations in the field of Latino politics, Leighley concludes that more research is needed specifically to measure the influence of Latino candidates on levels of Latino turnout and candidate preference. Latino turnout might be higher when co-ethnic candidates appear on the ballot because "minority candidates direct more resources toward mobilizing groups" or because "minority candidates change individuals' calculations of the (potential) benefits or costs of voting" (2001, 43). "No systematic evidence on the effects of political empowerment on Latino mobilization and participation has been documented" (43), suggesting the potential importance of the empirical findings contained in this chapter.

Studies of minority officeholding and its effect on minority political behavior demonstrate the importance of my research. At least since the publication of Browning, Marshall, and Tabb's seminal work (1984), we have known that cities with minority representation on city councils or in the mayor's office exhibit more policy responsiveness in terms of minority contracting and municipal employment. Espino (2007) has found that despite the institutional pressures of Congress, Latino members demonstrate a commitment to voting for pro-Latino policies. The argument that as minorities gain access to power in governing institutions, they obtain political representation provides a basis for understanding minority political behavior. Widely understood as the empowerment or incorporation hypothesis, this idea suggests similarly that minority communities are more likely to be involved in politics when minority candidates have a meaningful opportunity to be elected (Bobo and Gilliam 1990; Gilliam 1996).

Research on mayoral elections is the most relevant here. While many studies of Black mayoral candidates have been conducted, these examinations are frequently conducted in isolation from one another. For example, Pinderhughes (1987) finds that Harold Washington's candidacy led to greater political participation in predominantly Black wards and offers a rich contextual history of race relations in Chicago. Sonenshein (1993) documents the persistence of racial politics during the Bradley years in Los Angeles. Keiser (1990) estimates that Black voters uniformly supported Wilson Goode in 1983, making him Philadelphia's first Black mayor, but Keiser confines his theory and analysis to that city. Similar research on African American empowerment in mayoral elections exists for Atlanta, Cleveland, New Orleans, New York, San Francisco, Memphis, and many more cities. Despite the lack of cohesiveness, the literature on Black mayoral politics has established the premise that as a consequence of patronage, city contracts, and group pride, Black political representation resulted in a sense of Black empowerment and mobilization. Tate brings the scattered mayoral analyses together in her work on Black mobilization and the presidential candidacy of Jesse Jackson. Her review of previous mayoral elections, including those in Cleveland and Chicago, and Jackson's candidacy leads her to conclude that "blacks turn out and vote in greater numbers when a black is competing for elective office because of group loyalty, pride, and increased interest" (1991, 1161). Not only are black voters more interested and aware, but black candidates "often campaign more intensively and spend greater resources in black communities" (1161).

Far fewer studies of Latino political empowerment exist, with even less cohesiveness. Hill, Moreno, and Cue (2001) find that Cuban American mayoral candidates in Miami have resulted in greater mobilization and heightened ethnic politics, but the authors provide little in the way of comparisons outside of South Florida. In Denver, Hero and Clarke (2003) find evidence for a Black-Latino coalition in the elections of Federico Peña and Wellington Webb, the city's first Latino and Black mayors, respectively, but do not connect the findings to San Antonio, El Paso, or Miami, other major cities that have had Latino mayors. Brischetto and de al Garza (1985) and Fraga (1988) provide descriptive accounts of Chicano political mobilization in Henry Cisneros's 1981 election, while Manzano and Vega (2006) find continued evidence of ethnically polarized voting in Julian Castro's 2005 bid for the mayor's offce, but none of these analyses go beyond San Antonio. The closest we have come to a unifying theory of Latino empowerment is probably a descriptive article by Muñoz and Henry (1986) that compares Latino voting patterns in Denver and San Antonio mayoral elections, finding similarities in the ethnic-based mobilization of Latino voters.

The elections examined here help bridge the gaps in previous work. Most important to the research design is that in none of the five cities did a Latino Democrat face off against an Anglo Republican, a situation that would make it difficult to disentangle partisan and ethnic loyalties given Latinos' sustained preference for the Democratic Party (Cain, Kiewiet, and Uhlaner 1991). The Latino candidates in the analysis were members of the Democratic, Republican, and Green Parties, while in four of the five cities, their opponents were Democrats. (New York's mayoral election is not a partisan contest.) The non-Latino opponents were diverse in other respects, however: one was an African American, one was Jewish, and the others were Anglo Protestants. Given the differences among the cities, the elections included provide an ideal setting in which to test the effects of shared ethnicity on Latino voter mobilization and vote choice. Moreover, all five of the Latino candidates were viable, receiving important endorsements, donations, and media attention. Latino voters, like all voters, are unlikely to be mobilized by a poorly run campaign with few resources and little hope of success, regardless of a candidate's ethnicity. In addition, other important facets of the campaign, such as a scandal or unpopular policy positions, will likely mediate the impact of shared ethnicity or partisanship, as was the case for Cruz Bustamante in California's 2003 recall election (DeSipio and Masuoka 2006). However, if ethnicity appears to be a politically relevant variable in all five of these elections, held in different parts of the country with different Latino populations, we have something more than just anecdotal evidence. Indeed, we have a systematic and rigorous test of the shared-ethnicity hypothesis, which will inform new waves of research in Latino politics.

Hypotheses

Given the expectation that co-ethnic candidates will spur increased Latino participation among registered voters, we should also expect to find that Latinos will greatly support the co-ethnic candidacy. The two phenomena would seem to be inextricably linked. Despite the growth in the number of Latino candidates over the past three decades, however, few scholars have attempted to understand the impact of co-ethnic candidates on both turnout and voting preferences, even as a mountain of evidence pointing to racial bloc voting accumulates in VRA lawsuits (e.g., Grofman 1993; Engstrom and Brischetto 1997; Abosch, Barreto, and Woods 2007).

Given the combination of a politicized shared group experience and the presence of a co-ethnic candidate, Latinos should not be expected to pass up an opportunity to elect that candidate. Because four of the mayoral elections studied here are nonpartisan and the fifth is a partisan primary, it is possible to sidestep Graves and Lee's (2000) finding that the ethnicity effect is mediated by partisanship. If ethnicity influenced only partisanship, rather than directly influencing candidate preference, there would be no discernable difference between the number of Latino votes for each candidate when both are Democrats. And if the arguments advanced by Graves and Lee and Cain and Kiewiet (1984) remain true, when elections pit non-Latino Democrats against Latinos of other parties (in one case a Republican and in another a Green), Latinos should prefer the Democratic candidates.

This chapter explores two conceptual questions specifically oriented toward elections with top-of-ticket co-ethnic candidates. While Latino candidates are present on the ballot in many elections, my theoretical position is premised on the notion that top-of-ticket candidates are more important for ethnic mobilization. Such candidates garner more media attention and have higher name recognition, and holding such offices represents an important role for minority communities.[3] Chapter 6 explores the relationship between Latino candidates for legislative contests to determine whether the mobilization theory remains applicable.

First, are Latinos more likely to favor co-ethnic candidates over non-Latino alternatives in nonpartisan elections? Second, under the right circumstances, do Latinos vote at higher rates? For example, in an election with a top-of-the-ticket Latino candidate, are Latinos more likely to turn out than when a co-ethnic candidate is not present? Third, are Latino turnout rates higher than those of non-Latinos in elections with Latino candidates? Controlling for standard predictors of political participation such as partisanship, education, income, and age, this research tests the following hypotheses:

H1: *Latinos are significantly more likely to vote in favor of Latino candidates.*

H2: *Latinos will have significantly higher rates of voting in elections with co-ethnic candidates.*

H3: *Latinos will vote at higher rates than non-Latinos in elections with co-ethnic candidates.*

I examine these questions by estimating whether precincts with high percentages of Latino voters have higher or lower turnout rates when Latino candidates are running; whether turnout in these precincts is higher than in precincts with low percentages of Latino residents; and whether heavily Latino precincts favor co-ethnic candidates. The data employed in this chapter are aggregated at the precinct level, making interpretation about individual Latino voters difficult. Despite this limitation, this research presents an important analysis of the role of ethnicity in voter turnout and candidate preference in heavily Latino jurisdictions.

METHODOLOGICAL APPROACH AND DATA

The units of analysis are the individual precincts in Los Angeles, Houston, New York, San Francisco, and Denver. Table 5.1 provides a brief summary of the candidate and the elections studied. Each city analysis consists of two elections, one including a Latino mayoral candidate, one with no such candidate. Table 5.2 shows the elections used for each comparison. For each location, data were collected from three main sources—the county registrar of voters database, the city clerk's statement of votes cast, and the U.S. Census Bureau.

Data were merged together at the precinct level so that vote totals, candidate percentages, and the demographic characteristics of each precinct can be compared in a consistent fashion. The total number of observations stands at 6,776 precincts—all complete precincts in the five cities. Because the unit of

TABLE 5.1. Summary of Mayoral Candidates 2001–2003

City	Latino Candidate	Non-Latino Candidate	Winner (%)
Los Angeles	Antonio Villaraigosa Democrat	James Hahn Democrat	Hahn (53)
Houston	Orlando Sanchez Republican	Lee Brown Democrat	Brown (52)
New York—primary	Fernando Ferrer Democrat	Mark Green Democrat	Green (51)
San Francisco	Matt Gonzalez Green	Gavin Newsom Democrat	Newsom (53)
Denver	Don Mares Democrat	John Hickenlooper Democrat	Hickenlooper (65)

analysis is the precinct rather than the individual voter, this research offers more information about the institution of the precinct or political jurisdiction than about individual patterns of political behavior.

The ecological-inference problem, first noted by W. S. Robinson (1950), stems from the attempt to infer individual-level behavior from aggregate data. That is, if we find that high-density Latino precincts maintain a positive and significant relationship with voting, we cannot report with certainty that Latinos in general are voting at higher rates, even if such may be our underlying argument. Rather, we can only know that heavily Latino precincts demonstrate higher rates of overall turnout than precincts with few Latinos. To correct for this shortcoming, both Goodman (1953) and King (1997) have developed methods for dealing with ecological inference, but neither approach provides researchers with the ability to conduct multivariate analyses of turnout or candidate preference. To this extent, the first cut of data analysis employs a double-equation variation of King's ecological-inference technique to identify voting patterns by race and ethnicity in each city. While the courts have used these techniques in evaluating claims of racial bloc voting, they may not suffice for social scientists interested in voting patterns independent of partisanship, age, income, and education. For this reason, I also conduct a multivariate analysis with aggregate-level data to determine if race variables maintain a significant relationship after additional control variables are included. In addition, to get a spatial sense of the relationship between Latino candidates and the four main racial or ethnic groups in each city, scatterplots are presented for vote preference by precinct.

TABLE 5.2. Summary of Mayoral Data and Observations by City

City	Latino Mayoral Election	Comparison Election	Number of Observations
Los Angeles	June 5, 2001, mayoral runoff	March 3, 1997, mayoral general	1,730
Houston	November 2001 mayoral runoff	November 1999 mayoral general	614
New York	October 12, 2001, mayoral runoff (D)	November 4, 2001, mayoral runoff	3,449
San Francisco	November 2003 mayoral runoff	November 1999 mayoral runoff	561
Denver	December 2003 mayoral runoff	December 1999 mayoral runoff	422

Second, the basis for examining the percentage of Latinos within a precinct relies on data for both registered voters and voting-age population. Where possible, registered voter estimates are used to assess the Latino percentage within a precinct; however, such data were not available for all five cities, and U.S. Census voting-age population data were substituted. Thus, while the findings here may suggest that Latinos participate at higher rates than non-Latinos under certain electoral circumstances, this result applies only to the registered voting population. Previous studies of Latino politics have noted the low rates of voting vis-à-vis the adult population and adult citizen population (DeSipio 1996a; Pachon 1998, 1999; Sierra et al. 2000). Ramírez (2005, 2007) has recently demonstrated the effectiveness of registration and mobilization drives by Latino civic organizations, but additional studies are necessary to determine what impact, if any, the presence of Latino candidates has on narrowing the registration gap for Latinos.

The Need for a Comparison Election

A second, "base" election is useful to provide a point of comparison for the Latino electorate and is necessary to fully test my hypotheses. Thus, for each mayoral election with a Latino candidate, a second election without a Latino candidate is included.

In all five cases, the comparison election is a citywide mayoral election so that local dynamics remain constant (i.e., the same precinct boundaries and locations, uniformity in processing precinct-level results). For all cities except New York, the comparison election is the previous mayoral election—1997 in Los Angeles and 1999 in Houston, San Francisco, and Denver. In New York, the Latino candidate (Ferrer) did not win the primary, so the 2001 general election serves as the comparison election.[4] The main reason for including a comparison election is to test whether heavily Latino precincts turn out to vote at higher rates when a Latino candidate is present. However, we must also take into account the relative competitiveness of the elections, which may also influence turnout rates. I am concerned primarily with the change between elections in the standardized coefficient for the variable measuring the percentage Latino, holding citywide turnout constant.[5] We can also compare standardized coefficients for percentage Black and percentage White to determine whether the Latino candidate had a similar, greater, or lesser effect on other racial and ethnic groups.

Plan of Analysis and Description of the Data

To examine the hypotheses, I offer several approaches to test these expectations from a variety of analytical positions. Several estimates are presented, each specified with slightly different goals in mind. Two dependent variables, *Voter Preference* and *Voter Turnout,* are always used. In the first sequence of models, *Voter Preference* is the number of votes cast for the Latino candidate divided by the total number of votes cast for mayor within each precinct. In the second set of models, the dependent variable is *Voter Turnout,* measured simply as the number of total votes cast divided by the total number of registered voters within the precinct. In all vote-preference models, the two-person runoff election was used. Both *Voter Preference* and *Voter Turnout* are continuous variables, ranging theoretically from 0 to 100, and robust ordinary least squares regression techniques are used in the estimates of both.

I bring a variety of well-known measures to bear on the estimates of voter turnout and voter preference, and these independent variables are consistent for both models. The key predictor is *Percent Latino,* which is measured either (1) as the total number of Latinos registered to vote within each precinct divided by the total number of registered voters or (2) as the total number of Latino adults residing within each precinct divided by the total adult population.[6] I expect that as *Percent Latino* increases within a precinct, voter turnout and vote preference for the Latino candidate should be significantly and positively affected during the Latino mayoral elections. In comparison elections, the expectation is that the size of a precinct's Latino population is a less powerful (and perhaps negative) predictor because of the absence of a Latino candidate.

A number of control variables are included as well. Racial and ethnic variables include *Percent White, Percent Black,* and *Percent Asian,* all of which are based on voting-age population data. Additional demographic variables include *Percent Republican* and *Percent over Fifty.* Each of these measures is derived from the list of registered voters or Census Bureau data and is measured as the percentage within each precinct. Two additional demographic variables, *College* and *Income,* are taken from census-tract-level information. *College* is a calculation of the proportion of individuals within the census tract who have at least a college degree, and *Income* measures the median household income within the census tract. Finally, consistent with King's critique of Goodman related to heteroskedasticity and variance of unit size, I also control for total voter registration (*Registered*) within each precinct.

The results are presented according to the question asked—that is, *Voter Turnout* or *Voter Preference*—and the types of models employed to demonstrate the findings. I turn first to models of *Voter Preference*, initially evaluating scatterplots for precinct-level vote choice and race/ethnicity, then estimates using ecological inference, and finally multivariate ordinary least squares regression. *Voter Preference* models focus exclusively on the Latino mayoral election. Next, I examine *Voter Turnout* during the Latino mayoral election and the non-Latino mayoral election.

RESULTS: THE MOBILIZATION OF LATINO VOTERS

Vote Preference Scatterplots: Latino Candidates and Homogenous Precincts

For each of the five cities, data are brought together for percentage of the vote won by the Latino candidate and what percentage each racial or ethnic group comprises of the precinct. With these variables, it is possible to create a simple array depicting the relationship between Latino voters and Latino candidates. However, given that we have data for four major racial and ethnic groups, it is possible to disaggregate the non-Latino population to determine whether Latino candidates have a mobilizing, demobilizing, or indefinite effect on White, Black, and Asian American voters. These results are displayed in figures 5.1–5.5.

The first cut at the data is the simplest: an X–Y scatterplot that charts the percentage of the vote won by a Latino candidate (Y axis) and the percentage of Latinos within the precinct (X axis). I have superimposed homogenous racial precincts for White, Black, and Asian communities on the X axis, creating four types of precincts (heavily Latino, heavily White, heavily Black, and heavily Asian) that can be viewed on the same spectrum.[7] While this analysis is basic, it is very important. If no relationship can be found through a graphical presentation of the data, there is little value in more sophisticated ecological inference or multivariate regression techniques. The scatterplots enable us easily to compare data across all five cities, for four different ethnic groups, to determine whether there is consistency in elections with Latino candidates from the Democratic, Republican, and Green Parties.

Two trends may be observed. First, heavily Latino precincts tend to cluster together, exhibiting very similar patterns of candidate preference; second, heavily Latino precincts display high rates of support for Latino candidates, with few exceptions. Just as heavily Latino precincts tend to cluster together, so too do heavily Black and heavily White precincts. Non-Latino support for Latino candidates is not at all consistent, however, ranging from less than 10 percent to more than 80 percent. Beyond these generalizations, some interesting differences between the cities are also apparent and merit discussion.

In Los Angeles (figure 5.1), the seventy-seven heavily Latino precincts are clustered close together, all voting strongly in favor of the Latino candidate, Antonio Villaraigosa. Villaraigosa garnered between 72 percent and 91 percent of the vote in the Latino precincts, while his support in non-Latino precincts varied between 8 and 84 percent of the vote. Heavily Black precincts are clustered near the bottom left corner of the graph, almost universally providing less than 20 percent of their votes to Villaraigosa. White precincts in Los Angeles are also grouped together; support there for Villaraigosa was moderate, ranging between about 25 and 65 percent. The few heavily Asian American precincts are scattered. As the Latino population within a precinct increases, so too does the support for Villaraigosa, in a reasonably linear fashion.

Houston (figure 5.2) lacks the linear pattern found for Los Angeles. Precinct results are scattered, with the exception of heavily Latino parts of the city. Fifty-seven of the city's sixty-four heavily Latino precincts are clustered in the upper right portion of the scatterplot, signifying majority support for Orlando Sanchez. In only two heavily Latino precincts did Sanchez, a Republican, collect less than 35 percent of the vote. Among non-Latino precincts, the pattern is less clear, with Sanchez winning more than 90 percent of the vote in some but losing more than 90 percent of the vote in others. Here, Houston displays remarkably similar patterns to Los Angeles, despite the differences between the two Latino candidates. Sanchez drew strong support from both Latinos and Whites but received virtually no support in heavily Black precincts.

New York City's results (figure 5.3) conform to those of Los Angeles, at least at first glance. In the 134 high-concentration Latino precincts, the Latino candidate, Fernando Ferrer, received between 71 and 97 percent of the vote. There are no outliers among Latino precincts, with all precincts that are more than 65 percent Latino clustered closely together, demonstrating congruity in their voting patterns. Although the relationship between percentage Latino and vote for Ferrer is clearly linear, the non-Latino vote varies greatly. For example, in precincts with Latino populations of less than 10 percent, Ferrer received as little as 2 percent and as much as 97 percent of the vote. In sharp contrast to Los Angeles and Houston, a Latino-Black coalition supported New York's Latino candidate, with heavily White precincts offering little support for Ferrer. Overall, precincts are clustered tightly by race and ethnicity.

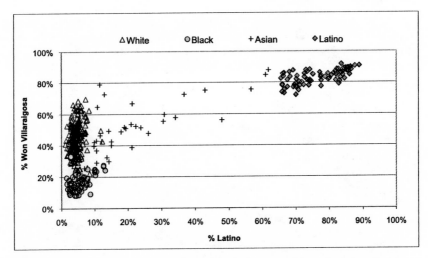

FIG. 5.1. Vote for Latino candidate by racial/ethnic composition of precinct, Los Angeles, 2001

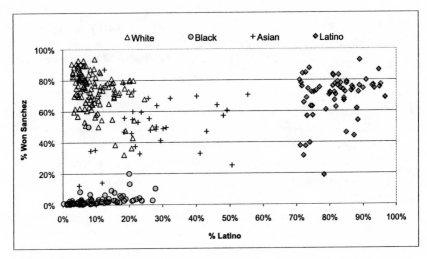

FIG. 5.2. Vote for Latino candidate by racial/ethnic composition of precinct, Houston, 2001

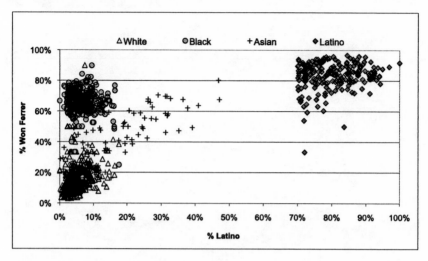

FIG. 5.3.   Vote for Latino candidate by racial/ethnic composition of precinct, New York City, 2001

San Francisco (figure 5.4) has fewer heavily Latino precincts than any of the other cities; however, the same pattern emerges there. All of the city's majority Latino precincts strongly supported the Latino candidate, Matt Gonzalez of the Green Party. In the 21 heavily Latino precincts, Gonzalez received between two-thirds and 83 percent of the vote. In fact, his highest vote totals came from heavily Latino precincts. Six Latino precincts gave Gonzalez more than 80 percent of the vote. In contrast, Gonzalez received 80 percent of the vote in only 2 of the 540 non-Latino precincts. San Francisco demonstrates less racial clustering than the cities discussed previously, although many patterns may be observed among non-Latinos. Most notably, heavily Black precincts tended to vote against Gonzalez. Only 1 of the city's 22 Black precincts voted for Gonzalez, and he only received 51 percent of the vote there. Only 3 of the 91 heavily Asian American precincts gave majority support for Gonzalez, and most gave him 45 percent or less. Heavily White precincts varied widely in their support for the Latino candidate. Precincts from the district that Gonzalez represents as a county supervisor, which are among San Francisco's most liberal, gave him strong support, while other heavily White precincts voted in favor of his White opponent.

In Denver (figure 5.5), high-concentration Latino precincts tended to vote in favor of the Latino candidate, Don Mares, although some precincts are out-

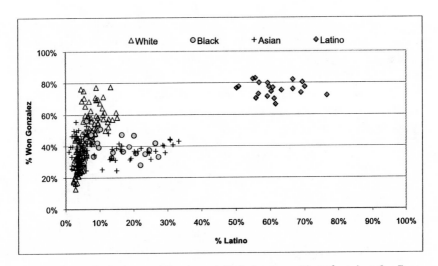

FIG. 5.4.   Vote for Latino candidate by racial/ethnic composition of precinct, San Francisco, 2003

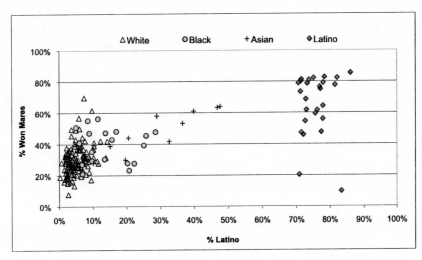

FIG. 5.5.   Vote for Latino candidate by racial/ethnic composition of precinct, Denver, 2003

liers. Twenty-seven of Denver's 34 heavily Latino precincts voted in favor of Mares. The Latino precincts generally are clustered together, and a linear pattern is present, with Mares's support level increasing along with the percentage of Latinos living there. Two heavily Latino precincts (shown in the lower right) reported very low levels of support for the Latino candidate. Nevertheless, Mares appears to have mobilized the Latino community despite trailing in the polls by more than 20 points throughout the campaign. Denver's Latino and White precincts are clustered in opposite corners of the graph. Only 3 of the city's 128 heavily White precincts supported Mares. Among Black precincts, support for Mares was moderate to low. In contrast, when Peña ran for the city's mayoralty, he received very high levels of support among the Black community (Hero 1992).

Vote Preference Regression Estimates for Latino Candidates

Figures 5.1–5.5 illustrate that heavily Latino precincts show consistent support for Latino candidates. However, these graphs do not readily indicate how Latinos in mixed or non-Latino precincts voted. Using ecological-inference techniques, we can provide point estimates for candidate support by race and ethnicity, thereby creating a sense of how each of the Latino candidates faired among Latino voters overall. Because we do not have accurate data on what percentage of the electorate was Latino in each city—the exact measure needed for precise vote-preference estimates—I used a double-equation version of King's ecological inference that takes nonvoting into account to fine-tune the independent variable, *Percent Latino*.[8] Table 5.3 shows the double-equation ecological inference results for the five cities.

Overall, Latino candidates received strong support from Latino voters, re-

TABLE 5.3. Double-Equation Ecological Inference Estimates of Support for Latino candidate (%)

	Los Angeles	Houston	New York	San Francisco	Denver
Latino	89	79	84	91	89
Non-Latino	27	43	30	40	29
Black	20	10	75	49	41
White	37	80	20	46	28
Asian	30	50	40	24	71
N	1,600	700	3,000	500	600

Note: Double-equation ecological inference employed (for more see Grofman and Merrill 2004).

gardless of party. The estimates indicate that Latino voters greatly preferred the Latino candidates in all five cities, while non-Latino support was mixed. In Los Angeles, Denver, and San Francisco, the Latino candidate received about 90 percent of the Latino vote. In New York, 84 percent of Latinos supported Ferrer, and in Houston, Sanchez received 79 percent of the Latino vote. As a general finding, the Latino population always preferred the Latino candidate, while non-Latinos as a group never voted in favor of the Latino.

Ethnicity is clearly important in understanding Latino political participation, and for a variety of reasons. First, the data are not limited to one geographic location but instead span five different cities. Second, the cities represent diverse Latino populations—Mexicans, Puerto Ricans, Dominicans, Salvadorans, and Colombians. Third, the candidates' varying Cuban, Mexican, and Puerto Rican ancestries also reflect the diversity of the Latino population. Fourth, none of the elections pitted a Latino Democrat against an Anglo Republican. Finally, Denver's inclusion means that the elections do not represent solely a series of first opportunities for Latinos to win the office of mayor.

In addition to the bivariate analysis reported in table 5.3, a more detailed multivariate regression was undertaken for each city to determine if the effects of ethnicity hold after controlling for age, education, income, and, most important, partisanship (table 5.4). For all five cities, heavily Latino precincts were statistically more likely to vote for Latino candidates, and the standardized beta coefficients suggest that ethnicity was a robust predictor of vote preference. This finding is consistent with Kaufmann's empowerment hypothesis—"In-group identification is a powerful electoral cue" (2003, 116).

In fact, *Percent Latino* is the only variable that is both statistically significant and positive across all five models. In comparison, *Percent Black* is negative in all of the models except New York, and *Percent White* is positive in Houston and San Francisco and negative or insignificant elsewhere. Thus, while Latinos consistently support Latino candidates, other coalition partners (African Americans or Anglos) may come and go depending on the local context. (The omitted racial category in the multivariate analysis is Asian and/or Other.) This finding strengthens the argument that ethnicity matters for Latinos, because other groups of voters do not show consistent results in elections when Latino candidates are present. However, this finding may also result from non-Latino opponents playing the race card and dampening Latino candidates' citywide appeal, as Reeves (1990) suggests.

Finally, the partisan dynamics in these elections provide assurances that party identification does not drive the results. In Los Angeles, New York, and

Denver, both runoff candidates were registered Democrats. Thus, it is possible that Latinos in these three cities were free to vote for the Latino candidate and that the results would not hold if a Republican candidate were present. However, if partisanship or ideology were the driving force, we would still expect Latino voters to evaluate both Democratic candidates with respect to the issues and policies at play, resulting in a more equal split between the two candidates. Multiple surveys of registered Latino voters have found strong ties to the Democratic Party but a split in ideological tendencies, with roughly equal thirds self-identifying as liberal, moderate, and conservative (Tomás Rivera Policy Institute 2000; Pew Hispanic Center 2004). Thus, we might expect conservative Latinos to select the more conservative Democrat, liberal Latinos to select the more liberal Democrat, and moderate Latinos to split their votes between the two Democrats, resulting in something close to a fifty-fifty split between the Latino and non-Latino candidates. The overwhelming Latino support for Villaraigosa, Ferrer, and Mares means that ethnicity should be

TABLE 5.4. Full Regression Model Predicting Support for Latino Candidate

	Los Angeles		Houston		New York		San Francisco		Denver	
	Coef.	Beta	Coef.	Beta	Coef.	Beta	Coef.	Beta	Coef.	Beta
Latino	.446***	.460	.224*	.188	.738***	.499	.464***	.396	.251**	.389
	(.017)		(.108)		(.024)		(.040)		(.101)	
Black	−.602***	−.693	−.376***	−.379	.289***	.313	−.156***	−.128	−.100	−.101
	(.017)		(.114)		(.020)		(.042)		(.108)	
White	.025	.046	.217*	.216	−.317***	−.390	.275***	.406	−.123	−.217
	(.014)		(.104)		(.018)		(.047)		(.102)	
Income	−.001*	−.051	.001**	.091	.048**	.027	−.001*	−.598	.001	.049
	(.000)		(.000)		(.022)		(.000)		(.001)	
College	.306***	.165	−.236***	−.168	.017	.011	.059	.073	−.229***	−.311
	(.047)		(.058)		(.018)		(.061)		(.047)	
Age (50)	−.219***	−.108	.284**	.122	−.108	−.062	−.681***	−.394	.051	.045
	(.023)		(.092)		(.095)		(.053)		(.034)	
Party (R)	−.795***	−.534	.452***	.363	−.003	−.002	−.141**	−.081	−.232***	−.161
	(.024)		(.059)		(.033)		(.051)		(.047)	
Registered	.001	.013	.001***	.096	−.001*	−.001	.001	.024	−.001*	−.058
	(.001)		(.000)		(.000)		(.001)		(.000)	
Constant	.676***	—	.156	—	.375***	—	.612	—	.587***	—
	(.019)		(.107)		(.017)				(.099)	
N	1,724		607		3,383		552		406	
Adj. R^2	.831		.766		.815		.678		.776	
Chi	3,069		890.4		5,707		633.5		616.2	

Note: Standard errors in parentheses.
*p < .05   **p < .01   ***p < .001

considered as a primary determinant of vote choice when a co-ethnic candidate is present.

In Houston and San Francisco, we would expect partisanship to work against the non-Democratic Latino candidates. Among the heavily Mexican American Latino populations in these two cities, recent literature would suggest that Democratic candidates would have the edge (Uhlaner and Garcia 2005). Indeed, evidence suggests that Latinos in Houston and San Francisco vote Democratic. In 2000, the Democratic presidential candidate, Al Gore, won 70 percent of the vote in Houston's heavily Latino precincts, and in 2002, Democratic governor Gray Davis won more than 80 percent of the vote in San Francisco's heavily Latino precincts. However, the results here show that, even after controlling for Democratic partisanship, heavily Latino precincts were statistically more likely to vote for the non-Democratic Latino candidates in these cities. This finding is consistent with recent work by Nuño (2007) that suggests that Latinos can be compelled to vote Republican only if they are mobilized by Latino Republicans, as was the case in Houston.

Voter Turnout: Comparing Latino and Non-Latino Elections

Tables 5.5 and 5.6 show the turnout results for the elections with and without Latino candidates. To assess Latino candidates' impact on turnout, two estimates are provided, similar to the candidate preference estimates. First, ecological inference is used to calculate the turnout rate among registered voters for each racial and ethnic group in all five cities. Second, for both elections, multivariate regression is performed, with coefficients and standardized beta estimates reported, to provide a comparison between the two elections. Such analysis provides answers to two compelling questions about Latino political participation. First, when Latino candidates are present, do heavily Latino precincts vote at rates higher than in elections with no Latino candidates? Second, in elections with Latino candidates, do heavily Latino precincts have higher turnouts than precincts that are predominantly White or Black? To answer the first question, we can compare standardized betas for *Percent Latino* in the two elections for each city. To answer the second question, we can compare standardized betas for different racial and ethnic groups in the election with the Latino candidate.

At first blush, table 5.5 confirms the hypotheses. In all five cities, Latino voter turnout is estimated to be higher in elections with Latino candidates. In contrast, no consistent pattern emerged for changes in turnout for non-Latinos. However, each election also reflects a different level of competitiveness and public interest; thus, we cannot read too much into the bivariate results. Table 5.6 provides a more accurate analysis. For each city, two regression models were estimated simultaneously—one for the election with no Latino candidate (E_{no}), and one for the election featuring a Latino candidate (E_{Lat}). Using Zellner's seemingly unrelated regression (1962), we can estimate both models together and then test for significant differences between coefficients and cross-equation parameter restrictions. For ease of comparability, standardized beta coefficients are reported in table 5.6. The betas allow us to make two important comparisons: (1) between the results for *Percent Latino* across time; and (2) between *Percent Latino* and *Percent Black* and *Percent White* at a single point in time.

Comparing coefficients across models further demonstrates that different electoral circumstances may lead to quite different results. Cross-model comparisons are often used to measure differences in institutions and political environments, most notably in Verba, Nie, and Kim (1978). Here, the two models contain the same independent variables, and both dependent variables measure voter turnout. Thus, comparisons across the two elections are accurate.

After controlling for a variety of other factors, heavily Latino precincts in all five cities had significantly higher voter turnout when Latino candidates were running for office. While this finding is consistent with the ecological inference analysis in table 5.5, comparing standardized beta coefficients neutralizes the potential bias of competitive elections in Latino candidate years by standardizing the slope of the equation. While the unstandardized coefficients might be misleading, the standardized betas represent the magnitude of the effect after normalizing all the independent variables within the model. In addition, using linear combinations of parameter tests, we can determine whether the change

TABLE 5.5. Estimates of Voter Turnout in Latino and Non-Latino Candidate Elections (in percentages)

	Los Angeles			Houston			New York			San Francisco			Denver		
	E_{no}	E_{Lat}	Change	E_{no}	E_{Lat}	Change	E_{no}	E_{Lat}	Change	E_{no}	E_{Lat}	Change	E_{no}	E_{Lat}	Change
Latino	29	41	12	16	22	6	19	34	15	39	44	5	25	29	4
Non-Latino	34	35	1	25	33	8	48	28	−20	44	56	12	27	23	−4
Black	32	35	3	26	35	9	29	32	3	35	35	0	25	25	0
White	34	35	1	24	30	6	54	27	−24	39	65	24	28	23	−5
Asian	25	27	2	18	18	0	18	14	−4	35	42	7	15	13	−2

Note: E_{no} represents the estimated turnout rate for each group in the election with no Latino candidate. E_{Lat} represents the estimated turnout rate for each group in the election with a Latino candidate.

TABLE 5.6.   Seemingly Unrelated Regression Model Predicting Voter Turnout in Two Elections

	Los Angeles			Houston			New York			San Francisco			Denver		
	E_{no}	E_{Lat}	E_{dif}	E_{no}	E_{Lat}	E_{dif}	E_{no}	E_{Lat}	E_{dif}	E_{no}	E_{Lat}	E_{dif}	E_{no}	E_{Lat}	E_{dif}
Latino	.185	.673	.488***	-.481	.001	.482***	-.279	.067	.346***	.056	.228	.172***	.322	.895	.573***
Black	.096	.393	.297**	.301	.329	.028**	-.220	-.017	.203***	-.193	-.231	-.040	.195	.208	.013
White	.589	.529	-.060	.425	.415	-.010**	.435	.184	-.251	.602	.551	-.051**	.862	.758	-.104**
Income	.163	-.213	-.376**	.232	.167	-.065	.266	.034	-.232	.105	.194	.089	.179	.291	.122
College	.144	.114	-.030	.099	.084	-.015	.075	.089	.014	.044	.062	.018**	.055	.074	.019
Age (50)	.175	.373	.198	.370	.119	-.261**	.234	.156	-.078	.209	.177	-.032	.298	.281	-.017
Party (R)	.073	.137	.064	.229	.112	-.117	.301	.282	-.019	.266	.183	-.083	.107	-.495	-.602
Registered	-.165	-.230	-.065	-.076	.051	.127	-.037	.203	.240	-.022	-.033	-.011	-.212	-.147	.065
Intercept	.402	.098	—	.146	.362	—	.368	.027	—	.331	.143	—	.178	.266	—
N	1,724	1,724		607	607		3,383	3,383		552	552		406	406	
Adj. R^2	.242	.348		.174	.183		.108	.135		.593	.717		.309	.284	
Chi	485.1	744.9		159.2	131.1		712.8	778.8		583.9	705.6		144.5	126.9	

Note: E_{no} represents the coefficient for each group in the election with no Latino candidate. E_{Lat} represents the coefficient for each group in the election with a Latino candidate. E_{dif} represents the difference in coefficient between the two elections.
**$p < .01$ ***$p < .001$

between betas is statistically significant. Even if the coefficients for a given variable in both model E_{no} and model E_{Lat} are significant, the difference between the two is not necessarily statistically significant, and the postestimation utilities employed allow us to conduct such a test. With this level of statistical analysis, we can say with certainty that as a precinct becomes more Latino, turnout is likely to increase greatly in elections with Latino candidates.

Without regard to the partisanship of the Latino candidates or to the local context surrounding the campaigns, Latino precincts in all five cities witnessed the largest and most consistent increases in voter turnout during elections with Latino candidates. In fact, none of the other variables in the models changed by as much or in as consistent a pattern from an election without a Latino candidate to one with a Latino candidate. While Latino candidates may have mobilizing or demobilizing effects on other groups of voters, these data reveal that shared ethnicity has a strong mobilizing effect on Latino voters.

These results contradict most research in this area but complement other studies (Gilliam and Kaufmann 1998; Kaufmann 2003) that show that Black voter turnout in Los Angeles is higher than average when a Black candidate is present and that Latinos in Denver vote at higher rates than non-Latinos when a Latino candidate is present. These findings also lend support to J. A. Garcia and Arce's suggestion that Latino turnout may be similar to and sometimes higher than that of non-Latinos as a result of "situational factors such as local personalities and ethnically defined political races, local issues compelling to Chicanos, historical patterns, and sophisticated organizational activities" (1988, 129).

In Los Angeles and Denver, the standardized betas for Latino precincts are the largest of any group, suggesting that their turnout rate was the highest. Latino voter turnout in Los Angeles had never before exceeded that of Blacks or Whites; in Denver, the Mares election saw high Latino turnout rates that echoed those found during the Peña elections in the 1980s. In New York and San Francisco, the betas for Latino precincts are higher than those for Black precincts but are only about half the size of the betas for White precincts. These two cities displayed opposite patterns with respect to the Black and White vote for the Latino candidates. Given the high levels of White voter participation, this finding might suggest either supportive or backlash mobilization in response to the Latino candidate. White voters in New York may have turned out to vote against Ferrer, while liberal Whites in San Francisco were part of the Gonzalez coalition. In contrast, highly Latino precincts in Houston reported far lower betas than those for highly Black or White precincts. While the Sanchez candidacy had a mobilizing effect on Latinos, the historically low turnout rates in Houston's Latino community may have prohibited record high turnout. Although Sanchez did well among Latino voters, a Latino Democrat might have been more successful at mobilizing Latino voters in a city where most Latino registered voters are Democrats.

Overall, the evidence from the elections featuring Latino candidates is mixed when viewed in a vacuum. Among heavily Latino precincts, voter turnout ranged from highest to lowest. However, when we compare the two elections, the picture is much clearer. In every instance, Latino precincts witnessed a significant increase in voter turnout in the elections with Latino candidates. Furthermore, even in Houston, where Latinos had lower voting rates than non-Latinos, the differential was substantially smaller when a Latino candidate was running.

Latino Candidates and Non-Latino Turnout

Although Latino precincts exhibit the clearest patterns of vote growth between E_{no} and E_{Lat}, patterns may also be observed in non-Latino precincts. In all five of the elections without Latino candidates, predominantly White precincts demonstrate the most robust standardized betas, suggesting that such precincts had the highest rates of turnout. This finding is consistent with extant literature that finds that Whites participate at higher rates than do Blacks, Latinos, or Asian Americans (e.g., Verba, Schlozman, and Brady 1995). However, heavily White precincts registered a net deficit in turnout in the elections with Latino candidates. When the interelection change in the standardized betas is calculated, White precincts demonstrated less robust betas in all five elections with Latino candidates, in part because of higher-than-average turnout in the elections without Latino candidates, a phenomenon that made it more difficult for Whites to raise their turnout rates in the Latino elections. However, this finding may also be the flip side of the coin that leads scholars to decry low rates of participation among Latinos. Co-ethnic candidates are an important mobilizing instrument because they help engage minority communities, increase minorities' opportunities to be mobilized, and perhaps increase the level of interest in elections. Elections that feature viable Latino (or Black) candidates may slightly reduce Whites' level of interest and participation rates. This finding is consistent with Barreto, Segura, and Woods's (2004) research, which showed that White turnout is lower in majority-Latino districts than in majority-White districts. This is not to say that White turnout will plummet in elections with

Latino candidates; rather, White turnout may be higher during elections featuring two White candidates—the inverse of the theory described here.

African Americans show less consistent patterns than Latinos or Whites in the ten elections under study. In Los Angeles and Houston, Latino candidates appear to have a mobilizing effect, although many pundits observed that Blacks were mobilized in opposition to the Latino candidacy in these two cities (Fleck 2001; Sonenshein and Pinkus 2002). This finding is consistent with the results of the scatterplots as well as table 5.4, all of which show heavily Black precincts voting against the Latino candidates. In Los Angeles, James Hahn had strong ties to the African American community, and his father, Kenneth Hahn, was a county supervisor in a traditionally black district. In Houston, the non-Latino candidate, Lee Brown, was an African American who was quite popular among Houston's Black community and leaders. If Black voters in these two cities viewed the Latino candidate as a potential threat to Black representation, it is reasonable to expect increased turnout in heavily Black precincts. In New York, a high percentage of Blacks supported Ferrer in the Democratic runoff; as with Latinos, the African American turnout rate dropped in the all-White general election between Mark Green and Michael Bloomberg. In San Francisco, highly Black precincts were marginally less likely to vote in the Gonzalez election, and in Denver, Black precincts exhibited an increase in turnout during the Mares election. Without a consistent pattern, it is difficult to expand significantly on the implications for Black-Brown political relationships. If anything, the data here suggest that in the absence of an overwhelming national issue that might unite or divide these two communities, Black-Brown dynamics are mediated by local context. The demographic control variables in the models perform as expected, with age, income, and education positive and significant predictors of turnout. Age and education are positive in all ten of the models estimated, while income is positive in nine.

CONCLUSION

During March, April, and May 2006, as many as 2 million Latinos took to the streets to protest immigration proposals passed by the U.S. House of Representatives and to call for respect and equality for documented and undocumented immigrants living in the United States. Without regard to nativity, immigrant status, generation, or age, Latinos of all backgrounds participated in these rallies. The implication was clear: shared ethnicity served as an overwhelming mobilizing force for many members of the Latino community. Similarly, shared ethnicity directly influences Latino vote choice. In addition, when a viable co-ethnic candidate is present, Latinos will turn out to vote at heightened rates—and in some instances, voting at rates greater than those of other ethnic and racial groups, including whites. Shared ethnicity thus serves as an important predictor of Latino political participation. Precincts with larger proportions of Latino registrants are more likely both to evidence high turnout rates when a Latino candidate is running for office and to vote for that candidate.

Under some circumstances, Latinos will turn out to vote, and race and ethnicity are less relevant determinants of candidate preference or ethnic political participation generally. Specifically, voter preferences may be directly influenced by ethnicity. As the empowerment literature (Bobo and Gilliam 1990; Tate 1993) contends, the presence of co-ethnic candidates influences minority electoral participation.

Forty years of research has suggested that Latino voter turnout cannot reach high levels. However, most of this work has involved elections that lacked viable Latino candidates at the top of the ticket, and Latino voters therefore may have felt out of touch with the predominantly Anglo candidates running for office. This study has shown that while heavily Latino precincts are unlikely to have high levels of turnout when no Latino candidate is running, the presence of a viable Latino candidate uniformly results in increased voter turnout.

The implications of these results should not be limited to the five cities discussed. The 2006 Current Population Survey reveals that minority populations are growing throughout the United States, and many large urban centers have (or will soon have) majority-minority populations. Future mayoral elections as well as statewide elections that feature co-ethnic candidates should be expected to mobilize the Latino electorate and thus have high levels of Latino voter turnout. Research has already demonstrated a mobilizing effect among Latino voters living in overlapping majority-Latino legislative districts, which are typically represented by Latino officeholders (Barreto, Segura, and Woods 2004). While ethnicity may have a stronger mobilizing effect in local (often nonpartisan) elections, when candidate attributes draw more attention from the media and voters, a mobilizing effect should also be present for Latino candidates for governorships, the U.S. Senate, and the presidency.

As the political landscape changes in the twenty-first century and Spanish-surnamed candidates become common in American elections, pundits and scholars alike will need to revisit the question of Latino and minority participation. The number of Latinos elected to U.S. municipal offices increased from 987 in 1984 to 1,624 in 2006 (64 percent). Phoenix, San Diego, Dallas, Jacksonville, Milwaukee, Boston, Las Vegas, and Washington, D.C., have growing Latino populations; each also has at least one prominent Latino elected municipal official. Other large cities, including San Antonio, El Paso, and Miami, have already documented Latino mobilization through the election of Latino mayors. However, as Latino candidates become more and more prominent, the salience of ethnicity may recede. Such changes are difficult to forecast because the politics of ethnicity is a two-way street, with both campaigns and individual voters relying on ethnic cues. Demographic projections suggest that immigration and naturalization among Latinos will continue, providing a growing Latino electorate with a sizable component of first-generation Americans. Further, given the perceived success of Spanish-language outreach and advertising by presidential candidates in 2000 and 2004, all campaigns are likely to continue using ethnic means to engage Latino voters. While Latino candidates may focus more on winning a coalition of voters through non-ethnic campaigns, their candidacies and campaigns are likely to continue to resonate with Latino voters.

Latino Candidates for State Legislature and Congress: How Multiple Co-Ethnic Candidates Affect Turnout

To this point, we have considered Latino candidates as individual political forces, running unique campaigns, and connecting with Latino voters. However, a given political candidate for office is never the only show in town. On the contrary, Americans typically go to the polls to elect numerous candidates for numerous offices, ranging from commissioner of the water board to state legislator to U.S. president. Wattenberg (2002) explains that one of the potential pitfalls of democracy is too much democracy—that is, too frequent elections with too many different political offices before the voter. Having to sort through ten or twelve different candidates for various public offices may confuse voters, resulting in roll-off or worse, nonvoting. However, a different possibility exists—particularly for Latino voters—when the multiple candidates on the ballot are co-ethnic candidates: they offer more mobilizing potential than just one co-ethnic candidate.

During the November 2002 election, Latino congressman Xavier Becerra distributed campaign mailers that supported Latino state senator Gil Cedillo, whose state senate district overlapped with Becerra's U.S. House district in Los Angeles. Cedillo, in turn, distributed campaign mailers endorsing Latino state assembly candidate Fabian Nuñez, whose district was nested within Cedillo's senate district. Each of the three Latino candidates had bilingual phone banks targeting Latino households and went door to door to talk to and rally Latino voters. To confound matters, the Republican challengers in this heavily Latino area were also Latino.[1] If one co-ethnic candidate has a mobilizing effect on Latino turnout, is this effect magnified by multiple co-ethnic candidates?

Verba, Schlozman, and Brady (1995) propose a model of political participation that moves beyond socioeconomic status and highlights the importance of civic skills, engagement, and recruitment. In addition to developing a set of civic skills that facilitate writing to Congress, volunteering for campaigns, and attending demonstrations, engagement and recruitment are important explanatory factors in political participation—specifically, voting. People lead busy lives and often have little time for political participation. However, when people become interested and engaged in political affairs or when they are asked or recruited to take part, they are more likely to be active citizens than passive bystanders.

While the Civic Participation Study extensively tests the impact of this model in self-reported acts of political participation, little work has extended the theory to official validated records of voter participation. Further, in the realm of minority politics, only recently has scholarship employed validated vote records in testing the effects of recruitment and engagement (Shaw, de la Garza, and Lee 2000; Pantoja, Ramírez, and Segura 2001; Ramírez 2007). Using county registrar of voter records, this chapter examines Latino voting patterns in California to determine whether Latino candidates affect recruitment and engagement and ultimately turnout. Specifically, I argue that Latinos are more likely to be psychologically engaged and recruited when more Latino candidates appear on the ballot, which in turn will result in a greater likelihood of voting. This effect may be even stronger for foreign-born citizens, who are less likely to be targeted by traditional campaigns and whose main interaction with politics may come from ethnically oriented media and mobilization.

UNDERSTANDING LATINO VOTER TURNOUT

Chapter 5 suggests that Latino candidates mobilize Latino voters; however, some scholars have recently called this idea into question. Manzano and Vega (2006) point out that as a result of the 2005 San Antonio mayoral election, many scholars and pundits concluded that Latino candidates do not mobilize the Latino electorate: Latino Julian Castro lost to Anglo candidate Phil Hardberger in a very competitive race, yet citywide turnout was just 19 percent. Using data from the 1996 election, Highton and Burris claim to "establish a persistent pattern of low Latino turnout" (2002, 285) even after controlling for citizenship. Some scholars even argued that low levels of Latino participation resulted from a cultural-ethnic rejection of civic participation (Nelson 1979).

Scholars have more recently attempted to reconcile the newly observed increases in Latino voting with the old theories. One of the main factors explaining Latino turnout today is mobilization. Shaw, de la Garza, and Lee (2000) find that Latinos are more likely to turn out when they are mobilized by other Latinos. Both Michelson (2003) and Ramírez (2005, 2007) demonstrate that Latinos vote at high rates when exposed to ethnic-based get-out-the-vote campaigns. Other studies have found that Latino voters in multiple and overlapping majority-Latino districts are more likely to turn out to vote (Barreto, Segura, and Woods 2004). However, that research focused only on the population dynamics within political districts, not on the presence of Latino candidates on the ballot. This chapter answers the questions of whether Latino candidates for state legislature and U.S House mobilize Latinos to vote and whether multiple Latino candidates have an additive effect.

The conventional wisdom in studies of voting suggests that minorities turn out at lower rates than Whites. Generally speaking, this deficit has been explained by minorities' lower levels of education and income and less interest in political affairs. However, many studies of participation have focused too heavily on individual-level measures such as demographic characteristics that do not go far enough in explaining Latino participation. While socioeconomic factors are a starting point for predicting both non-Latino and Latino political behavior, they explain less of the variance in models of Latino turnout, suggesting that additional variables are at play. Leighley (2001) argues that socioeconomic-status-based models are inadequate for studying Latino voting and that scholars instead should consider contextual characteristics. Although she focuses on group size and elite mobilization, candidates themselves are also an important consideration. In explaining Latino turnout, Shaw, de la Garza, and Lee argue that "resource models alone fail to account for declining turnout" (2000, 339). If traditional models fail to explain racial and ethnic minorities' political participation, scholars must turn to better methods of measurement.

Moving beyond socioeconomic status, studies have looked to community-level and mobilization variables to understand Latino participation. Following the traditional rational-choice turnout model of benefits minus costs, research on Latino voting has suggested that community mobilization rather than individual characteristics may increase the perceived benefits or reduce the costs associated with voting.

Most recently, Shaw, de la Garza, and Lee (2000) have found ethnic mobilization to be a significant explanatory factor in Latino voter turnout. In addition to socioeconomic status controls, the authors included specific measures of political contact: Latinos who had been contacted by Latino organizations were significantly more likely to vote. However, Latinos contacted by non-Latino organizations were no more likely to vote, suggesting that traditional voter mobilization does not work among Latinos and that ethnic-based outreach is the way to go. Given Leighley's assertion that ethnic candidates direct more mobilization resources toward ethnic communities, Latinos in geographic areas with more Latino candidates on the ballot should be more likely to be targeted and hence more likely to vote.

LATINO CANDIDATES, ENGAGEMENT, AND RECRUITMENT

Latinos in the United States have high immigrant numbers and low levels of political participation (DeSipio 1996a; Lien 2001). Campaign managers target get-out-the-vote drives in communities where voter payoff is likely to result, not in communities with large numbers of newly naturalized citizens or noncitizens and low numbers of registered voters. Thus, because of gaps in citizenship and voter registration, traditional campaigns often ignore potential Latino voters (Bike 1998; Shaw, de la Garza, and Lee 2000; Mendelberg 2001; Shea and Burton 2001). While the 2000 presidential election marked a watershed year in courting the Latino vote, less than 2 percent of spending on campaign ads was dedicated toward mobilizing Latinos (Doyle 2002).

If minority voters are not actively recruited through the established political avenues, it is not surprising that they show less interest and engagement with mainstream politics. However, as Dahl notes, a key component of ethnic politics is the presence of co-ethnic candidates for office, which alters the stakes for minority voters. "Politicians themselves, in fact, were often ethnics who knew from personal experience the problems of an out group" and were more likely to appeal to voters of their ethnic minority (Dahl 1961, 33). Moreover, the findings in chapter 3 demonstrate that Latino candidates increase the level of recruitment in Latino neighborhoods.

Also relevant to the argument that ethnic candidates attract more ethnic voters is Downs's (1957) economic theory of democracy. Voters often have difficulty calculating the relative utilities associated with various candidates, making the benefits of voting seem low. Thus, citizens should be expected to vote when the costs are low and the benefits are clear. Building on the idea that ethnic candidates are more closely linked to voters' ethnic groups, these candidates should reduce the costs and increase the benefits of voting for citizens of the same ethnic group.

When ethnic candidates target voter-mobilization campaigns toward co-ethnic voters, information-gathering costs are lower. Indeed, Downs outlines, one of the primary sources of political information is material distributed by candidates. Second, the information that is received may ease the decision calculus (again reducing costs) when voters learn that co-ethnic candidates are running for office and assign shared policy interests to those candidates. Because voters constantly struggle to reduce the costs of voting, information shortcuts such as candidates' race or ethnicity may represent a reliable and easy guide to determining candidate differential. When the candidate differential is calculated and the benefits associated with voting become clear, citizens become more likely to vote than to abstain. Those Latino voters who emphasize ethnic representation may be more likely to abstain in an election between two Anglo candidates if they perceive the candidate differential to be zero but may be more likely to vote when the candidate differential is clear because a Latino is running for office. Each successive co-ethnic candidate on the ballot increases the likelihood that minority voters will receive free or subsidized information from candidates and will estimate that candidate differentials exist in multiple contests. Indeed, one study has found that Latinos who have at least one Latino representative are more likely to report receiving voter mobilization during the 2000 election (Barreto et al. 2003).

Empirical studies on racial minority groups have demonstrated that minority voters become more psychologically engaged and interested in politics with co-ethnics on the ballot. Numerous studies of Black political participation have found psychological engagement to increase when Black politicians compete in elections. Bobo and Gilliam's (1990) seminal study found that Blacks in high-Black-empowerment areas (as defined by a mayor in office) are more active than both Blacks in low-empowerment areas and Whites with similar characteristics. Similarly, Dawson (1994) argues that members of racial minority groups are more likely to trust and vote for members of their groups because they share the same racialized experiences and can therefore understand and represent their interests. Looking at Black participation in the 1980s, Tate (1993) also found a direct correlation between the number of Black candidates and voter registration. As the number of Black mayors grew, Black voters began to feel a greater sense of efficacy in the political process, augmenting a sense of political optimism within the Black community. Behind this psychological engagement lay recruitment. Tate notes that Black candidates "often campaign more intensively and spend greater resources in black communities" (1991, 1161).

Similar arguments have been made with respect to Latino and Asian voting patterns. Pantoja (2005) argues that the level of interest in politics increases when Latino identities are cued. Examining LNPS data, Pantoja finds that Latinos pay more attention to elections, gather more political information, and show a higher level of political knowledge when Latino candidates are running for office. Asian Americans have also been found to turn out at higher levels with fellow Asian Americans on the ballot (Cho 1995; Ichinose and Tan 2001). Data from the 2000 elections demonstrate that Asians are likely to vote for Asian candidates regardless of partisanship (Ichinose and Tan 2001). Looking at the election for the Forty-fourth District of the California State Assembly, Ichinose and Tan have found that Asian voters overwhelmingly voted for the Democratic Chinese American candidate, Carol Liu, despite their party affiliation. However, the differences between the effects of "ethnicity" and "race" on Asian turnout become blurred as a consequence of the ethnic and cultural diversity of the Asian racial category, which raises questions about which factor has more saliency (Tam 1995; Saito 1998). However, Latinos are more cohesive than Asian Americans, and differences in national origin should not prevent group mobilization in light of Latinos' common language and heritage.

Most studies of minority candidates, however, have focused exclusively on the effects of a single minority candidate in a given election, such as for mayor (Kaufmann 2003), Congress (Cain and Kiewet 1984), or U.S. Senate (Graves and Lee 2000). Because independent elections do not take place for each level of political office, however, we must take account of the full range of minority candidates running for office, from governorships to seats on school boards. If the presence of one minority candidate has a mobilizing effect on minority voters by increasing psychological engagement and opportunities for recruitment, multiple minority candidates should have an additive mobilizing effect. In political jurisdictions that have Latino candidates, co-ethnic registered voters should be more psychologically engaged and have more opportunities to be recruited. "In other words, people may be inactive because they lack *resources*, because they lack psychological *engagement* with politics, or because they are outside of the *recruitment* networks that bring people into politics" (Verba, Schlozman, and Brady 1995, 269). While co-ethnic candidates cannot help overcome resource deficits, they may greatly increase Latino voters' engagement and recruitment.

For example, Latino candidates are running for office in Congressional District 34, State Senate District 21, and Assembly District 51, but no Latino candidates are running in Senate District 20 or Assembly District 50. If *Latino Voter 1* lives in Congressional District 34, Senate District 21, and Assembly District 51,

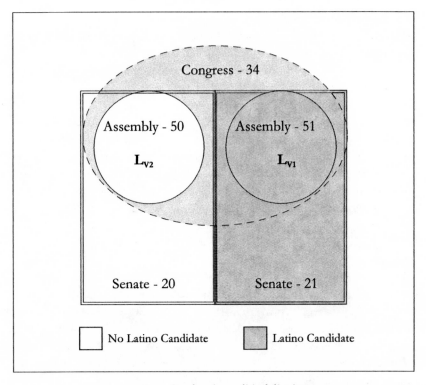

FIG. 6.1. Overlapping political districts

he or she has a chance to be engaged and recruited by three Latino candidates. Because of overlapping political boundaries, *Latino Voter 2* lives in Congressional District 34 but lives in Senate District 20 and Assembly District 50; he or she has only one Latino candidate and thus has less opportunity to be engaged and recruited (figure 6.1). To this end, this chapter tests the effect of the full range of Latino candidates on an individual voter's ballot.

Using individual-level data for the universe of more than 5 million registered voters in California's Los Angeles and Orange Counties, regression models are estimated for voter turnout in the November 2002 general election. A unique measure for engagement and recruitment is introduced: the number of Latino candidates—both incumbents and challengers—who appear on the ballot for each jurisdiction in the data set. This information is then matched to individual voters based on their state assembly, state senate, and U.S. House districts, providing a unique count of the number of Latinos each voter had the opportunity to elect (engagement) and be contacted by (recruitment). I also include the degree of newspaper readership for each precinct, providing a level of political knowledge and information for each household.

Using these variables as proxies for engagement and recruitment, I expect that the probability of Latino voting will increase along with the number of co-ethnic candidates on the ballot. Further, the effect may be stronger among foreign-born naturalized voters, who are the most likely to be linguistically segregated from the general political process as well as the most likely to gather most of their political information from within their ethnic communities. A co-ethnic candidate will likely use social networks with which foreign-born voters come into contact, thereby encouraging greater engagement.

DATA AND METHODOLOGY

This chapter brings together a unique combination of official government records, election results, and lists of Spanish surnames to identify Latino citizens' voting patterns. While Verba, Schlozman, and Brady (1995) employ survey data, their results suffer from two common methodological problems that this chapter avoids. First, survey data rely on self-reported accounts of political participation, and people tend to overreport, thereby confusing models that seek to predict acts of participation, especially voting. Second, most surveys have very small samples of Latino respondents. In fact, the Voice and Equality data set provides only 300 Latino interviews, and the 2000 American National Election Study includes only 110 Latino observations. In contrast, the data used here employ real voting records for more than 5 million registered voters in Southern California, including 1.2 million Latinos.[2] The large data set is important because it circumvents potential problems related to multicollinearity of interaction variables from which smaller data sets suffer. Variance inflation tests were run for each estimate, and in all cases, the tolerance levels are well above levels associated with problematic multicollinearity.[3]

In examining voter turnout in the November 2002 general election, databases of registered voters with vote history were acquired from the Los Angeles and Orange County registrars of voters. An ideal study site, the Southern California area is home to the largest Latino community in the United States—5.5 million people as of 2002. Examining the November 2002 election in Southern California is significant for many reasons. First, the area featured more than thirty Latino candidates running for many different levels of federal and state offices. Second, because of the plethora of ethnic community networks, ethnic candidates can easily locate avenues through which to attempt to engage and mobilize Latino voters. Third, because no presidential election took place in 2002, no strong national media attention on two major candidates entered voters' households. Mobilization in midterm elections is usually left to individual candidates. In particular, the November 2002 election in California attracted scant attention because voters had little enthusiasm for either major candidate for governor and expressed low levels of interest in the gubernatorial election (Barabak 2002a; Barabak 2002b; Brownstein 2002; Pasco and LeTran 2002). This lack of attention and interest increases our confidence that the mobilizing effects of ethnic candidates within their ethnic groups resulted from the candidates themselves rather than external contextual factors. And the lack of interest and controversial ballot initiatives pressured ethnic candidates to mobilize their voter bases. Further, as more co-ethnic candidates are options on Latino voters' ballots, more mobilization efforts should be channeled into their neighborhoods and households. The type and context of this election, therefore, help augment the environment to test whether ethnic candidates have a mobilizing effect on co-ethnic voters.

To identify Latino registered voters, lists of ethnic surnames were merged with voting records, a practice common in studies of ethnic voting (Himmelfarb, Loar, and Mott 1983; Uhlaner, Cain, and Kiewiet 1989; Tam 1995; Pantoja and Woods 2000; Barreto, Segura, and Woods 2004). Latino registrants are identified via the U.S. Census Spanish Surname Database.[4] In addition, Asians are identified by way of lists of Chinese, Korean, Japanese, Vietnamese, Indian, and Filipino surnames.[5] The registration data also include place of birth and allows us to flag foreign-born naturalized citizens. In addition, age, gender, marital status, date of registration, and party affiliation are included from the registration database at the individual level.

To supplement this data, socioeconomic variables from the U.S. Census, Summary File 3, are merged into the database at the census-tract level. Median income and percentage of those with college educations are based on the averages for the census tract in which the registrant resides and assigned to each person within the tract. Further, to identify African American registrants, I include a variable that estimates the probability that a voter is Black (see Barreto, Segura, and Woods 2004). After excluding all registered voters with Latino and Asian surnames, it is possible to assign the Black percentage of the population in the precinct to all remaining voters. To control for level of information and interest in politics, per capita newspaper readership is included, at the zip code level, for four large regional publications (the *Los Angeles Times,* the *Orange County Register,* the *Los Angeles Daily News,* and *La Opinión*).[6] Despite declining levels of newspaper readership in American cities today (Putnam 2000, 219–20), interest in news and political affairs remains one of the best predictors of political participation (Wattenberg and Brians 1999; Milner 2001). When working with individual-level voter records, contextual data such as per capita newspaper readership is an innovative and appropriate way to control for this known predictor of turnout (Dill 1995). Previous research in Wichita, Kansas, found that, "where the Wichita Eagle has heavy readership, voter turnout increased, even as it decreased across the state" (Dill 1995).

Finally, the key independent variable, which seeks to tap psychological engagement and recruitment into politics, is the list of ethnic candidates running for each level of office in the 2002 election. Election results from the California secretary of state and both county election offices provided the necessary information on the candidates to reconstruct the ballot that each voter received on Election Day. The number of Latino candidates was counted for three key levels of public office: U.S. House, state senate, and state assembly.[7] The number of ethnic candidates running for more than forty different elected offices was counted to determine how many Latino candidates each individual voter had a chance to elect (table 6.1). Because the 2002 midterm election included statewide offices, the candidates for U.S. Congress and the state legislature drew more attention and were better equipped to mobilize voters.

To gauge Latino candidates' effect on Latino voters, an interaction variable was created for voters' ethnicity and the number of ethnic candidates. The interaction variable, when combined with the original ethnicity variable and the direct effect for number of candidates, yields the net effect of ethnic candidates on Latino voters. In the two-county area, the number of Latino candidates on voters' ballots ranged considerably. Table 6.2 shows the distribution of voters and candidates by ethnicity. As expected, Latino voters are more likely to live in areas where more ethnic candidates are running for office. For example, 24 percent of Latinos had four high-level Latino candidates on their ballot, whereas only 7 percent of non-Latinos lived in areas where so many Latinos were running for office.

Because the dependent variable—turnout—is dichotomous, probit regression is used to estimate the relationship between ethnic candidates and voter turnout. The resulting probit coefficients are not readily interpretable in the same manner as ordinary least squares results. Thus, postestimation analysis is used to transform the coefficients into predicted probabilities, and minimum-

TABLE 6.1. Summary of Latino
Candidates by Office

Office	Number of Latinos
U.S. House	11
State senate	5
State assembly	15
Total	31

TABLE 6.2. Distribution of Latino
Voters by Number of Latino Candidates

Federal/State Latino Candidates		
Number	Non-Latino (%)	Latino (%)
0	52.1	31.1
1	23.5	13.7
2	9.5	13.8
3	7.8	16.1
4	6.6	23.7
5	0.5	1.6
Total		
15	100	100

to-maximum-change estimates are reported (Long 1997; Long and Freese 2001).

While this chapter employs a unique data set containing the complete universe of registered voters in Southern California, the data have limitations. First, although lists of Latino and Asian surnames are frequently used, they are not exact measures of race and ethnicity. Interracial marriage and multiraciality may result in some citizens with "ethnic" surnames who do not self-identify as either Latino or Asian or in citizens with nonethnic surnames who do self-identify as one of those minorities. However, the large number of immigrants in the Latino and Asian communities in Los Angeles and Orange Counties means that the surname lists may be more accurate in this environment than elsewhere. Further, the results are limited by the geographic focus of Southern California; different patterns of ethnic voting may be found elsewhere. Segura and Woods (2007) have found a similar mobilizing effect for Latinos in majority-minority districts in New York. Further, focusing only on U.S. House election, Barreto and Branton (2006) suggest that Latino congressional candidates mobilize Latinos in contexts outside of California. Thus, although the data presented in this chapter are limited to California, similar patterns are beginning to emerge across the nation.

MORE LATINO CANDIDATES EQUALS MORE MOBILIZATION

The regression results provide additional evidence that Latino candidates mobilize Latino voters. While Latinos tended to vote at lower rates than non-Latinos, the presence of Latino candidates greatly increased Latino turnout in California, with each subsequent ethnic candidate providing an additional expected increase in the turnout rate.

Latinos generally were less likely than non-Latinos to turn out in the 2002 election, as indicated by the negative and statistically significant coefficient for *Latino* in table 6.3. The presence of Latino candidates, however, had a clear mobilizing effect on Latino voters, and that effect did not hold for non-Latinos. This finding suggests that the presence of additional Latino candidates continues to increase the likelihood that Latinos will vote and demobilizes non-Latinos. When the interaction term (*Latino × Latino Candidates*) is included, the coefficient for *Latino Candidates* (the direct effect) assumes that the remainder of the electorate in the district is non-Latino, and its negative coefficient tells us that non-Latinos are less likely to vote when more Latinos appear on the ballot.[8]

Because of the nonlinearity of the equation, the coefficient results cannot easily be interpreted without postestimation analysis. In addition to probit coefficients, changes in predicted probability are presented for each variable to allow us to assess the relative weight of each independent variable (Long and Freese 2001). Based on these calculations, registered Latino voters who had five Latino candidates on their ballot were 15.2 percent more likely to vote than if they had no Latino candidates on their ballots.[9]

Beyond the ethnic-candidate explanation, the resource, life cycle, and political variables also predict Latino voter turnout. Voting history for 1998, age, marital status, and party affiliation are all positively related to voter turnout in 2002. The newspaper readership contextual variable is also a good predictor of turnout, with high-readership zip codes 15 percent more likely to vote. Overall, the model performs well, correctly predicting 70 percent of cases.

While the regression results and postestimation analysis in table 6.3 are informative, predicted probabilities were estimated to consider the full effect of each successive Latino candidate on Latino and non-Latino voter turnout (figure 6.2). The solid line represents the estimated or predicted turnout rate for Latinos given the number of Latino candidates on their ballots. The dashed line represents the predicted turnout rate for non-Latinos under the same circumstances. On the left side of the figure, when zero Latino candidates are present, non-Latinos have a much higher rate of voting than do Latinos. However, with the addition of each successive Latino candidate, the expected rate of non-Latino voting goes down, ultimately falling by more than 10 points. In contrast, the expected Latino turnout rate increases; the two lines converge when two co-ethnics are running, and as the number of co-ethnic candidates further in-

TABLE 6.3. Probit Regression Estimates with Latino Interactions of Voter Turnout in 2002

	Coef.	MinMax
Voted in 1998	.876	.244
	.001	
Latino	−.085	−.088
	.002	
Latino candidates	−.055	−.099
	.001	
Latino × Latino	.043	.152
candidates	.001	
Asian	−.102	−.026
	.003	
Probability Black	−.133	−.037
	.003	
Female	−.027	−.014
	.001	
Age	.011	.333
	.001	
Registration date	.005	.271
	.001	
Percent college	−.181	−.066
	.009	
Median income	−.001	−.050
	.000	
Democrat	.113	.024
	.002	
Republican	.164	.048
	.002	
Married	.281	.083
	.001	
Newspaper readership	.003	.154
	.000	
Constant	−12.026	
	.191	
N		4,602,439
ML R^2		.175
Percentage predicted correctly		.699
Prop. reduction error		.319

Note: All values are significant at $p < .001$.

The Min/Max value reports the predicted probability that the dependent value will take on a value of 1 (i.e., the registrant voted) rather than 0 when the independent variable is adjusted from its minimum to its maximum value.

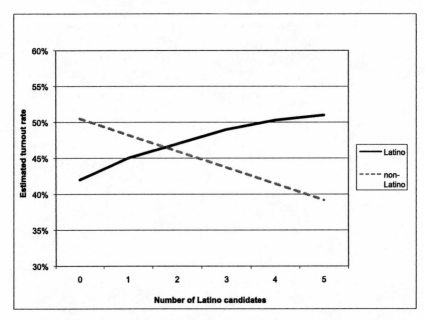

FIG. 6.2. Effect of Latino candidates on Latino and non-Latino turnout, November 2002 election, Southern California

creases, Latinos outvote non-Latinos. When five Latinos are running for office (the situation in three heavily Latino districts), Latinos are expected to turn out at rates 10 points higher than those for non-Latinos, a finding that is consistent with previous work focusing on majority-Latino districts, not necessarily the candidates (Barreto, Segura, and Woods 2004).

To investigate the dynamics within the Latino community, I now analyze Latino voters alone. The mobilizing effects of ethnic candidates are expected to be stronger for naturalized citizens and in Spanish-dominant neighborhoods. Immigrants are likely to have higher levels of ethnic attachment and to be more open to minority candidates' ethnic appeals. Latino candidates are more likely to campaign in Spanish, creating opportunities to mobilize Spanish-speaking Latinos that English-only campaigns miss. I use two models for predicting Latino turnout that examine the interactions between the number of Latino candidates and (1) foreign birth and (2) the percentage of Spanish speakers in the census tract (table 6.4). In both models, foreign-born and Spanish-dominant Latinos are significantly more likely than native-born Latinos to vote. This result is counterintuitive, running contrary to a plethora of research on Latino voting patterns (Pachon 1991; de la Garza, Menchaca, and DeSipio 1994; DeSipio 1996a; Shaw, de la Garza, and Lee 2001; Mollenkopf, Olson, and Ross 2001; Cassel 2002). Higher voting rates for naturalized Latinos may result from political attacks during the 1990s on California's Latino immigrants—three statewide ballot initiatives, Pete Wilson's 1994 reelection bid for governor, and multiple legislative attempts to restrict immigrants' rights. The results included an increase in citizenship, voter registration, and voter mobilization drives within the foreign-born Latino community (Pantoja, Ramírez, and Segura 2001). Many immigrants gained a new appreciation for the ballot box during this contentious period (Segura, Pachon, and Falcon 1997; Barreto and Woods 2005). In fact, Ramírez (2007) has found that those immigrants who first registered to vote during this period are much more likely to sustain high levels of participation than other cohorts of Latino voters. Antonio Villaraigosa's 2001 mayoral campaign in Los Angeles also witnessed massive registration and get-out-the-vote campaigns targeted at foreign-born, first-time Latino voters. Labor unions as well as nonprofit groups such as the Southwest Voter Registration and Education Project and the National Association of Latino Elected and Appointed Officials put thousands of hours into mobilization campaigns targeted at naturalized citizens. The 2002 contest was mild compared to the previous eight years of campaigns. Native-born Latino voters may have acted in a traditional manner, consistent with the full California electorate, which posted a record low level of voter turnout in 2002 (Barabak 2002b; Brownstein 2002). However, foreign-born voters, potentially more appreciative of the right to vote, may have cared less about the dull candidates for governor and more about the Latino candidates for state legislature and Congress. Indeed, the groups that conducted get-out-the-vote efforts targeted at naturalized Latino voters in 2001 increased their efforts in 2002, which in turn may have heightened foreign-born voters' interest in ethnic campaigns.

Latino immigrant voters also experienced higher levels of turnout where co-ethnic candidates were on the ballot. In the first model, Foreign Born, the interaction term for *Latino Foreign* × *Latino Candidates* is positive for naturalized Latino voters. For foreign-born Latino voters, increases in the number of Latino candidates on the ballot increase the likelihood of turnout by 7.6 percent. In contrast, the direct effect for the variable *Latino Candidates,* which assumes the result for native-born Latinos, is negative. While table 6.3 suggests that Latino voters were more mobilized by Latino candidates than were non-Latino voters, table 6.4 suggests that among Latinos, the effect was much

TABLE 6.4. Probit Regression Estimates of Voter Turnout in 2002 among Latinos Only, Foreign Born × Latino Candidate and Percent Spanish × Latino Candidate Interactions

Independent Variables	Foreign Born		Percent Spanish	
	Coef.	MinMax	Coef.	MinMax
Voted in 1998	.735	.238	.734	.237
	.003		.003	
Latino candidates	−.019	−.029	−.032	−.046
	.001		.002	
Latino foreign	.210	.051	.223	.015
	.004		.003	
Latino foreign × Latino candidates	.007	.076	—	—
	.002			
Percent Spanish	.286	.067	.179	.057
	.011		.015	
Percent Spanish × Latino Candidates	—	—	.043	.089
			.004	
Female	.023	.021	.024	.021
	.003		.003	
Age	.012	.418	.012	.416
	.001		.001	
Registration date	.013	.177	.013	.177
	.001		.001	
Percent college	.060	.032	.010†	.009
	.026		.026	
Median income	.005	.039	.005	.036
	.001		.001	
Democrat	.250	.045	.249	.044
	.003		.003	
Republican	.198	.019	.198	.019
	.004		.004	
Married	.207	.064	.205	.062
	.003		.003	
Newspaper readership	.003	.111	.003	.112
	.000		.000	
Constant	−27.669		−27.477	
	.475		.475	
N	1,157,676		1,157,676	
ML R^2	.145		.142	
Percentage predicted correctly	.722		.714	
Lambda–P	.285		.277	

Note: All values are significant at $p < .001$, except †.

stronger for the foreign-born. Looking at the second model, Percent Spanish, the same results emerge. Independent of nativity, Latinos residing in census tracts that are Spanish-dominant were far more mobilized by Latino candidates than were Latinos in English-dominant census tracts.

DISCUSSION

In their study of psychological engagement and recruitment in politics, Verba, Schlozman, and Brady (1995) find that minorities are less likely to be engaged or asked to participate and as a result are less politically active. Engagement with the political process and recruitment into its formal and informal channels are important factors in predicting whether an individual eventually will participate. Given the appropriate political context, such as the presence of ethnic candidates for office, minorities are likely to be engaged and recruited and ultimately to participate. As Dahl (1961) noted more than forty years ago in New Haven, Connecticut, ethnic candidates are likely to target their campaigns at ethnic voters. His finding holds true for a new wave of ethnic candidates in 2002 in Los Angeles and Orange Counties. Specifically, Latino candidates for office have a mobilizing effect for Latino registered voters. Further, the result is stronger for foreign-born and Spanish-dominant Latino voters, who may have a higher degree of ethnic attachment and be more persuaded to vote when co-ethnic candidates are on the ballot.

Chapter 5 demonstrates that mayoral elections with Latino candidates have significant mobilizing effects on Latino voters, and the results in this chapter confirm that this pattern of mobilization holds for state legislative and congressional elections. In addition to the governorship, control of the state legislature was on the line in 2002, and Latino legislative candidates spent more than $10 million on their campaigns. In addition, a record eleven Latinos ran for the U.S. House in Southern California alone, while twenty Latinos ran for the state legislature. These thirty-one Latino candidates seemed to carry great influence with Latino voters but no influence with non-Latinos. These candidates were generally well funded and well organized, allowing them to direct more campaign resources toward voters. Since 1994, a fund-raising and mobilization network has solidified among California's Latino elites, especially as more Latinos run for and win elected office (Pachon 1999; National Association of Latino Elected Officials 2002).

CHAPTER 7

¿Viva Bill Richardson? Latino Voters and the 2008 Presidential Election

"I won't be running as a Hispanic candidate, I am running as an American—proud to be Hispanic, proud of my heritage. Ours is a growing, dynamic community in America. But I won't just be focusing on Hispanic issues or only trying to get the Hispanic vote."
—BILL RICHARDSON, April 2007

On January 20, 2007, William Blaine Richardson III made history by announcing his intention to run for president of the United States. Richardson, the governor of New Mexico, became the first credible Latino candidate for the U.S. presidency. After the first few "exploratory" months of the campaign, Richardson returned to Los Angeles, his birthplace, on May 21 to announce his official candidacy in a bilingual address delivered while Richardson was surrounded by prominent Latino officials. Standing on the same stage at the Biltmore Hotel where John F. Kennedy had accepted the 1960 Democratic presidential nomination, Richardson opened his speech with the words, "Con orgullo, espero ser el primer presidente latino de los Estados Unidos [With pride, I hope to be the first Latino president of the United States]." The heavily Latino crowd erupted in cheers before Richardson had said anything in English.

The notable Latinas and Latinos on stage with Richardson included Gloria Molina, the first Latino elected to the Los Angeles County Board of Supervisors and chair of the 2000 Democratic National Convention; California state senator Gilbert Cedillo; and Edward Romero, former U.S. ambassador to Spain. Henry Cisneros, the former mayor of San Antonio and former U.S. secretary of housing and urban development, and other prominent Latinos sent their congratulations and endorsements. While Richardson was certain to elicit interest, enthusiasm, and support from the Latino community, he also faced a significant obstacle in mobilizing Latino voters for his long-shot presidential bid—Senator Hillary Rodham Clinton. Despite a long career in public service, Richardson lacked the name recognition possessed by prior minority candidates such as the Reverend Jesse Jackson, who garnered between 80 and 90 percent of the African American vote in 1984 and 1988 (Tate 1993). In 1988, when Jackson won eleven state primaries, he was not campaigning against a Democratic candidate already well known and popular among Blacks, as Clinton was. Richardson thus faced a far more significant challenge. Although he garnered attention as a Latino candidate, many observers questioned whether he would mobilize the Latino community. Would Latinos throw their support to Richardson in the way Blacks had supported Jackson? Would Richardson's Anglo surname create confusion and questions for Latino voters? In Richardson's words, he had "a slight problem . . . with the electorate—Hispanics don't know I'm Hispanic." Further, against the backdrop of growing anti-immigrant sentiment, would a Latino candidate be able to campaign as a Latino, or would he shy away from the Latino vote? This chapter explores the role of shared ethnicity in presidential politics, a question that has never before been addressed vis-à-vis the Latino electorate. Some scholars have argued that ethnic politics is limited to local elections, where patronage and ethnic loyalties are more likely to be visible (see chapter 5). However, as the Jackson candidacy demonstrated and as Tate (1993) makes very clear, ethnic politics may have a place in the presidential arena as well. Analysis of Richardson's presidential campaign, policy positions, and support from Latino voters suggests that shared ethnicity played an important and mobilizing role in the first Latino presidential bid. Although he did not win the nomination, his candidacy highlights the importance of the Latino electorate and Richardson's status as a newly established national Latino leader.

¿QUIÉN ES BILL RICHARDSON?

William Blaine Richardson III was born in Pasadena, California, in 1947 but moved to Mexico City as a newborn. Richardson's mother, María Luisa López-Collada, was born and still resides in Mexico. His father, William Blaine Richardson Jr., a banker originally from Massachusetts, had settled in Mexico, where he met and married López-Collada. Although many accounts describe Richardson as "half" Latino, his paternal grandmother, Rosaura Ojeda Medero, was also Mexican, and his father was born in Nicaragua and lived there until he reached age fifteen, when he moved to Boston for high school and college. Bill

Richardson's paternal grandfather, however, could trace his ancestry to the Mayflower Pilgrims. William Richardson Sr. was a well-known naturalist who studied plants and animals in Central America, where he met and married Ojeda Medero. Bill Richardson describes his upbringing in Mexico as bicultural and bilingual and as rooted in strong family ties. Each year, the Richardson family would host a large Fourth of July with hamburgers, hotdogs, and fireworks. In addition, the family proudly celebrated September 16, the Mexican Independence Day. Both Bill Richardson and his sister, Vesta Luisa, were raised as Mexican Americans, not as Americans living in Mexico.

Richardson returned to the United States to attend Middlesex High School in Concord, Massachusetts. An outstanding high school baseball player, he had the opportunity to play in the minor leagues but instead chose to follow in his father's footsteps and attend Tufts University, where he earned a bachelor's degree in French and political science and a master's degree in international studies. Richardson subsequently took jobs with the State Department and the Senate Foreign Relations Committee, developing a keen interest in foreign affairs and electoral politics. In 1978, Richardson moved to Santa Fe, New Mexico, and took on Republican incumbent Manuel Lujan in the First Congressional District. Despite his complete anonymity in New Mexico, Richardson came close to defeating Lujan. When redistricting took place after the 1980 census, northern New Mexico received a new congressional district, and Richardson won the seat in 1982 with 65 percent of the vote. Richardson served in Congress for the next fifteen years, distinguishing himself as a strong advocate for civil rights and civil liberties and as a proponent of issues involving Latinos and Native Americans, New Mexico's two significant minority groups. Richardson was elected chair of the Hispanic Caucus during his first term in the House, and in 1990, he became the first chair of the Subcommittee on Native American Affairs. According to Richardson, "My heritage was central to my identity, and I was proud of it." In 1993, during debates on the North American Free Trade Act, Richardson gave a speech on the House floor criticizing H. Ross Perot's anti-Mexican rhetoric as "outrageous and an insult to Mexico and an insult to Hispanic Americans.... [T]he Hispanic American community ... will not sit back and let Ross Perot get away with his racist rhetoric anymore." As he gained seniority, Richardson became more involved in foreign affairs. In the summer of 1994, he began negotiations with Haitian general Raoul Cédras to allow the democratically elected Jean-Bertrand Aristide to return to power. In December 1994, Richardson negotiated the release of two U.S. helicopter pilots shot down in North Korea; two years later, North Korean officials called him back to discuss another American prisoner release. In 1995, he traveled to Baghdad and arranged the release of two American aerospace workers who had been captured by Saddam Hussein's government.

In 1997, President Bill Clinton appointed Richardson as the U.S. ambassador to the United Nations, a post for which he won unanimous Senate confirmation. A year later, he became secretary of energy, remaining in that position until the end of Clinton's second term. Richardson subsequently became a senior fellow at the U.S. Institute of Peace and served as a negotiator with North Korea on issues of nuclear energy. In 2002, Richardson handily defeated Republican John Sanchez to become governor of New Mexico. It was the first time two Latino candidates had faced off in a gubernatorial general election, and the campaign included a Spanish-language debate between the two men. While serving as governor, Richardson maintained his influence in international affairs. President George W. Bush capitalized on Richardson's ties to North Korea by asking him to continue in his negotiating role with officials from that country, and a delegation from Pyongyang visited a mountain retreat in Santa Fe in 2003. In 2005, Bush again asked Richardson to lead a diplomatic mission to North Korea for discussions regarding nuclear energy. In November 2006, Richardson was reelected to the New Mexico governorship, taking 68 percent of the vote to John Dendahl's 32 percent, the largest margin of victory in the state's history. Ten weeks later, Richardson announced the formation of his presidential exploratory committee.

THE LATINO VOTE IN 2008

The 2008 presidential election promised to be the most significant to date for Latino voters. Latinos were the fastest-growing segment of the American electorate; Latinos had an important presence in battleground states such as New Mexico, Florida, Nevada, and Colorado; and Richardson was making a bid to become the first Latino president. In addition, the front-loaded primary schedule offered Richardson an opportunity to mobilize Latino voters early.

The first contest, the Iowa caucus, was held on January 3; within the first thirty-six days of the year, twenty states held their primaries, meaning that the nomination might be decided as early as Super Tuesday, February 5, a full eight months before the November general election. Some pundits argued that shortening the primary season did voters a disservice, leaving them with less time to get to know the candidates and become informed. However, the plethora of early primaries gave Latino voters a meaningful say in nominating the candidate. Many states with significant Latino populations moved up their primary dates, leading Richardson and the other seven Democratic hopefuls to begin a vigorous campaign for Latino votes a full year and a half before the general election. In previous elections, both Democratic and Republican candidates had seemed to ignore the Latino vote until the final months of the campaign (DeSipio and de la Garza 2004). Nevertheless, Latinos were among the most prized swing voters in the 2004 presidential election. The candidates spent more than $10 million on Spanish-language television commercials alone, a remarkable figure considering that the contest was not competitive in California, Texas, and New York (Segal 2006).

In Iowa, New Hampshire, and South Carolina, the states that traditionally hold the first primaries, Latino voters account for less than 1 percent of the electorate. In 2008, however, the other states that moved up their primaries included Nevada (where Latinos comprise 15 percent of the electorate), Arizona (18 percent), California (30 percent), Colorado (16 percent), New Mexico (35 percent), and New York (10 percent) (table 7.1).[1] The revised primary system required candidates in the primary election to campaign for Latino votes, hire Latino staff and consultants, and air Spanish-language campaign commercials. And Richardson was uniquely positioned to conduct outreach to Latino voters. His biggest obstacle was getting his name and his story to Latino voters. Candidates began to court Latino voters during the summer and fall of 2007, and Univision televised a Democratic debate entirely in Spanish. This new early focus on Latino voters enabled Richardson to move from relative obscurity to a household name among Latino voters.

TABLE 7.1.   Early States with Significant
Latino Population in 2008

State	Primary Date	Percentage Latino of Democratic Vote
Nevada	Jan. 19	15
Florida	Jan. 29	11
Arizona	Feb. 5	18
California	Feb. 5	30
Colorado	Feb. 5	16
Illinois	Feb. 5	10
New Jersey	Feb. 5	12
New Mexico	Feb. 5	35
New York	Feb. 5	10

MI FAMILIA CON RICHARDSON

On July 20, 2007, Bill Richardson made his tenth visit to Nevada and unveiled his plan to target Latino voters, Mi Familia con Richardson (figure 7.1). The first of the candidates to devise such a plan, Richardson announced this initiative in a bilingual address to supporters and the media at Bally's Hotel in Las Vegas, where the Democratic National Committee was hosting the Joint Unity Summit on minority issues. Following the announcement, Richardson visited a union labor site and delivered a thirty-minute speech entirely in Spanish asking Latinos to support his candidacy, outlining plans for immigration reform, and promising to champion equality for immigrants.

Instead of promoting a generic "Latinos por . . ." slogan, as previous campaigns had done, Richardson used his Latino heritage to make a more authentic campaign connection. On the one hand, Mi Familia showed insight into the Latino community by promoting a family-based message; on the other hand, it reminded Latino voters that Richardson is part of *la familia*—that he is Latino. As Christine Trujillo, a senior Richardson adviser, explained, Richardson "can come up here and do his job and he can be Mi Familia. He represents us well." Richardson represented the Latino community without showing off his ethnicity and without the pomp and circumstance that usually accompanies non-Latino candidates who campaign in the barrio. In an August 2007 speech in Iowa, Richardson lamented traditional campaigns' lack of understanding of Latino voters: "The Democratic leaders would ask me, 'Well, how are we going to appeal to Latinos?' And you know they had the traditional way of doing things, they'd get rallies together, they'd get mariachis, the Mexican food, a lit-

FIG. 7.1. Richardson's family-based campaign to target Latino voters

tle dancing, and that was it. That's not the way to appeal to Latinos. You've got to talk issues. You have to appeal to Latinos as mainstream Americans and also as bilingual and bicultural Americans."

When the campaign unveiled its Latino outreach plan, Richardson outlined the importance of Mi Familia, oscillating between English and Spanish and between generic and ethnic appeals. Television cameras from Univision and CBS recorded the speech, and reporters from the Associated Press and *La Prensa* jotted down notes. After Trujillo's introduction, Richardson began speaking: "*Muchisimas gracias—que viva* Mi Familia con Richardson. *Que honor que esta con ustedes, con latinos de todos estados unidos.* What Mi Familia is, it's real, it's authentic and it's the future—the Latino community in America is the future." Richardson went on to explain his qualifications for the presidency, including his Hispanic heritage on the list because, as he frequently explained, his bicultural tradition was a unique asset in twenty-first-century multicultural America. "Some of the presidential candidates say they represent change. Other presidential candidates say they represent experience. With me, you get change and experience. As an ambassador, as a former congressman, as a secretary of energy, as a governor, and as a Latino, all my life I've tried to bring people together."

Richardson and other Latino candidates for higher-level office frequently face the charge that they represent only Latinos. Thus, such campaigns face the challenge of resonating with all voters yet maintaining a special appeal to Latinos. Richardson's announcement made clear his status as more than just the Latino candidate: "I'm running for president because I believe I can bring people together. I'm running for president for all Americans, but I'm proud of being Latino, I'm enormously proud of being Latino. . . . *Y yo se porque los Latinos vamos a ganar este eleccion* [And it is because of Latinos that I am going to win this election]. And I am looking forward to a very strong Latino turnout in some of the early states." Richardson repeatedly described himself as a candidate for all Americans, with a campaign focusing on all fifty states and Americans from all walks of life. But he also did not avoid Latino outreach. While other campaigns paid lip service to Latino voters, making a few speeches but sometimes failing to follow through by organizing and mobilizing Latinos, Richardson declared that his campaign staff would "do everything we can to reach out to Latino voters, and with Mi Familia, the concept of family, *familia*, neighborhood, church, bringing America together. We are going to organize family units all around this country." Richardson closed the announcement by urging Latinos to unite and asking them to support him, invoking the familiar and popular image of the American Dream: "*La razon porque estamos aqui es para que todos latinos en American se junten con mi familia con Richardson, les pido su apoyo.* The American Dream is for everyone."

In addition, many of Richardson's top campaign advisers and staff were Latino. Ray Martinez served as the Nevada state campaign chair, and Rick Hernandez held the post of senior adviser. Trujillo, president of the AFL-CIO of New Mexico and a longtime Richardson supporter, managed both Latino and non-Latino union outreach. California state senator Alex Padilla, formerly president of the Los Angeles City Council, also served as a senior adviser. Padilla explained the importance of co-ethnic candidate, "As a Latino growing up in Los Angeles, we were looking for role models and political leaders to look up to, and as long as I can remember, my parents would point out Bill Richardson when he was on TV. . . . We support him because of his qualifications, we support him because of his experience, but we're proud of him as a fellow Latinos." Pete Gallego, a member of the Texas State House and chair of the Mexican American Legislative Caucus, served as another of Richardson's senior advisers.

The presence of so many Latinos shaped Richardson's overall campaign. For example, unlike most campaigns, which are run by people who believe that Latinos lack the money to contribute, Richardson hosted Latino-targeted fundraisers. Not surprisingly, therefore, Richardson received a higher percentage of his funding from Latinos than did any other candidate, although he lagged far behind Hillary Clinton and Barack Obama in total money raised. Lucy Casado, a prominent Latino businesswoman and activist, hosted two "Latino fund-raisers" for Richardson. Others who hosted Richardson fund-raisers included Mickey Ibarra, an official in the Bill Clinton administration who had become a lobbyist; a Latino who had previously served as a Georgia state senator; Ed Romero, a former U.S. ambassador to Spain; and Latino leaders in Dallas (Castro 2007; Scherer 2007).

Richardson gave bilingual speeches before Latino audiences and talked about the issues, instead of using props such as mariachi bands on stage (Barack Obama in San Antonio) or speaking at taco stands (Hillary Clinton in Los Angeles). Rather than beating Latino voters over the head with overtly ethnic themes, Richardson connected in a more authentic and perhaps meaningful manner. Furthermore, Richardson was the only candidate to have a complete Spanish-language Web site, www.richardsonparapresidente.com, rather than simply a part of a regular Web site "en Español."

Finally, Richardson and his campaign team promoted policy positions consistent with Latino preferences. He strongly opposed the Iraq war and called for an immediate troop withdrawal. He favored changes to national education policy that included expanded access to bilingual education. He insisted that any immigration reform effort include a pathway to citizenship for the estimated 12 million undocumented immigrants in the United States in 2007. He continually challenged anti-immigrant sentiment, calling it racist, just as he had challenged Perot nearly fifteen years earlier: "You're watching television, and they're talking about immigration, and they show somebody jumping over a wall or swimming across a river. Why don't they show the backbreaking work of maids who are taking care of a hotel, or why don't they recognize the backbreaking work of farm workers who have no protection, or the thousands of immigrants who are giving their lives in Iraq? Nobody should be demonized. My blood boils when I get these questions. There has to be a return to civility."

BACK TO SANTA FE

Despite his long résumé, Richardson was never able to compete with what he described as the "rock star" candidacies of Hillary Clinton, Barack Obama, and John Edwards. Preelection polls gave Richardson about 10 percent of the Iowa vote, but the 15 percent viability rule prevented him from reaching double digits, and he finished a very distant fourth.[2] In the New Hampshire primary on January 8, Richardson again finished fourth. A day later, his money having run out, Richardson returned home to Santa Fe and announced that he was dropping out of the presidential race. Before any of the major Latino states had voted, Richardson was no longer a candidate. He decided to remain neutral through Super Tuesday and the Texas primary on March 4.[3] Despite the fact that he withdrew before voting took place in any of the states in which Latinos had significant influence, both the media and Hillary Clinton's campaign had painted Richardson as solely the Latino candidate. On March 21, Richardson broke his neutrality and endorsed Obama. The Associated Press reported that "Richardson's endorsement could help Obama pick up support among Hispanics," but Clinton campaign chief Mark Penn suggested that Richardson's only appeal was among Latinos, most of whom had voted by March 4: "The time when he could have been most effective has long since passed." In endorsing Obama, Richardson told his story as a Hispanic American who had a Mexican mother, grew up in a bicultural community, and hoped to achieve the American Dream. Given Richardson's lengthy foreign policy experience and his popularity in many Mountain West states predicted to be competitive in the November election, many pundits anointed him a leading vice presidential candidate (Maass 2008). Although Obama ultimately did not select Richardson, he continued to play an important role on the campaign trail, helping Obama court the Latino vote, delivering speeches in Spanish and English, and signaling to Latino voters that Obama was the best candidate on Latino issues. Richardson campaigned extensively in such previously Republican states as New Mexico, Nevada, Colorado, and Florida, where the Latino vote ultimately helped Obama win.

BILL RICHARDSON VERSUS JESSE JACKSON

In 1984 and 1988, respectively, Jesse Jackson won an estimated 77 percent and 92 percent of the African American vote during the Democratic primaries, providing strong evidence that race matters during presidential campaigns (Tate 1993). According to Tate, "Jackson's presidential bids mobilized new Black voters and stimulated Black interest in presidential campaigns" (1993, 15). Chapter 5 demonstrates that Latinos and Blacks offer similar rates of support for co-ethnic/co-racial candidates; however, Jackson's vote totals do not represent a fair comparison for Richardson's 2008 tally for two reasons.

First, Richardson lacked the national prominence that Jackson had enjoyed prior to his presidential bid. In 1983, Jackson was recognized as the most visible leader of the African American community: 95.7 percent of Blacks knew who Jackson was, more than 70 percent had a favorable impression of him, and a majority viewed him as a national leader for the Black community (Tate, Brown, and Jackson 1989; Tate 1993). In contrast, Richardson, the governor of a small state, was relatively unknown among both Latinos and non-Latinos, and he was not viewed as a national leader on Latino issues: whereas Latinos who had heard of Richardson recognized him as the governor of New Mexico, Blacks who had heard of Jackson recognized him as a social, political, and civil rights leader.

Second, the two men faced very different opponents. The 1984 Democratic front-runner, former vice president Walter Mondale, a Minnesotan, had no track record with the Black community. On the Republican side, President Ronald Reagan was a very popular incumbent against whom any Democrat would have had a hard time mounting a successful campaign; thus, few viable Democratic challengers were willing to enter the 1984 race. Jackson consequently faced John Glenn and Gary Hart, neither of whom had a history of support from the Black community, and was considered among the top tier of candidates. Jackson therefore had the benefits of high name recognition and low competition, at least within the Black community. For Richardson, the opposite held true: he had low name recognition and faced what analysts called the "most qualified" field ever of Democratic candidates (Greenhouse 2007). Hillary Clinton started the campaign with a clear majority of the Latino vote as a result of her high profile and her husband's immense popularity among Latinos. In 1996, Bill Clinton had won 70 percent of the Latino vote; when he left office, 80 percent of Latinos had a favorable opinion of him.

Often using Jackson as a yardstick, some pundits declared that Richardson had "failed to generate much excitement, especially among Latino constituencies" (Castro 2007). But in light of this analysis, we should take a more careful approach to evaluating the role of shared ethnicity in the 2008 presidential election. My examination of Richardson's campaign, of Mi Familia, and of his policy issues has already reinforced the importance of shared ethnicity. Moreover, a closer inspection of Latino voters' attitudes and opinions suggests that ethnic attachment was salient in 2008.

In this chapter, I test two hypotheses:

H1: *Latinos who recognized Richardson as a Latino candidate were significantly more likely to support him for president.*

H2: *Latinos who followed ethnic cues were significantly more likely to support Richardson for president.*

DID SHARED ETHNICITY MATTER?

To answer the question of whether the Richardson campaign's outreach resonated with and mobilized Latino voters, I turn to public opinion data collected at different stages of the 2008 presidential campaign. The starting point is a March 2007 national survey in which the Latino Policy Coalition asked Latino registered voters their opinions about Richardson, Hillary Clinton, Obama, and the rest of the field. I then turn to preelection surveys of registered Latino voters in Nevada, the first state with a significant Latino population to hold a primary, to determine how voters there responded to Richardson's candidacy.

Table 7.2 shows registered Latino voters' opinions of various presidential candidates twenty months before the election. Nationwide, 45.7 percent of those polled had no opinion of Richardson; only the governor of another small state, Massachusetts Republican Mitt Romney, had lower name recognition. In contrast, only 7.5 percent of respondents had no opinion of Hillary Clinton, and 4.1 percent had no opinion of President Bush. More than two-thirds of those Latinos who had an opinion of Richardson viewed him favorably. However, for Hillary Clinton and Barack Obama, that margin was even higher—nearly three of every four Latino voters who had opinions of those two candidates viewed them in a positive light. Richardson's low profile clearly provided him with a challenge even among Latino voters.

The Latino Policy Coalition survey also found that 60.3 percent of Latinos nationwide planned to support Clinton, 11.9 percent planned to support Obama, 8.6 percent planned to vote for Richardson, and 6.9 percent intended to vote for Edwards. The fifty-point gap between Clinton and her rivals was the widest gulf reported for any demographic segment of the American electorate in the early stages of the campaign. These findings do not prove that shared ethnicity did not matter in 2008 but make finding such effects more difficult.

I also employed multivariate regression to determine whether Latinos supported Richardson as a result of unique ethnic cues or of more traditional factors such as policy issues. I used data from the Latino Policy Coalition survey and from the Latino Decisions survey of Latino registered voters in Nevada. I examined two dependent variables: (1) intended vote for Richardson; and (2) favorability ratings for Richardson. The surveys asked respondents who were Democratic partisans or who leaned toward the party which candidate they intended to support in the primary. In addition, the surveys asked all respondents to rate the favorability of each candidate, with 0 representing a very unfavorable rating, 1 representing unfavorable, 2 representing don't know, 3 representing favorable, and 4 representing very favorable.

I used two different measures to assess the importance of shared ethnicity based on the availability of questions on each survey. The Latino Policy Coali-

TABLE 7.2. Latino Ratings of Presidential Candidates, March 2007

	Favorable	Unfavorable	No Opinion	Favorability Ratio
Hillary Clinton	68.1	24.5	7.5	2.78
Barack Obama	48.5	16.7	34.9	2.90
Bill Richardson	37.8	16.6	45.7	2.28
John Edwards	43.5	24.8	31.7	1.75
Rudy Giuliani	44.5	30.7	24.8	1.45
John McCain	37.0	32.4	30.6	1.14
Mitt Romney	14.4	20.9	64.8	0.69
George Bush	*31.4*	*64.5*	*4.1*	*0.49*

Source: Latino Policy Coalition, national survey of Latino voters, March 2007.

Note: "No opinion" includes respondents who answered "Don't Know" or who had never heard of the candidate.

tion survey asked whether respondents knew if a Latino was among the presidential candidates. Respondents who answered in the affirmative were asked to name the candidate. Twenty-six percent of registered Latino voters identified Richardson, and an additional 11 percent knew that a Latino was running but could not provide his name. I coded members of both groups as 0, along with respondents who did not know of any Latino candidate. If shared ethnicity mattered, those Latinos who were able to identify Richardson as Latino would be expected to be significantly more likely to vote for him. The Nevada survey did not ask this question; instead, voters there were asked whether they would be more or less likely to support a candidate if he or she had received an endorsement from Antonio Villaraigosa.[4] Again, if shared ethnicity mattered, Latino voters who responded positively to co-ethnic endorsements would be expected to support co-ethnic candidates. Forty percent of Nevada's Latinos stated that a Villaraigosa endorsement would make them more likely to support a presidential candidate, while 16 percent said that an endorsement would make them less likely to support the candidate, and 44 percent said that the endorsement would have no effect.

In contrast to these direct measures of ethnic cues, the traditional literature suggests that policy issue congruence matters to presidential vote choice (Wattier 1983; Abramowitz 1989). To this end, I include measures of Latino policy preferences on the Iraq war and on immigration reform, the two issues found to be the most salient to Latino voters. With the possible exception of Dennis Kucinich, who polled at less than 1 percent, Richardson had the strongest antiwar stance among the Democratic candidates. He routinely stated that he would end the Iraq war immediately and leave no residual troop presence in Iraq, and he had the fastest timeline for bringing all U.S. soldiers home. Observers consistently called Richardson the Democrats' strongest antiwar candidate (Ambinder 2007). When asked if the United States had made a mistake in sending troops to Iraq, 66 percent of Latinos nationwide and 76 percent in Nevada said yes. If policy congruence mattered, Latinos opposed to the war would be expected to be more likely to support Richardson.

Richardson also staked out a more consistent pro-immigration position than did other Democratic candidates, calling for immediate immigration reform to provide a pathway to citizenship. Richardson criticized Clinton, Obama, and Edwards as not going far enough on immigration. Latinos who favored some sort of amnesty for undocumented immigrants should be significantly more likely to support Richardson based on his policy stance. Further, the increased salience of immigration in the Latino community may make it both a policy issue and an ethnic issue, creating a convergence of shared policy preference and shared ethnicity.

Descriptive Results

Shared ethnicity appears to have influenced support for Richardson. In the Latino Policy Coalition survey, stated vote preference for Richardson jumped from 8.6 percent to 29.2 percent when shared ethnicity was taken into account. Figure 7.2 shows the stated vote preferences for Clinton and Richardson based on certain attitudinal and demographic characteristics of Latino voters. Among all Latino voters, Clinton had a substantial advantage over Richardson (60.3 percent to 8.6 percent). However, as ethnic variables are added, support for Richardson rises. Among respondents who knew that Richardson was Latino and who were interviewed in Spanish, 17.8 percent would vote for Richardson. In the subgroup of voters who knew that Richardson was Latino, who were interviewed in Spanish, and who supported citizenship for immigrants, the gap between Clinton and Richardson narrowed markedly. Even at this very early stage in the election, when Clinton enjoyed extremely high levels of name recognition and favorability among Latinos, ethnic cues caused significant movement toward Richardson.

The data from Nevada tell the same story (figure 7.3). Richardson's vote share among Latinos started out low but increased dramatically as additional ethnic cues were taken into account and as those voters who had no opinion of Richardson were excluded. (Excluding these Latinos is a fair point of departure because nearly all Latinos had heard of and had opinions on Clinton.) When all ethnic cues were added and Latinos with no opinion of Richardson were excluded, Richardson became the choice of 45.2 percent of those surveyed, compared to only 39.4 percent who backed Clinton. The margin of error grows rapidly as the cell sizes get smaller, and statistical significance is impossible to infer using only descriptive tables and charts. However, the pattern both in Nevada and nationwide is clear: Latinos who valued shared ethnicity or who relied on ethnic cues were much more likely to support Richardson.

Regression Results

Saying that either shared ethnicity or the presence of ethnic cues was a statistically significant predictor of support for Richardson requires multivariate regression analysis, which enables us to control for multiple factors, including

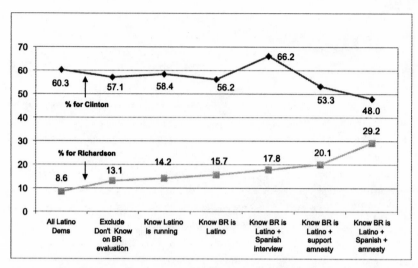

FIG. 7.2. Percentage vote for Clinton vs. Richardson among Latino Democrats, March 2007, Latino Policy Coalition survey

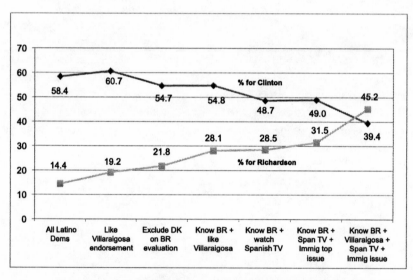

FIG. 7.3. Percentage vote for Clinton vs. Richardson among Nevada Latino Democrats, July 2007, Latino Decisions survey

those presented in figures 7.2 and 7.3 as well as other important variables such as age, education, income, and gender. When all the control variables are plugged into the regression models, the key measures of ethnicity are in fact statistically significant predictors of voting for Richardson and higher favorability ratings.

Table 7.3 presents the vote choice results among Democratic Latino voters in both the national and Nevada samples. Nationwide, *Identify Richardson (as Latino)*, the key variable in figure 7.2, is a positive and significant predictor of voting for Richardson. Likewise, in the Nevada sample, *Villaraigosa Endorsement*, the key variable in figure 7.3, is a positive and significant predictor of voting for Richardson. In both cases, Latino voters who are more interested in ethnic politics or who rely on ethnic cues are significantly more likely to prefer Richardson. However, there is no support for the hypothesis that Latinos who oppose the Iraq war will prefer Richardson. In both samples, Latinos who believe the Iraq war to be a mistake are significantly less likely to back Richardson.

TABLE 7.3.   Predictors of Vote for Bill Richardson in Democratic Primary

	National		Nevada	
	Coef.	S.E.	Coef.	S.E.
Identify Richardson (as Latino)	0.4197	0.1719*	1.3698	0.3127***
Villaraigosa positive			0.4696	0.2401*
Candidate knowledge	0.1708	0.0881*	−0.4306	0.1346***
Iraq was mistake	−0.3313	0.1919†	−0.5528	0.2783*
Path to citizenship	−0.0943	0.1719	0.0695	0.2513
Party ID (7 point)	−0.0612	0.1229	0.2194	0.2927
Southwestern state	0.1369	0.2514		
Clark County (Vegas)			−0.2274	0.2184
Spanish interview	0.2097	0.1914	0.6600	0.3266*
Mexican	0.3595	0.1770*	−0.0430	0.2509
First generation	0.1747	0.1918	−0.2412	0.3395
Third generation	0.0033	0.2215	0.6228	0.3897
Age	0.0104	0.0053*	0.0000	0.0000
Education	−0.0629	0.0317*	0.0979	0.1110
Income	0.0570	0.0413	0.0462	0.0782
Female	−0.2442	0.1673	−0.4684	0.2223*
Married	−0.0392	0.1923		
Constant	−1.8532	0.6439**	−1.6493	0.7455*
N	548		297	

Note: S.E. = standard error.
*p < .05   **p < .01   ***p < .001   †p < .10

And no statistically significant differences were detected among Latinos who supported citizenship for undocumented immigrants. Finally, Nevada respondents interviewed in Spanish were significantly more likely to vote for Richardson, a finding consistent with the descriptive results in figure 7.3; no such effect was found in the national sample.

Richardson's favorability ratings show a similar pattern (table 7.4). Here, the data include all Latinos in the sample, not just Democrats, and the findings for shared ethnicity are consistent and statistically significant. In the national sample, Latinos who identify Richardson as the Latino candidate are significantly more likely to rate him favorably, while in Nevada, Latinos influenced positively by a Villaraigosa endorsement also rate Richardson significantly more favorably.

However, some differences emerge with respect to policy issues. Latinos who believe that the Iraq war was a mistake rate Richardson more favorably in

Table 7.4. Bill Richardson Favorability Ratings among All Latinos

	National		Nevada	
	Coef	S.E.	Coef	S.E.
Identify Richardson (as Latino)	0.5252	0.0899***	1.1011	0.1416***
Villaraigosa positive			0.1781	0.0609**
Candidate knowledge	0.1240	0.0355***	−0.1893	0.0705**
Iraq was mistake	0.1999	0.0846*	0.0036	0.1488
Path to citizenship	0.0301	0.0781	0.2240	0.1342†
Party ID (7 point)	−0.0410	0.0199*	−0.1426	0.0871†
Southwestern state	0.0159	0.1216		
Clark County (Vegas)			−0.0285	0.1161
Spanish interview	−0.0182	0.0929	0.2331	0.1572
Mexican	0.1202	0.0767	−0.2024	0.1284
First generation	0.0221	0.0866	−0.1905	0.1673
Third generation	−0.0156	0.0952	0.0428	0.1872
Age	0.0012	0.0023	0.0000	0.0000
Education	0.0075	0.0147	0.1095	0.0627†
Income	−0.0115	0.0186	−0.0085	0.0440
Female	−0.0553	0.0758	0.0460	0.1174
Married	−0.0141	0.0832		
Cut1	−0.8571	0.2724	−1.2165	0.4250
Cut2	−0.3441	0.2678	−0.7469	0.4179
Cut3	0.9010	0.2675	0.7976	0.4180
Cut4	1.9149	0.2752	1.8059	0.4262
N	843		387	

Note: S.E. = standard error.
$*p < .05$ $**p < .01$ $***p < .001$ $†p < .10$

the national sample but not in Nevada, and Latinos who support a pathway to citizenship for immigrants rate Richardson higher in the Nevada sample. Thus, policy consistency predicts candidate favorability but does not transfer into vote support. Vote support is obviously a more clear test because voters can select only one candidate even if they have favorable opinions of several others. Proxy measures of ethnic cues carry the most weight in the area of vote support, overshadowing the measures of policy congruence.

CONCLUSION

Although Bill Richardson's dominance among Latinos in 2008 did not match Jesse Jackson's levels among Blacks in 1988, Richardson's historic presidential bid still highlighted the importance of shared ethnicity within the Latino community during a presidential election. Although Richardson dropped out of the Democratic race early on, his candidacy unquestionably resonated with Latinos, and he took on important issues that non-Latino candidates avoided. Richardson's main obstacle was not his lack of support among Latino voters but rather his overall low level of name recognition and his inability to raise money when competing against better-known and better-connected candidates. Though he ultimately turned down a cabinet position as secretary of commerce under Obama in 2009, Richardson may once again return to the national stage, either as an eventual member of Obama's cabinet, as an adviser on immigration reform, or as an international broker of nuclear agreements with North Korea. If he is able to return once again to the national stage he may be able to increase his name recognition and favorability, and he may well consider a second run at the White House in 2016 or beyond. If there is one thing about Bill Richardson that rings true, he is definitely not one to give up.

CHAPTER 8

Ethnic Cues and the New American Voter: Implications and Conclusion

In May 2005, Los Angeles elected its first Latino mayor in more than 130 years. Once a Mexican city in Alta California, the City of Angels has the largest percentage Latino population of any U.S. city. However, Whites still comprise about 50 percent of the Los Angeles electorate, with Latinos constituting about 25 percent, Blacks 17 percent, and Asian Americans 7 percent. Thus, Antonio Villaraigosa's victory was not a Latino-only phenomenon. In addition to an estimated 85 percent of the Latino vote, Villaraigosa won a majority of White and Black votes in defeating incumbent James Hahn by a margin of 59 percent to 41 percent (Guerra et al. 2005). A week after the election, Villaraigosa graced the cover of *Newsweek* magazine with the headline, "Latino Power!" Latino candidates may mobilize and energize Latino voters anew, but voters from all walks of life and all racial groups feel their presence. For twenty-first-century voters across the United States, Latino candidates and ethnic politics will become commonplace. Latinos are running for office and winning in places such as Milwaukee, Boston, Atlanta, and Wichita, Kansas. Scholars must observe these elections and examine the impact of the Latino candidacy on both Latino and non-Latino voters.

During the 1960s and 1970s, Latino elected officials and Latino voters were not visible to the mainstream. Pachon and DeSipio note that, "while there were Hispanic elected officials and Latino community activism, no one spoke of 'Latino' politics or the 'Hispanic' vote in national politics" (1992, 212). In 1973, an enumeration of Spanish-surnamed elected officials counted just 10 Latinos elected to office in New York and just 13 in Florida (Lemus 1973). In 2006, the

National Association of Latino Elected and Appointed Officials counted 66 in New York and 125 in Florida, among the more than 6,000 Latinos who held elected office in the United States. Thousands of others had run unsuccessful campaigns for office. While the electoral landscape has clearly changed, our understanding of ethnic politics has evolved less rapidly.

My research shows that Latino candidates have a mobilizing effect among Latino voters, resulting in heightened levels of voter turnout and strong support for the Latino candidate. Among non-Latinos, coalition politics is not guaranteed. In some cases, Blacks are positively mobilized by Latino candidates and support their candidacies, while in other cases Blacks vote solidly against Latino candidates. White voters generally appear less inclined to vote in elections with Latino candidates and will only sometimes support Latino candidates. For example, in the 2001 New York Democratic primary, Fernando Ferrer won more than 80 percent of the Latino and Black vote but only 20 percent of the White vote. In Houston's 2001 mayoral runoff, Orlando Sanchez won an estimated 80 percent of the Latino and White vote but received less than 20 percent of the Black vote. The only constant in the five mayoral elections analyzed here was the Latino vote. In every election, Latino voters were mobilized by the presence of Latino candidates.

The state legislature is an important threshold for Latino politics because such representatives have both a regional and a state presence and can use the position as a stepping-stone to higher public office, including service as mayors, members of the U.S. House or Senate, and governors. In 1990, fifteen states had elected Latinos to their legislatures, including not only Arizona, California, Florida, New York, and Texas but also such surprises as Washington, Kansas, Indiana, and Rhode Island (figure 8.1), all of which had burgeoning Latino populations. Fourteen years later, that number had more than doubled, and thirty-six states—including newcomers Georgia, Wisconsin, Nebraska, and Idaho—now had Latinos serving in their legislatures (figure 8.2). Latinos have clearly become relevant to U.S. politics.

This book has established a framework for an ethnic-candidate paradigm of twenty-first-century U.S. politics. Table 8.1 illustrates the circumstances under which this ethnic-candidate model will apply to future elections. The model is appropriate only when a confluence of two significant factors occurs: the relevant political entity must have both a viable Latino candidate running for office and a growing or sizable Latino electorate. Such an electorate is difficult to define, but a rough measure might be either Latinos comprising 10 percent of the voting electorate or a Latino population that has grown by 50

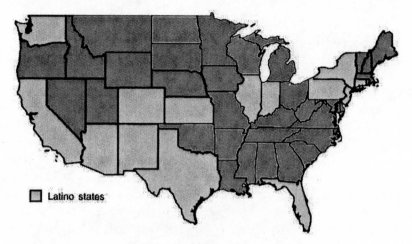

Latino states

FIG. 8.1.   States with Latinos elected to the state legislature in 1990

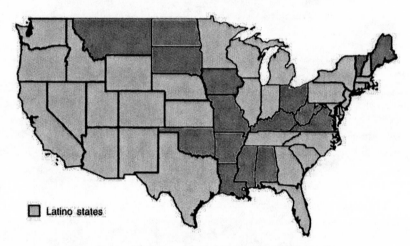

Latino states

FIG. 8.2.   States with Latinos elected to the state legislature in 2004

TABLE 8.1.   Applying the Ethnic Candidate Model

	Candidate = Viable Latino	Candidate = Not Latino
Growing or sizable Latino electorate	Ethnic model	No—unless Ethnic "issue"
No significant Latino electorate	No	No

percent or more in ten years. In these circumstances, I would expect viable Latino candidates to mobilize the Latino community, resulting in elevated voter turnout and strong support for the ethnic candidate.

However, ethnic politics may also emerge when Latino-related issues are present. While the main focus of this book has been on co-ethnic candidates as mobilizing agents, prior research finds that perceived ethnic ballot initiatives or campaign issues mobilize Latino voters where a growing or sizable Latino electorate exists (Segura, Falcon, and Pachon 1997; Tolbert and Hero 2001; Barreto and Woods 2005). Moreover, the mobilizing effect of Latino candidates on Latino voters may not be limited to a first-time effect, as some scholars have speculated. Indeed, when a viable Latino candidate represents the first Latino elected to a given office, we might expect more excitement and interest among Latinos (and among the media). However, chapter 6 reveals that Latino candidates have a lasting effect on voters. In the analysis of Los Angeles and Orange Counties, California, Latinos were significantly more likely to vote if they resided in jurisdictions that featured greater numbers of Latinos running for office. Many of the areas with multiple Latino candidates are heavily Latino districts in East Los Angeles, San Fernando, or Santa Ana that have elected Latinos to office for ten or even twenty years. Further, the general elections in heavily Latino districts are typically uncompetitive, with winners decided months earlier during Democratic primaries. Thus, Latino voters' elevated turnout rates are likely the result of Latino candidates' lasting mobilizing effects.

In addition, this study offers several insights into racial and ethnic politics more broadly, although many questions remain about whether racial and ethnic minorities will form political coalitions or whether intragroup differences will create a competitive environment. Much more research is needed in the area of electoral coalitions to derive a new theory of minority politics that will help understand and even predict when Latinos, Blacks, Whites, and Asians will be partners and when they will be foes. Less than a month after Villaraigosa used a Latino-White coalition to win his mayoral victory, San Antonio's Julian Castro won more than 70 percent of the Latino vote but less than 30 percent of the White vote and lost a mayoral runoff. How can we account for the differing levels of White support for mayoral candidates in the two cities? San Antonio had previously elected several Latinos to the city's top office, including Henry Cisneros, whose 1981 victory represented the first time a Latino had been elected mayor of a major city. Furthermore, the outgoing incumbent in San Antonio was a Latino, Ed Garza, who had served two terms. The excitement that accompanied the "first-Latino" candidacies of Cisneros and Villaraigosa

TABLE 8.2. Potential Locations for Ethnic-Candidate Model to Emerge

City	Latino 2000	2000 Percentage Latino	Latino 1990	Total Growth	Percentage Growth	Potential Candidate
Atlanta	18,582	4.5	7,640	10,942	143	Pedro Marin, state legislature
Benton / Washington, AR	26,323	8.5	2,805	23,518	838	Rey Hernandez, school board
Boston	85,199	14.5	59,692	25,507	43	Felix Arroyo, city council
Charlotte, NC	40,008	7.4	5,261	34,747	660	John Herrera, city council
Detroit	47,257	5.0	27,157	20,100	74	Juan Jose Martinez, school board
Kansas City	30,374	6.9	16,819	13,555	81	CiCi Rojas, county commission
Milwaukee	71,032	11.9	37,420	33,612	90	Peggy West, county board
Minneapolis–St. Paul	51,781	7.7	17,627	34,154	194	Edgardo Rodriguez, state Chicano council
Nashville	25,291	4.6	4,131	21,160	512	Gabriela Coto, neighborhood liason
Omaha	29,006	7.4	9,703	19,303	199	Mark Martinez, school board
Philadelphia	128,300	8.5	84,186	44,114	52	Juan Ramos, city council
Washington, DC	45,015	7.9	31,358	13,657	44	Victor Reinoso, school board

Source: U.S. Census Bureau 1990–2000, Summary File 3.

may not have been present for Castro. Just 19 percent of San Antonio's registered voters turned out for the 2005 election, less than half the 43 percent who cast ballots in 1981 but more than the record low 13.5 percent who voted during Garza's first candidacy, in 2001. Castro's candidacy thus illustrates Latino mobilization—but not hypermobilization—as a result of a viable Latino candidate.

This project has revealed that Latino voter turnout is not necessarily doomed to perennially low levels, as most of the research over the past forty years has suggested. In most of the previous research, no viable Latino candidates were present at the top of the ticket, and Latino voters may not have felt connected to Anglo or Black candidates. My findings show, however, that although heavily Latino precincts are unlikely to have high levels of turnout when no Latino candidate is running, the presence of a viable Latino candidate uniformly results in increased voter turnout among Latinos.

Given these results and the models presented here, we can anticipate future pockets of Latino mobilization as a consequence of Latino candidates. Based on Latino population growth and the subsequent increases in voter registration, it is reasonable to expect the expansion of ethnic politics across the country. Table 8.2 offers some possibilities for such expansion. As more Latino candidates emerge, so too will more data points for our models of ethnic politics. Over the next ten to fifteen years, these cities will witness rapid growth in Latino population, citizenship, and voter registration, potentially resulting in a healthy Latino electorate that all political candidates will need to court. However, when Latino candidates are present, we should expect serious mobilization efforts in the Latino community as well via Spanish-language media and Latino civic organizations. The result may very well be a sharp increase in the number of Latinos elected to prominent positions. It is as yet unclear whether Latino politics will remain ethnic politics, but the theory and evidence provided here suggest that Latino candidates go far in energizing and mobilizing Latino voters.

Notes

CHAPTER 1

1. Throughout this book, I use the terms *Hispanic* and *Latino* interchangeably to refer to persons of descent from Spanish-speaking Latin America.

2. In addition to the four Latinos elected from U.S. states, Baltasar Carrada was Puerto Rico's nonvoting delegate in the U.S. House.

3. An implicit argument is that Latino candidates can win public office. If every Latino who ran for office lost, there would be no reason to suspect that Latinos' candidacies would "energize" the Latino community.

4. Rather than replace existing models of voter turnout and candidate preference, I use them as a base and introduce additional explanatory variables. The models include such standard predictors as age, education, income, gender, marital status, political efficacy/interest, partisanship, and mobilization, among others.

5. For example, more than two-thirds of all Cuban Americans reside in Florida, while two-thirds of all Mexican Americans live in two states (California and Texas) and more than 60 percent of Dominicans reside in New York.

CHAPTER 2

1. The term *Latino* was first used on the decennial census in 2000. In 1980 and 1990, the census form used the language *Hispanic or Spanish ancestry.* In 1970, the census asked about Spanish origin.

2. Notable exceptions include Lyndon B. Johnson and Robert Kennedy, both of whom actively campaigned for Mexican American votes. However, non-Latino elected officials rarely courted, let alone connected with, the Latino community. Some observers view these early attempts to court the Latino vote as symbolic gestures to attract white liberals, given the small number of Latino voters in the 1950s and 1960s.

3. This book describes *Latinos* or *Hispanics* as those persons living (permanently) in the United States whose ancestry can be traced to any of the Spanish-speaking countries of North, Central, or South America and excludes those of European descent. This definition of *Latinos* is consistent with most scholarly research.

4. In fact, the official 1950 census form asked census takers to report a person's race as White, Negro, American Indian, Japanese, Chinese, or Filipino.

5. I searched the Lexis-Nexis news database for the terms *Latino* and *Hispanic* in the headlines of stories about elections and politics. Overall, *Latino* seems to be more popular in the press, although regional variations exist, with some parts of the country favoring *Hispanic*.

CHAPTER 4

1. Rather than replace existing models of voter turnout and candidate preference, I use them as a base and introduce additional explanatory variables. The models include such standard predictors as age, education, income, gender, marital status, political efficacy/interest, partisanship, and mobilization, among others.

2. Stokes-Brown (2006) did not test crossover voting among Latinos but rather the extent to which Latinos preferred a Latino candidate when the two candidates are equally qualified. While her findings are important, her dependent variable from the 2004 Pew Hispanic Survey may be too easy a test of ethnic voting. Here, we do not present the candidates as equally qualified but rather as from opposing ideological or partisan camps.

3. A 2003 TRPI survey of Latinos in California found that a majority of Latino registered voters picked Latinos as group that receives the most discrimination, ahead of African Americans, Asian Americans, and Arab Americans.

4. The LIF data are for California Latinos, most of whom are of Mexican origin. Among survey respondents, 77 percent self-identified as being of Mexican ancestry. To determine the differences among Latino subgroups, I include in the models a dummy variable for Mexican origin.

5. The survey did not follow a strict experimental design. A better approach would have been to switch the names *Smith* and *Hernandez* for half of the respondents to determine more accurately ethnic attachment's effects on vote choice. However, because Hernandez is portrayed as the Republican candidate and California Latinos have strong ties to the Democratic Party, this approach provides considerable insight into ethnicity's role in Latino vote choice.

6. Among respondents, 25 percent chose Smith, 48 percent chose Hernandez, 5 percent chose Neither, 16 percent chose Both, and 7 percent said Don't Know (Arteaga 2000).

7. The trichotomous dependent variable takes a value of 0 when Smith is preferred, 1 when voters are undecided, and 2 when Hernandez is preferred. The Neither, Both, and Don't Know voters can be considered undecided between the two candidates and placed between the options on the three-point index, as opposed to taking a value of 0.

8. Twenty-six percent of respondents chose the Latino nonpartisan, 40 percent chose the non-Latino partisan, 29 percent said that their choice would depend on the candidate, and 5 percent did not know which one they would choose.

9. Elsewhere in the LIF survey, respondents were asked a series of issue questions, and the salience of each issue was determined. Respondents were asked if each issue was very important, somewhat important, not too important, or not at all important. The salience indicators for "improving public education" and "increasing affordable housing" were combined and recoded as *Smith Issues*. Similarly, "preserving family values"

and "reducing crime" were combined and recoded as *Hernandez Issues*. Each variable ranges from 2 to 8.

10. The variable *Ethnic Mobilization* is based on a set of three questions about whether certain electoral circumstances would increase or decrease the likelihood that a respondent might cast a ballot. Latino registered voters were asked, "Would you be more or less likely to vote in an election where (1) there was a viable Latino candidate; (2) issues important to Latinos had been discussed in depth over the course of the election; and (3) Latino organizations and community leaders were urging Latinos to vote?" Although the variable specifically addresses mobilization, it also taps the underlying importance of ethnicity with regard to political behavior (Lien 1994; Pantoja and Woods 2000). Using Cronbach's alpha, we can determine the internal consistency of the scale based on the average interitem correlation. The variable ranges from 3 to 15. Overall, the test produces an alpha reading of .7799, which is quite high for a four-item scale. The variable *Ethnic Attachment* combines the responses to a series of four questions about whether different ethnic-based characteristics would attract support among Latino voters. For example, the survey asked, "Would you vote for a candidate who [characteristic], or would the information make no impact on your decision to vote?" The characteristics are (1) is bilingual in English and Spanish; (2) has a Latino surname; (3) is endorsed by a Latino organization or group; (4) is Latino and speaks Spanish as his/her native language. The variable ranges from 4 to 20. Unlike the previous variable, this measure directly addresses ethnic identity's role in candidate preference. If the ethnic association hypothesis is correct, both variables should reveal a significant and positive relationship with voting for the co-ethnic candidate, Hernandez. For this measure, Cronbach's alpha is .7758—again, a high degree of reliability.

11. The specific candidate attributes in this hypothetical election are less important. Voters who stated a preference for a White Democrat are less likely to prefer Hernandez in the probit analyses, but this relationship is not statistically significant.

12. Respondents in the TRPI survey were asked, "Just thinking about groups living in the United States, how much do you think you have in common with other Latinos? Is it a great deal, a fair amount, only a little, or do you think you have nothing in common?" The *Shared Commonality* variable ranges from 1 to 4.

13. The *Ethnic Attachment* variable is based on three items: (1) the importance of Latino representation; (2) identifying an ethnic theme as the most important issue (i.e., immigration or race relations); (3) a feeling that Latinos have too little power. The variable ranges from 0 to 3.

CHAPTER 5

1. The lack of empirical evidence persists despite numerous instances of expert witness testimony in court that strongly support the idea that Latino candidates mobilize Latino voters (e.g., *Garza v. Los Angeles County; Ruiz v. Santa Maria; Martinez v. Bush*).

2. In Denver, the first-ever Latino candidates for the U.S. Senate and Congress may have helped generate this feeling.

3. Thus, we would expect similar findings with respect to Latino turnout and candidate preference when a Latino candidate is running for president (or vice president),

U.S. senator, governor, or mayor. In addition, this assumption may hold true for lower-ballot offices in a community where a Latino candidate would be the first Latino elected to an office. This analysis appears in chapter 6.

4. In the case of New York, the turnout bias should be in favor of the general election instead of the Democratic primary. For decades, scholars have found that turnout is significantly lower in primary elections than in general or runoff elections.

5. For example, if the standardized coefficient for percentage Latino in the 1999 Houston mayoral election was –.1052 and –.0672 in 2001, the net change would be positive .0380. Even if the constant was 25 in 1999 and was 40 in 2001, the standardized coefficient reports the normalized contribution for the percentage Latino variable, independent of the constant (or turnout rate citywide) for both elections.

6. Percentage Latino is based on registration in Los Angeles and New York and is based on voting-age population in Houston, Denver, and San Francisco. For the first method, voter registration records were merged with a list of Spanish surnames that is based on the 1990 census and is constructed by tabulating the responses to the question regarding Hispanic origin. Each surname is categorized by the percentage of individuals who identified themselves as Hispanic. Each surname is then given a numeric value for the probability that persons with the surname are Hispanic. The list contains more than twenty-five thousand surnames and is reliable at 94 percent confidence. For the second method, U.S. census voting-age population data were gathered at the census tract level for each city and merged in with precinct boundaries.

7. Heavily White and heavily Black precincts are those with populations 80 percent or more homogenous. Heavily Asian American precincts are those with populations 50 percent or more Asian; I used the lower number because of small sample size considerations. Heavily Latino precincts are those with populations 80 percent or more Latino in all cities except San Francisco, where I use 50 percent or more as a consequence of the small number of observations.

8. In ecological inference involving estimating levels of racial bloc voting, data on the racial composition of the electorate are often missing (at the precinct level), but data are available (at the precinct level) on surrogate variables such as Spanish surname registration and the racial proportions among the total population or among the voting-age population. For several decades, scholars have debated how to adjust ecological techniques to compensate for such systematic measurement errors in the independent variable (see, e.g., discussion in Kousser 1973; Grofman, Migalski, and Noviello 1985; Grofman and Migalski 1988; Loewen and Grofman 1989). The availability of a computer program to implement King's (1997) ecological inference method has sparked a renaissance of ecological studies, especially in political science, leading to a renewed interest in this adjustment question (see esp. King 1997, 71–72; Cho, Judge, and Cain 2002; Zax 2002). The problem is that single-equation ecological inference techniques often assume a linear relationship between the data for voting-age population (which are easily accessible) and for actual voting population (which are difficult to track down). In reality, the relationship is not linear. Differences in citzenship rates, registration rates, and voter participation rates greatly affect the bottom line (i.e., the independent variable)—in this case, percentage Latino. Rather than just plugging in percentage Latino among voting-

age population, the double-equation technique first takes into account turnout rates of Latinos and non-Latinos and reestimates the x variable (percentage Latino). Then, given that many members of the voting-age population did not vote, we recast the dependent variable (percentage vote won by Latino candidate Y) as percentage vote won among voting-age population. Then we create a second dependent variable for percentage vote won among voting-age population by the non-Latino candidate. Finally, we regress the new, more appropriate independent variable, percentage Latino, against both dependent variables (thus the double equation) to determine the percentage of the vote won by the Latino candidate among Latino voters. In comparing actual election results, exit poll results, and single- and double-equation techniques, Grofman and Barreto (2009) find that the double-equation method most closely approximates the actual election results. For more on this technique, see also Grofman and Merrill 2004.

CHAPTER 6

1. Becerra ran against Luis Vega, and Nuñez ran against Manuel Aldana Jr. Cedillo ran unopposed.

2. The full data set includes 5,221,306 registered voters in Los Angeles and Orange Counties, of which 1,228,466 (23.5 percent) are Latino.

3. For each of the regressions, the variance inflation factor for each independent variable was estimated, and in all cases the score fell well below the traditional cutoff level of 20.0; the corresponding tolerance values never fall below 0.05. For more on multicollinearity and variance inflation, see Farrar and Glauber 1967; Wesolowsky 1976; Cohen and Cohen 1983; Morrow-Howell 1994.

4. The Spanish surname list is based on the 1990 census and is constructed by tabulating the responses to the question regarding Hispanic origin. Each surname is categorized by the percentage of individuals who identified themselves as Hispanic. Each surname is then given a numeric value for the probability that persons with that surname are Hispanic. The list contains more than twenty-five thousand surnames and is considered 94 percent accurate. For a full explanation on the methodology of the list, see Word and Perkins 1996.

5. In addition to Tam 1995, see also Lauderdale and Kestenbaum (2000), who developed the list of Asian surnames used here.

6. Circulation records were provided by the Audit Bureau of Circulations, a nonprofit, third-party auditing organization specifically focusing on major media industries. The variable included is the total newspaper household coverage within the zip code for the twelve months ending on March 31, 2002. They reflect, by zip code, the number of both paid daily and Sunday-only household newspaper subscriptions in Los Angeles and Orange Counties. The four largest newspapers in Southern California were used to assess newspaper readership levels in the study area.

7. For partisan offices, only major-party Latino candidates were counted.

8. Because I am interested in testing the effect of Latino candidates on Latino (rather than non-Latino) voters, split-sample analysis that estimates separate models for Latinos and non-Latinos is not appropriate for this test. When non-Latinos are not included

in the model, it is not possible to assess the impact of ethnic candidates on Latinos relative to non-Latinos. However, in subsequent tests, I split the sample and focus only on Latino registrants.

9. The interaction term cannot be interpreted in isolation from its components. Assessing the predicted probability that a Latino or non-Latino would vote, given the presence of Latino candidates, requires taking into account race, ethnic candidates, and the interaction term. These results are shown in figure 6.2.

CHAPTER 7

1. These estimates are taken from entrance and exit polls conducted during the 2008 primary contests and report the percentage of Democratic voters in each state that was Latino. These estimates can be found at http://www.cnn.com/POLITICS/2008/.

2. In the Iowa Democratic caucuses, a candidate must receive at least 15 percent of the vote in the caucus precinct to win delegates. Supporters of candidates who receive less than 15 percent are asked to vote for their second choice or remain undeclared. News accounts from Iowa suggested that most Richardson supporters voted for Obama in the second round, likely contributing to Obama's seven-point win over Edwards.

3. Some political blogs suggested that Richardson was leaning toward endorsing Obama before Super Tuesday. As a result, Bill Clinton, a close Richardson friend, invited himself to the governor's mansion in Santa Fe to watch the Super Bowl on February 3, just two days before Super Tuesday. The former president encouraged Richardson to endorse Hillary Clinton or to stay neutral, and the governor made no endorsement.

4. Los Angeles mayor Antonio Villaraigosa ultimately endorsed Hillary Clinton and was named a national Latino cochair of the Clinton campaign. However, when the survey was conducted, Clinton had not yet begun campaigning with Villaraigosa.

References

Abosch, Yishaiya, Matt A. Barreto, and Nathan D. Woods. 2007. "An Assessment of Racially Polarized Voting for and against Latino Candidates in California." In *Voting Right Act Reauthorization of 2006: Perspectives on Democracy, Participation, and Power,* ed. Ana Henderson. Berkeley: Berkeley Public Policy Press.

Abrajano, Marisa, R. Michael Alvarez, and Jonathan Nagler. 2005. "Race Based vs. Issue Voting: A Natural Experiment." *Political Research Quarterly* 58:203–18.

Abramowitz, Alan I. 1989. "Viability, Electability, and Candidate Choice in a Presidential Primary Election: A Test of Competing Models." *Journal of Politics* 51:977–92.

Affigne, Tony. 2000. "Latino Politics in the United States: An Introduction." *PS: Political Science and Politics* 33:523–27.

Affigne, Tony, Manuel Avalos, and Njeri Jackson. 1999. "Latino Politics in the United States: Building a Race-Conscious, Gendered and Historical Analysis." Paper presented at the annual meeting of the American Political Science Association, Atlanta.

Aldrich, John H., John L. Sullivan, and Eugene Borgida. 1989. "Foreign Affairs and Issue Voting: Do Presidential Candidates 'Waltz before a Blind Audience?'" *American Political Science Review* 83:123–41.

Alt, James. 1994. "The Impact of the Voting Rights Act on Black and White Voter Registration in the South." In *Quiet Revolution in the South: The Impact of the Voting Rights Act, 1965–1990,* ed. C. Davidson and B. Grofman. Princeton: Princeton University Press.

Ambinder, Marc. 2007. "Richardson's Anti-War Bet." *Atlantic* blog on politics, September 25.

Ambrecht, Biliana, and Harry Pachon. 1974. "Ethnic Political Mobilization in a Mexican American Community: An Exploratory Study of East Los Angeles, 1965–1972." *Western Political Quarterly* 27:500–519.

Appiah, A. 1994. "Identity, Authenticity, Survival: Multicultural Societies and Social Reproduction." In *Multiculturalism: Examining the Politics of Recognition,* ed. A. Gutmann. Princeton: Princeton University Press.

Arteaga, Luis. 2000. "Are Latinos Pro-Democrat or Anti-Republican? An Examination of Party Registration and Allegiance in the 2000 Election and Beyond." In *The California Latino Vote 2000.* San Francisco: Latino Issues Forum.

Arteaga, Luis. 2002. "To Vote or Not to Vote? An Examination of Latino Voting Patterns and Motivations to Vote." *Civic Participation Report* (Latino Issues Forum), October.

Arvizu, John R., and F. Chris Garcia. 1996. "Latino Voting Participation: Explaining and Differentiating Latino Voting Turnout." *Hispanic Journal of Behavioral Sciences* 18:104–28.

Barabak, Mark Z. 2002a. "Limping to the Finish Line: Record-Low Turnout Is Predicted after Californians Endure Relentless Negative Ads in Eight-Month General Election Campaign." *Los Angeles Times,* November 5.

Barabak, Mark Z. 2002b. "Negative Campaign Repelled Some Voters: A Times Exit Poll Finds Alienation of Latinos and African Americans Also Kept Turnout Low." *Los Angeles Times,* November 11.

Barreto, Matt, and Regina Branton. 2006. "Unifying Minority Political Participation: Black, Latino, and Asian American Turnout in Primary and General Elections." Paper presented at the 2006 annual meeting of the Midwest Political Science Association, Chicago.

Barreto, Matt A., and Alejandro Esparza. 2001. *2001 Post-Election Analysis: LA Mayoral Race.* Claremont, Calif.: Tomás Rivera Policy Institute.

Barreto, Matt A., Rodolfo Espino, Adrian Pantoja, and Ricardo Ramírez. 2003. "Selective Recruitment or Empowered Communities? The Effects of Descriptive Representation on Latino Voter Mobilization." Paper presented at the annual meeting of the American Political Science Association, Philadelphia.

Barreto, Matt A., and José A. Muñoz. 2003. "Reexamining the 'Politics of In-Between': Political Participation among Mexican Immigrants in the United States." *Hispanic Journal of Behavioral Sciences* 25:427–47.

Barreto, Matt, and Francisco Pedraza. 2009. "The Renewal and Persistence of Group Identification in American Politics." *Electoral Studies* 28:595–605.

Barreto, Matt A., Gary M. Segura, and Nathan D. Woods. 2004. "The Mobilizing Effect of Majority-Minority Districts on Latino Turnout." *American Political Science Review* 98:65–75.

Barreto, Matt A., and Nathan D. Woods. 2000. *Voting Patterns and the Dramatic Growth of the Latino Electorate in Los Angeles County, 1994–1998.* Claremont, Calif.: Tomás Rivera Policy Institute.

Barreto, Matt A., and Nathan D. Woods. 2005. "The Anti-Latino Political Context and Its Impact on GOP Detachment and Increasing Latino Voter Turnout in Los Angeles County." In *Diversity in Democracy: Minority Representation in the United States,* ed. Gary Segura and Shawn Bowler. Charlottesville: University of Virginia Press.

Berelson, Bernard, Paul F. Lazarsfeld, and William N. McPhee. 1954. *Voting.* Chicago: University of Chicago Press.

Bike, William. 1998. *Winning Political Campaigns: A Comprehensive Guide to Electoral Success.* Juneau, Alaska: Denali.

Bobo, Lawrence, and Frank D. Gilliam. 1990. "Race, Sociopolitical Participation, and Black Empowerment." *American Political Science Review* 84:377–94.

Bonomi, Patricia. 2008. "Religious Pluralism in the Middle Colonies." Religion in American History. National Humanities Center.

Branton, Regina. 2007. "Latino Attitudes towards Public Policy: The Importance of Acculturation." *Political Research Quarterly* 60:293–303.

Brischetto, Robert R., and Rodolfo de la Garza. 1985. "The Mexican American Electorate:

Political Opinions and Behavior across Cultures in San Antonio." Occasional Paper 5, Southwest Voter Registration Project, San Antonio.

Browning, Rufus P., Dale Rogers Marshall, and David H. Tabb. 1984. *Protest Is Not Enough*. Berkeley: University of California Press.

Brownstein, Ronald. 2002. "Stakes High but Interest Low at Polls." *Los Angeles Times*, November 4.

Bullock, Charles S. 1984. "Racial Crossover Voting and the Election of Black Officials." *Journal of Politics* 46:238–51.

Cain, Bruce E., and D. Roderick Kiewiet. 1984. "Ethnicity and Electoral Choice: Mexican American Voting Behavior in the California 30th Congressional District." *Social Science Quarterly* 65:315–27.

Cain, Bruce E., D. Roderick Kiewiet, and Carole Uhlaner. 1991. "The Acquisition of Partisanship by Latinos and Asian Americans." *American Journal of Political Science* 35:390–422.

Calvo, Maria A., and Steven J. Rosenstone. 1989. *Hispanic Political Participation*. San Antonio: Southwest Voter Research Institute.

Cameron, Charles, David Epstein, and Sharyn O'Halloran. 1996. "Do Majority-Minority Districts Maximize Substantive Black Representation in Congress?" *American Political Science Review* 90:794–812.

Campbell, Angus, Philip Converse, Warren Miller, and Donald Stokes. 1960. *The American Voter*. New York: Wiley.

Campbell, Cameron. 2000. *Intermediate Statistical Methods: Interpreting Coefficients for Transformed Variables*. Los Angeles: University of California. www.soc.ucla.edu/faculty/campbell/210b_Winter2000/210B_Winter2000_class_8.PDF.

Cano, Gustavo. 2002. "The Chicago-Houston Report: Political Mobilization of Mexican Immigrants in American Cities." Center for US-Mexican Studies, University of California, San Diego, October 30.

Carmichael, Stokely, and Richard Hamilton. 1967. *Black Power*. New York: Vintage.

Cassel, Carol A. 2002. "Hispanic Turnout: Estimates from Validated Voting Data." *Political Research Quarterly* 55:391–408.

Castro, Tony. 2007. "Can Richardson Steal the Thunder? New Mexico Gov. Seeks to Make It a Latino White House." *Los Angeles Daily News*, April 14.

Cho, Wendy Tam, George C. Judge, and Bruce Cain. 2002. "Some Empirical Evidence on the Impact of Measurement Errors in Making Ecological Inferences." Manuscript.

Clemente, Peter C. 1998. *State of the Net: The New Frontier*. New York: McGraw-Hill.

Cohen, J., and P. Cohen. 1983. *Applied Multiple Regression/Correlation Analysis for Behavioral Sciences*. Hillsdale, N.J.: Erlbaum.

Cohen, Jonathan, Thad Kousser, and John Sides. 1999. "Sincere Voting, Hedging, and Raiding: Testing a Formal Model of Crossover Voting in Blanket Primaries." Paper presented at the 1999 meeting of the American Political Science Association, Atlanta.

Cook, Elizabeth A. 1994. "Voter Responses to Women Candidates." In *The Year of the Woman: Myths and Realities*, ed. E. A. Cook, S. Thomas, and C. Wilcox. Boulder, Colo.: Westview.

Current Population Survey. 2006. "Voting and Registration in the Election of November 2006." P20-557. United States Census Bureau.

Dahl, Robert. 1961. *Who Governs? Democracy and Power in an American City*. New Haven: Yale University Press.

Dalton, Russell. 2002. *Citizen Politics: Public Opinion and Political Parties in Advanced Industrial Democracies*. 3rd ed. New York: Chatham House.

Davis, Darren W. 1997a. "The Direction of Race of Interviewer Effects among African-Americans: Donning the Black Mask." *American Journal of Political Science* 41:309–22.

Davis, Darren W. 1997b. "Nonrandom Measurement Error and Race of Interviewer Effects among African Americans." *Public Opinion Quarterly* 61:183–207.

Dawson, Michael. 1994. *Behind the Mule: Race and Class in African-American Politics*. Princeton: Princeton University Press.

DeFrancesco Soto, Victoria. 2006. "Partisanship with Accents: When Does Ethnicity Trump Partisanship?" Paper presented at the 2006 American Political Science Association annual meeting, Philadelphia.

DeFrancesco Soto, Victoria. 2007. "Do Latinos Party All the Time? The Role of Shared Ethnic Group Identity on Political Choice." Ph.D. diss., Duke University.

DeFrancesco Soto, Victoria, and Jennifer Merolla. 2006. "Vota por tu Futuro: Partisan Mobilization of Latino Voters in the 2000 Presidential Election." *Political Behavior* 28:285–304.

De Leon, Richard. 2003. "Some Graphical Studies of the Nov 2003 SF Mayoral Precinct Vote." Usual Suspects blog, November 25, http://www.sfusualsuspects.com/re sources/docs/DeLeonMarch04/DeLeon_GraphicalAnalysis_of_Nov03_Election.pdf.

de la Garza, Rodolfo. 1988. "Chicano Elites and National Policy Making, 1977–1980." In *Latinos and the Political System*, ed. F. Chris Garcia. Notre Dame, Ind.: University of Notre Dame Press.

de la Garza, Rodolfo. 2005. "The Latino Vote across Time." Paper presented at the Woodrow Wilson International Center for Scholars.

de la Garza, Rodolfo O., Louis DeSipio, F. Chris Garcia, John Garcia, and Angelo Falcon. 1992. *Latino Voices: Mexican, Puerto Rican, and Cuban Perspectives on American Politics*. Boulder, Colo.: Westview.

de la Garza, Rodolfo, Louis DeSipio, and David Leal, eds. 2010. *Beyond the Barrio: Latinos in the 2004 Elections*. South Bend, Ind.: University of Notre Dame Press.

de la Garza, Rodolfo O., Charles W. Haynes, and Jaesung Ryu. 2002. "An Analysis of Latino Voter Turnout Patterns in the 1992–1998 General Elections in Harris County, Texas." *Harvard Journal of Hispanic Policy* 14:77–95.

de la Garza, Rodolfo O., Martha Menchaca, and Louis DeSipio, eds. 1994. *Barrio Ballots: Latino Politics in the 1990 Elections*. Boulder, Colo.: Westview.

Delli Carpini, Michael, and Scott Keeter. 1996. *What American Know about Politics and Why It Matters*. New Haven: Yale University Press.

DeSipio, Louis. 1996a. *Counting on the Latino Vote: Latinos as a New Electorate*. Charlottesville: University of Virginia Press.

DeSipio, Louis. 1996b. "Making Citizens or Good Citizens? Naturalization as a Predictor of Organizational and Electoral Behavior among Latino Immigrants." *Hispanic Journal of Behavioral Sciences* 18:194–213.

DeSipio, Louis, and Rodolfo de la Garza. 2004. "Between Symbolism and Influence:

Latinos and the 2000 Election." In *Muted Voices: Latinos and the 2000 Elections,* ed. Rodolfo de la Garza and Louis DeSipio. Boulder, Colo.: Rowman and Littlefield.

DeSipio, Louis, and Natalie Masuoka. 2006. "Opportunities Lost? Latinos, Cruz Busta-mante, and California's Recall." In *Clicker Politics,* ed. Shaun Bowler and Bruce Cain. Upper Saddle River, N.J.: Pearson.

Diaz, William. 1996. "Latino Participation in America: Associational and Political Roles." *Hispanic Journal of Behavioral Sciences* 18:154–75.

Dill, Sheri. 1995. "Wichita Reverses a Trend." *Civic Catalyst Newsletter,* Spring, http://www.pewcenter.org/doingcj/civiccat/displayCivcat.php.

Downs, Anthony. 1957. *An Economic Theory of Democracy.* New York: Harper and Row.

Doyle, Michael. 2002. "Spanish Election Ads Hit Record—$16 Million Spent on Spanish Television Advertising This Year." *Fresno Bee,* November 22.

Engstrom, Richard L. 1992. "Modified Multi-Seat Election Systems as Remedies for Mi-nority Vote Dilution." *Stetson Law Review* 21:743–70.

Engstrom, Richard L., and Robert B. Brischetto. 1997. "Cumulative Voting and Latino Representation: Exit Surveys in Fifteen Texas Communities." *Social Science Quarterly* 78:973–91.

Espino, Rodolfo. 2007. "Is There a Latino Dimension to Voting in Congress?" In *Latino Politics: Identity, Mobilization, and Representation,* ed. Rodolfo Espino, David Leal, and Ken Meier. Charlottesville: University of Virginia Press.

Farrar, D., and R. Glauber. 1967. "Multicollinearity in Regression Analysis: The Problem Revisited." *Review of Economics and Statistics* 49:92–107.

Fleck, Tim. 2001. "Runoff Worries: Brown Duplicates 1997 Showing, but Sanchez Has the Momentum." *Houston Press,* November 15.

Fraga, Luis R. 1988. "Domination through Democratic Means: Nonpartisan Slating Groups in City Electoral Politics." *Urban Affairs Quarterly* 23:528–55.

Fraga, Luis, John Garcia, Rodney Hero, Michael Jones-Correa, Valerie Martinez-Ebers, and Gary Segura. 2006. "Su Casa Es Nuestra Casa: Latino Politics Research and the Development of American Political Science." *American Political Science Review* 100:515–21.

Fraga, Luis, and Fernando Guerra. 1996. "Theory, Reality, and Perpetual Potential: Lati-nos in the 1992 California Election." In *Ethnic Ironies: Latino Politics in the 1992 Elec-tions,* ed. Rodolfo O. de la Garza and Louis DeSipio. Boulder, Colo.: Westview.

Fry, Brian. 2001. "Anti-Immigrant Backlash." In *Encyclopedia of American Immigration,* ed. James Ciment. New York: Sharpe.

Frymer, Paul. 1999. *Uneasy Alliances: Race and Party Competition in America.* Princeton: Princeton University Press.

Gaddie, Ronald K., and Charles S. Bullock. 1994. "Voter Turnout and Candidate Partici-pation Effects of Affirmative Action Districting." Paper presented at the Citadel Sym-posium on Southern Politics, Charleston, S.C.

Garcia, F. Chris. 1988. *Latinos and the Political System.* Notre Dame, Ind.: University of Notre Dame Press.

Garcia, F. Chris, and Rodolfo O. de la Garza. 1977. *The Chicano Political Experience: Three Perspectives.* North Scituate, Mass.: Duxbury.

Garcia, F. Chris, John Garcia, and Rodolfo O. de la Garza. 1991. *Latinos and Politics: A Se-lect Research Bibliography.* Austin: University of Texas Press.

Garcia, John A., and Carlos H. Arce. 1988. "Political Orientations and Behaviors of Chicanos: Trying to Make Sense out of Attitudes and Participation." In *Pursuing Power: Latinos and the Political System,* ed. F. Chris Garcia. Notre Dame, Ind.: University of Notre Dame Press.

Garcia, John A., and Rodolfo O. de la Garza. 1985. "Mobilizing the Mexican Immigrant: The Role of Mexican-American Organizations." *Western Political Quarterly* 38:551–64.

García-Bedolla, Lisa. 2000. "They and We: Identity, Gender, Politics among Latino Youth in Los Angeles." *Social Science Quarterly* 81:106–21.

Garza v. Los Angeles County. 1990. 918 F.2d 763 (9th Cir.).

Gay, Claudine. 2001a. "The Effect of Black Congressional Representation on Political Participation." *American Political Science Review* 95:589–602.

Gay, Claudine. 2001b. *The Effect of Minority Districts and Minority Representation on Political Participation in California.* San Francisco: Public Policy Institute of California.

Gilliam, Frank D. 1996. "Exploring Minority Empowerment: Symbolic Politics, Governing Coalitions and Traces of Political Style in Los Angeles." *American Journal of Political Science* 40:56–81.

Gilliam, Frank D., and Karen M. Kaufmann. 1998. "Is There an Empowerment Life Cycle? Long-Term Black Empowerment and Its Influence on Voter Participation." *Urban Affairs Review* 33:6741–66.

Glazer, Nathan. 1997. *We Are Multiculturalist Now.* Cambridge: Harvard University Press.

Godfrey, L. G., Michael McAleer, and C. R. McKenzie. 1988. "Variable Addition and Lagrange Multiplier Tests for Linear and Logarithmic Regression Models." *Review of Economic and Statistics* 70:492–503.

Godfrey, L. G., and Michael R. Wickens. 1981. "Testing Linear and Log-Linear Regressions for Functional Form." *Review of Economic Studies* 48:487–96.

Gonzalez-Juenke, Eric, and Anna Sampaio. 2008. "Deracialization and Latino Politics: The Case of the Salazar Brothers in Colorado." *Political Research Quarterly* online, December 24.

Goodman, Leo. 1953. "Ecological Regression and the Behavior of Individuals." *American Sociological Review* 18:663–64.

Gordon, Milton M. 1964. *Assimilation in American Life: The Role of Race, Religion, and National Origins.* New York: Oxford University Press.

Gosnell, Harold. 1935. *Negro Politicians: The Rise of Negro Politics in Chicago.* Chicago: University of Chicago Press.

Graves, Scott, and Jongho Lee. 2000. "Ethnic Underpinnings of Voting Preference: Latinos and the 1996 U.S. Senate Election in Texas." *Social Science Quarterly* 81:227–36.

Greenhouse, Steven. 2007. "Labor Sets Stage for a Democratic Forum." *New York Times,* caucus blog, August 7.

Grofman, Bernard. 1993. "Voting Rights in a Multi-Ethnic World." *Chicano-Latino Law Review* 13:15–37.

Grofman, Bernard, and Matt A. Barreto. 2009. "A Reply to Zax's (2002) Critique of Grofman and Migalski (1988): Double Equation Approaches to Ecological Inferences." *Sociological Methods and Research* 37:599–617.

Grofman, Bernard, and Lisa Handley. 1989. "Minority Population Proportion and Black and Hispanic Congressional Success in the 1970s and 1980s." *American Politics Quarterly* 17:436–45.

Grofman, Bernard, Lisa Handley, and David I. Lublin. 2001. "Drawing Effective Minority Districts: A Conceptual Framework and Some Empirical Evidence." *North Carolina Law Review* 79:1383–1430.

Grofman, Bernard, and Samuel Merrill. 2004. "Ecological Regression and Ecological Inference." In *Ecological Inference: New Methodological Strategies*, ed. Gary King, Ori Rosen, and Martin A. Tanner. Cambridge, U.K.: Cambridge University Press.

Grofman, Bernard, and Michael Migalski. 1988. "Estimating the Extent of Racially Polarized Voting in Multicandidate Elections." *Sociological Methods and Research* 16:427–54.

Grofman, Bernard, Michael Migalski, and Nicholas Noviello. 1985. "The 'Totality of Circumstances' Test in Section 2 of the 1982 Extension of the Voting Rights Act: A Social Science Perspective." *Law and Policy* 7:209–23.

Guerra, Fernando. 1992. "Conditions Not Met: California Elections and the Latino Community." In *From Rhetoric to Reality: Latino Politics in the 1988 Election*, ed. Rodolfo de la Garza and Louis DeSipio. Boulder, Colo.: Westview.

Guerra, Fernando, Matt Barreto, Mara Marks, Nathan Woods, and Stephen Nuño. 2005. City of Los Angeles Mayoral Exit Poll. Center for the Study of Los Angeles, Loyola Marymount University.

Guerra, Fernando, and Mara Marks. 2002. *Survey of Public Opinion a Decade after the Los Angeles Riots*. Los Angeles: Center for the Study of Los Angeles.

Guinier, Lani. 1994. *The Tyranny of the Majority: Fundamental Fairness in Representative Democracy*. New York: Free Press.

Gurin, Patricia, Arthur Miller, and Gerald Gurin. 1980. "Stratum Identification and Consciousness." *Social Psychology Quarterly* 43:30–47.

Gutmann, Amy, ed. and intro. 1994. *Multiculturalism*. Princeton: Princeton University Press.

Haeberle, Steven H. 1997. "Exploring the Effects of Single Member Districts on an Urban Political System." *Urban Affairs Review* 33:287–97.

Hegstrom, Edward. 2003. "Little Latino Activism Here." *Houston Chronicle*, June 22.

Hendricks, Tyche. 2003. "Latino Vote Hotly Contested in S.F.'s Mayoral Runoff." *San Francisco Chronicle*, December 1.

Herberg, Will. 1955. *Catholic—Protestant—Jew*. New York: Doubleday.

Hero, Rodney. 1992. *Latinos and the U.S. Political System: Two-Tiered Pluralism*. Philadelphia: Temple University Press.

Hero, Rodney, and Anne Campbell. 1996. "Understanding Latino Political Participation: Exploring the Evidence from the Latino National Political Survey." *Hispanic Journal of Behavioral Sciences* 18:129–41.

Hero, Rodney, and Susan Clarke. 2003. "Latinos, Blacks, and Multiethnic Politics in Denver: Realigning Power and Influence in the Struggle for Equality." In *Racial Politics in*

American Cities, ed. Rufus P. Browning, Dale Rogers Marshall, and David H. Tabb. White Plains, N.Y.: Longman.

Hero, Rodney, F. Chris Garcia, John Garcia, and Harry Pachon. 2000. "Latino Participation, Partisanship, and Office Holding." *PS: Political Science and Politics* 33:529–34.

Highton, Benjamin, and Arthur Burris. 2002. "New Perspectives on Latino Voter Turnout in the United States." *American Politics Research* 30:285–306.

Hill, Kevin, Dario Moreno, and Lourdes Cue. 2001. "Racial and Partisan Voting in a Tri-Ethnic City: The 1996 Dade County Mayoral Election." *Journal of Urban Affairs* 23:291–307.

Hill, Tony. 2003. "Discovering Racism in Election Results: Methodology and Case Study, Minneapolis, 1997." Paper presented at the annual meeting of the Midwest Political Science Association.

Himmelfarb, Harold S., Michael Loar, and Susan H. Mott. 1983. "Sampling by Ethnic Surname: The Case of American Jews." *Public Opinion Quarterly* 47:247–60.

Hogg, M. A., and G. M Vaughn. 2002. *Social Psychology.* 3rd ed. London: Prentice-Hall.

Hotelling, Harold. 1929. "Stability in Competition." *Economic Journal* 39:41–57.

Houston Chronicle. 1999. "Election '99: Voting at a Glance." November 3.

Hritzuk, Natasha, and David K. Park. 2000. "The Question of Latino Political Participation: From SES to a Social Structural Explanation." *Social Science Quarterly* 81:151–65.

Huckfeldt, Robert, and John D. Sprague. 1995. *Citizens, Politics, and Social Communication: Information Influence in an Election Campaign.* New York: Cambridge University Press.

Ichinose, Daniel K., and Dennis Tan. 2001. "Findings from the November 2000 Southern California Voter Survey." Asian Pacific American Legal Center, Los Angeles.

Jacobson, Gary C. 1987. *The Politics of Congressional Elections.* 2nd ed. Boston: Little, Brown.

Jackman, Robert W. 1987. "Political Institutions and Voter Turnout in the Industrial Democracies." *American Political Science Review* 81:405–24.

Jones-Correa, Michael. 1998. *Between Two Nations: The Political Predicament of Latinos in New York City.* Ithaca: Cornell University Press.

Jupp, James. 1997. "New Politics and Social Movements: The Ethnic Dimension." *Journal of Australian Studies,* no. 54–55:200–206.

Kaufmann, Karen. 2003. "Black and Latino Voters in Denver: Responses to Each Other's Political Leadership." *Political Science Quarterly* 118 (April):107–26.

Kaufmann, Karen. Forthcoming. "Exploring the Effects of Minority Empowerment: How Black and Latino Voters Respond to Each Other's Political Leadership." *Urban Affairs Review.*

Keiser, Richard. 1990. "The Rise of a Biracial Coalition in Philadelphia." In *Racial Politics in American Cities,* ed. Rufus P. Browning, Dale Rogers Marshall, and David H. Tabb. White Plains, N.Y.: Longman.

Key, V. O. 1949. *Southern Politics in State and Nation.* New York: Vintage.

Kinder, Donald R., and David O. Sears. 1985. "Public Opinion and Political Behavior." In *Handbook of Social Psychology,* 3rd ed., ed. Gardner Lindsey and Elliot Aronson. New York: Random House.

King, Gary. 1997. *A Solution to the Ecological Inference Problem: Reconstructing Individual Behavior from Aggregate Data.* Princeton: Princeton University Press.

King, Gary, Michael Tomz, and Jason Wittenburg. 2000. "Making the Most of Statistical Analyses: Improving Interpretation and Presentation." *American Journal of Political Science* 44:347–61.

Kohler, Judith. 2004. "Beer Baron, Hispanic Lawyer Fight for Colorado Senate Seat." Associated Press, October 27.

Kornblut, Anne. 2007. "Richardson's Bid Is Now Official: 'I've Got to Appeal to All Voters.'" *Washington Post,* May 22.

Kousser, Morgan J. 1973. "Ecological Regression and Analysis of Past Politics." *Journal of Interdisciplinary History* 4:237–62.

Kymlicka, Will. 1995. *Multicultural Citizenship: A Liberal Theory of Minority Rights.* Oxford: Clarendon.

Landa, Janet, Michael Copeland, and Bernard Grofman. 1995. "Ethnic Voting Patterns: A Case Study of Metropolitan Toronto." *Political Geography* 14:435–49.

Lauderdale, Diane S., and Burt Kestenbaum. 2000. "Asian American Ethnic Identification by Surname." *Population Research and Policy Review* 19:283–300.

Lazarsfeld, Paul F., Bernard Berelson, and Hazel Gaudet. 1948. *The People's Choice.* 2nd ed. New York: Columbia University Press.

Leighley, Jan E. 2001. *Strength in Numbers? The Political Mobilization of Racial and Ethnic Minorities.* Princeton: Princeton University Press.

Lester, Will. 2001. "The Dynamic of Ethnic Loyalty." *Puerto Rico Herald,* December 7.

Lien, Pei-te. 1994. "Ethnicity and Political Participation: A Comparison between Asian and Mexican Americans." *Political Behavior* 16:237–64.

Lien, Pei-te. 2001. *The Making of Asian America through Political Participation.* Philadelphia: Temple University Press.

Lindlaw, Scott. 2004. "Bush Reaches Out to Hispanics." *Miami Herald,* July 8.

Linz, Juan J., and Alfred Stepan. 1996. *Problems of Democratic Transition and Consolidation: Southern Europe, South America, and Post-Communist Europe.* Baltimore: Johns Hopkins University Press.

Loewen, James, and Bernard Grofman. 1989. "Comment on Recent Developments in Methods Used in Voting Rights Litigation." *Urban Lawyer* 21:589–604.

Logan, John. 2001. *The New Latinos: Who They Are, Where They Are.* Albany, N.Y.: Lewis Mumford Center for Comparative Urban and Regional Research, University at Albany.

Long, J. Scott. 1997. *Regression Models for Categorical and Limited Dependent Variables.* Advanced Quantitative Techniques in the Social Sciences. Vol. 7. Thousand Oaks, Calif.: Sage.

Long, J. Scott, and Jeremy Freese. 2001. *Regression Models for Categorical Dependent Variables Using Stata.* College Station, Tex.: Stata Press.

Los Angeles City Clerk. 2003. "Statement of Votes Cast (OFFICIAL)—by Council District." March 4, 2003, Primary Election.

Los Angeles County Registrar of Voters. 2002. "November 2002 Election Results: Statement of Votes Cast by Precinct." Los Angeles.

Lublin, David I. 1997. *The Paradox of Representation.* Princeton: Princeton University Press.

Lublin, David I. 1999. "Racial Redistricting and African-American Representation: A Critique of 'Do Majority-Minority Districts Maximize Substantive Black Representation in Congress?'" *American Political Science Review* 93:183–86.

Lublin, David I., and Katherine Tate. 1992. "Black Office Seeking and Voter Turnout in Mayoral Elections." Paper presented at the annual meeting of the American Political Science Association, Chicago.

Lupia, Arthur. 1994. "Shortcuts versus Encyclopedias: Information Voting and Behavior in California Insurance Reform Elections." *American Political Science Review* 88:63–76.

Maass, Dave. 2008. "Guv Looks Good as Obama's Running Mate." *This Week in Print,* April 17, http://maassive.com/?p=549.

Macias, Elsa, Richard Cutler, and Sara Jones. 2001. *Promoting Access to Network Technologies in Underserved Communities: Lesson Learned.* Claremont, Calif.: Tomás Rivera Policy Institute.

MacManus, Susan, and Carol Cassel. 1982. "Mexican Americans in City Politics: Participation, Representation and Policy Preferences." *Urban Interests* 4:57–69.

Mansbridge, Jane. 1986. *Why We Lost the ERA.* Chicago: University of Chicago Press.

Manzano, Sylvia, and Arturo Vega. 2006. "I Don't See Color, I Vote for the Best Candidate: The Persistence of Ethnic Polarized Voting." Paper presented at the annual meeting of the Western Political Science Association.

Marquez, Benjamin, and James Jennings. 2000. "Representation by Other Means: Mexican American and Puerto Rican Social Movement Organizations." *PS: Political Science and Politics* 33:541–46.

Martinez v. Bush. 2002. 234 F. Supp. 2d 1275 n.4 (S.D. Fla).

Masuoka, Natalie. 2006. "Together They Become One: Examining Predictors of Panethnic Group Consciousness among Asian Americans and Latinos." *Social Science Quarterly* 87:993–1011.

Masuoka, Natalie. 2008. "Political Attitudes and Ideologies of Multiracial Americans." *Political Research Quarterly* 61:253–67.

Menchaca, Martha. 2002. *Recovering History, Constructing Race: The Indian, White, and Black Roots of Mexican Americans.* Austin: University of Texas Press.

Mendelberg, Tali. 2001. *The Race Card: Campaign Strategy, Implicit Messages, and the Norm of Equality.* Princeton: Princeton University Press.

Michelson, M. 2003. "Getting out the Latino Vote: How Door-to-Door Canvassing Influences Voter Turnout in Rural Central California." *Political Behavior* 25:247–63.

Michelson, Melissa. 2005. "Does Ethnicity Trump Party? Competing Vote Cues and Latino Voting Behavior." *Journal of Political Marketing* 4:1–25.

Miller, Arthur, Patricia Gurin, Gerald Gurin, and Oksana Malanchuk. 1981. "Group Consciousness and Political Participation." *American Journal of Political Science* 25:494–511.

Milner, Henry. 2001. *Civic Literacy: How Informed Citizens Make Democracy Work.* Hanover, N.H.: University of Press of New England.

Mollenkopf, John, David Olson, and Tim Ross. 2001. "Immigrant Political Incorporation in New York and Los Angeles." In *Governing American Cities: Interethnic Coalitions, Competition, and Conflict,* ed. Michael Jones-Correa. New York: Sage.

Montoya, Lisa J., Carole Hardy-Fanta, and Sonia Garcia. 2000. "Latina Politics: Gender, Participation, and Leadership." *PS: Political Science and Politics* 33:555–61.

Moore, Joan, and Harry Pachon. 1985. *Hispanics in the United States.* Englewood Cliffs, N.J.: Prentice-Hall.

Morrow-Howell, N. 1994. "The M Word: Multicollinearity in Multiple Regression." *Social Work Research* 18:247–51.

Muñoz, Carlos, and Charles P. Henry. 1986. "Rainbow Coalitions in Four Big Cities: San Antonio, Denver, Chicago, and Philadelphia." *PS: Political Science and Politics* 19:598–609.

Muñoz, Carlos, and Charles P. Henry. 1990. "Coalition Politics in San Antonio and Denver: The Cisneros and Peña Mayoral Campaigns." In *Racial Politics in American Cities,* ed. Rufus P. Browning, Dale R. Marshall, and David H. Tabb. White Plains, N.Y.: Longman.

Murray, Richard. 2003. "Houston Politics in City Elections." University of Houston Center for Public Policy.

Myrdal, Gunnar. 1944. *An American Dilemma: The Negro Problem and Modern Democracy.* New York: Harper and Row.

National Survey on Latinos in America. 2000. Questionnaire and Toplines. Washington Post/Kaiser Family Foundation/Harvard University Survey Project no. 3023. Menlo Park, Calif.: Kaiser Family Foundation.

National Association of Latino Elected and Appointed Officials. 2000. 17th Annual Conference, Denver.

National Association of Latino Elected and Appointed Officials. 2001. *The 2001 Directory of Latino Elected Officials.* Los Angeles: National Association of Latino Elected and Appointed Officials.

National Association of Latino Elected and Appointed Officials. 2002. *The 2002 National Roster of Hispanic Officials.* Los Angeles: National Association of Latino Elected and Appointed Officials.

National Association of Latino Elected and Appointed Officials. 2007. *Directory of Latino Elected and Appointed Officials.* Los Angeles: National Association of Latino Elected and Appointed Officials.

National Association of Latino Elected and Appointed Officials. 2008. *The 2008 National Roster of Hispanic Officials.* Los Angeles: National Association of Latino Elected and Appointed Officials.

National Election Study. 1952. The 1952 National Election Study (data set). Ann Arbor, Mich.: University of Michigan, Center for Political Studies (producer and distributor). www.electionstudies.org.

National Election Study. 1958. The 1958 National Election Study (data set). Ann Arbor, Mich.: University of Michigan, Center for Political Studies (producer and distributor). www.electionstudies.org.

National Election Study. 1980. The 1980 National Election Study (data set). Ann Arbor, Mich.: University of Michigan, Center for Political Studies (producer and distributor). www.electionstudies.org.

National Election Study. 2000. The 2000 National Election Study (data set). Ann Arbor, Mich.: University of Michigan, Center for Political Studies (producer and distributor). www.electionstudies.org.

National Telecommunications and Information Administration. 1995. *Falling through the Net: A Survey of the "Have Nots" in Rural and Urban America.* U.S. Department of Commerce.

National Telecommunications and Information Administration. 1998. *Falling through the Net II: New Data on the Digital Divide.* U.S. Department of Commerce.

National Telecommunications and Information Administration. 1999. *Falling through the Net: Defining the Digital Divide.* U.S. Department of Commerce.

National Telecommunications and Information Administration. 2000. *Falling through the Net: Toward Digital Inclusion.* U.S. Department of Commerce.

Nelson, Brent A. 1994. *America Balkanized: Immigration's Challenge to Government.* Monterey, Va.: American Immigration Control Foundation.

Nelson, Dale. 1979. "Ethnicity and Socioeconomic Status as Sources of Participation: The Case for Ethnic Political Culture." *American Political Science Review* 73:1024–38.

Nuño, Stephen. 2007. "Latino Mobilization and Vote Choice in the 2000 Presidential Election." *American Politics Research* 35:273–93.

O'Hanlon, Michael. 2001. "GOP Picks Gonzalez to Run in 49th: Newcomer to Politics and District Targets Mostly Democratic Hispanic Vote." *Washington Post,* July 22.

Olson, Mancur. 1970. *The Logic of Collective Action: Public Goods and the Theory of Groups.* Cambridge: Harvard University Press.

Omi, Michael, and Howard Winant. 1989. *Racial Formation in the United States: From the 1960s to the 1980s.* 2nd ed. New York: Routledge.

Pachon, Harry. 1987. "An Overview of Citizenship in the Hispanic Community." *International Migration Review* 21:299–310.

Pachon, Harry. 1988. "Hispanic Underrepresentation in the Federal Bureaucracy: The Missing Link." In *Latinos and the Political System,* ed F. Chris Garcia. Notre Dame, Ind.: University of Notre Dame Press.

Pachon, Harry. 1991. "U.S. Citizenship and Latino Participation in California." In *Racial and Ethnic Politics in California,* ed. Byran O. Jackson and Michael B. Preston. Berkeley, Calif.: Institute of Governmental Studies Press.

Pachon, Harry. 1998. "Latino Politics in the Golden State: Ready for the 21st Century?" In *Racial and Ethnic Politics in California,* ed. Byran O. Jackson and Michael B. Preston. Berkeley: Institute for Governmental Studies, University of California.

Pachon, Harry. 1999. "California Latino Politics and the 1996 Elections: From Potential to Reality." *In Awash in the Mainstream,* ed. Rodolfo O. de la Garza and Louis DeSipio. Boulder, Colo.: Westview.

Pachon, Harry, Matt A. Barreto, and Frances Marquez. 2004. "Latino Politics Comes of Age in the Golden State." In *The Latino Electorate in 2000,* ed. Rodolfo O. de la Garza and Louis DeSipio. Boulder, Colo.: Westview.

Pachon, Harry, and Louis DeSipio. 1992. "Latino Elected Officials in the 1990s." *PS: Political Science and Politics* 25:212–16.

Padilla, Felix M. 1985. "On the Nature of Latino Ethnicity." In *The Mexican-American Experience,* ed. Rodolfo O. de la Garza. Austin: University of Texas Press.

Pantoja, Adrian. 2005. "A Vigilant Spirit? Exploring Political Knowledge among the Latino Electorate." In *Minority Representation: Institutions, Behavior, and Identity,* ed. Gary Segura and Shawn Bowler. Charlottesville: University of Virginia Press.

Pantoja, Adrian D., Ricardo Ramírez, and Gary M. Segura. 2001. "Citizens by Choice, Voters by Necessity: Patterns in Political Mobilization by Naturalized Latinos." *Political Research Quarterly* 54:729–50.

Pantoja, Adrian D., and Gary M. Segura. 2003a. "Does Ethnicity Matter? Descriptive Representation in Legislatures and Political Alienation Among Latinos." *Social Science Quarterly* 84:441–60.

Pantoja, Adrian D., and Gary M. Segura. 2003b. "Fear and Loathing in California: Contextual Threat and Political Sophistication among Latino Voters." *Political Behavior* 25:265–86.

Pantoja, Adrian D., and Nathan D. Woods. 2000. "Latino Voter Turnout in Los Angeles County: Did Interest Group Efforts Matter?" *American Review of Politics* 20:141–62.

Papadakis, Maria C. 2001. *The Application and Implications of Information Technologies in the Home: Where Are the Data and What Do They Say?* Arlington, Va.: National Science Foundation, Division of Science Resources Studies.

Parenti, Michael. 1967. "Ethnic Politics and the Persistence of Ethnic Identifications." *American Political Science Review* 61:717–26.

Pasco, Jean O., and Vivian LeTran. 2002. "Orange County Elections 2002: Problems Few—Just Like Voters; an Estimated 30% of the Electorate Casts Ballots, about Half the Rate of Four Years Ago." *Los Angeles Times,* November 6.

Perez-Rivas, Manuel. 2001. "Bloomberg, Giuliani Confer on Transition." CNN.com, November 7.

Petrocik, John. 1989. "An Expected Party Vote: New Data for an Old Concept." *American Journal of Political Science* 33:44–66.

Pew Hispanic Center. 2004. *2004 National Survey of Latinos.* Washington, D.C.

Pinderhughes, Dianne. 1987. *Race and Ethnicity in Chicago Politics: A Re-examination of Pluralist Theory.* Urbana: University of Illinois Press.

Piven, Frances F., and Richard A. Cloward. 1979. *Poor People's Movements: Why They Succeed, How They Fail.* New York: Vintage.

Pliagas, Linda. 2005. "The Politics of Life." *Latino Leaders,* February 1.

Pollock, Jefrey, and Jeffrey Plaut. 2002. "The Latino Vote: Lessons from New York and New Jersey." *Campaigns and Elections,* 9.

Popkin, Samuel. 1991. *The Reasoning Voter.* Chicago: University of Chicago Press.

Portes, Alejandro, and Rafael Mozo. 1985. "The Political Adoption Process of Cubans and Other Ethnic Minorities in the United States." *International Migration Review* 19:35–63.

Portes, Alejandro, and Rubén G. Rumbaut. 1996. *Immigrant America: A Portrait.* 2nd ed. Berkeley: University of California Press.

Portes, Alejandro, and Rubén G. Rumbaut. 2001. *Legacies: The Story of the Immigrant Second Generation.* Berkeley: University of California Press; New York: Sage.

Putnam, Robert. 2000. *Bowling Alone: The Collapse and Revival of American Community.* New York: Simon and Schuster.

"Race, Ethnicity and California Politics." 1998. *California Journal,* November.

Ramírez, Ricardo. 2002a. "The Changing Landscape of California Politics, 1990–2000." Ph.D. diss., Stanford University.

Ramírez, Ricardo. 2002b. "Getting Out the Vote: The Impact of Non-Partisan Voter Mobilization Efforts in Low Turnout Latino Precincts." Paper presented at the annual meeting of the American Political Science Association.

Ramírez, Ricardo. 2005. "Giving Voice to Latino Voters: A Field Experiment on the Effectiveness of a National Non-Partisan Mobilization Effort." *Annals of the American Academy of Political and Social Science* 601:66–84.

Ramírez, Ricardo. 2007. "Segmented Mobilization: Latino Non-Partisan Get out the Vote Efforts in the 2000 General Election." *American Politics Research* 35:155–75.

Rath, Jan, and Shamit Saggar. 1992. "Ethnicity as a Political Tool in Britain and the Netherlands." In *Ethnic and Racial Minorities in the Advanced Industrial Democracies,* ed. Anthony Messina. Westport, Conn.: Greenwood.

Redmond, Tim. 2003. "Matt's Momentum: The Gonzalez Campaign Could Represent a Pivotal Movement in the Fight to Take Back San Francisco." *San Francisco Bay Guardian,* December 17.

Reeves, Keith. 1990. *Voting Hopes or Fears?* New York: Oxford University Press.

Reeves, Keith. 1997. *Voting Hopes or Fears? White Voters, Black Candidates, and Racial Politics in America.* New York: Oxford University Press.

Robinson, Randall N. 1999. *The Debt: What America Owes to Blacks.* New York: Dutton.

Robinson, W. S. 1950. "Ecological Correlations and the Behavior of Individuals." *American Sociological Review* 15:351–57.

Rocco, Raymond. 1977. "A Critical Perspective on the Study of Chicano Politics." *Western Political Quarterly* 30:558–73.

Ruiz v. City of Santa Maria. 160 F.3d 543 (9th Cir. 1998).

Rusk, Jerrold G. 1970. "The Effect of the Australian Ballot Reform on Split Ticket Voting: 1876–1908." *American Political Science Review* 64:1220–38.

Rytina, Nancy. 2002. "IRCA Legalization Effects: Lawful Permanent Residence and Naturalization Through 2001." Paper presented at conference on "The Effects of Immigrant Legalization Programs on the United States," the Cloister, Mary Woodward Lasker Center, National Institutes of Health Main Campus, Bethesda, Md., http://www.dhs.gov/xlibrary/assets/statistics/publications/irca0114int.pdf.

Saito, Leland. 1998. *Race and Politics: Asian Americans, Latinos, and Whites in a Los Angeles Suburb.* Champaign: University of Illinois Press.

Salces, Luis, and Peter Colby. 1988. "Mañana Will Be Better: Spanish-American Politics in Chicago." In *Latinos and the Political System,* ed F. Chris Garcia. Notre Dame, Ind.: University of Notre Dame Press.

Sanchez, Gabriel. 2006. "The Role of Group Consciousness in Political Participation among Latinos in the United States." *American Politics Research* 34:427–50.

Sanchez, Gabriel. 2008. "Latino Group Consciousness and Perceptions of Commonality with African Americans." *Social Science Quarterly* 89:428–44.

Santiago, Esmeralda, and Joie Davidow. 1998. *Las Christmas: Favorite Latino Authors Share Their Holiday Memories.* New York: Knopf.

Scherer, Michael. 2007. "Bill the Greek. Raising Funds for His Run at Presidency, Bill Richardson Has an Unlikely Role Model—Michael Dukakis." *Salon,* March 15.

Schmidt, Ronald, Edwina Barvosa-Carter, and Rodolfo Torres. 2000. "Latina/o Identities: Social Diversity and U.S. Politics." *PS: Political Science and Politics* 33:563–67.

Segal, Adam. 2003. *The Hispanic Priority: The Spanish Language Television Battle for the Hispanic Vote in 2000 U.S. Presidential Election.* Washington, D.C.: Hispanic Voter Project, Johns Hopkins University.

Segal, Adam. 2006. "Total Spanish-Language TV Spending by Market in 2004 Presidential Election. The Hispanic Voter Project." Johns Hopkins University, February.

Segura, Gary M., Denis Falcon, and Harry Pachon. 1997. "Dynamic of Latino Partisanship in California: Immigration, Issue Salience, and Their Implications." *Harvard Journal of Hispanic Politics* 10:62–80.

Segura, Gary M., and Nathan D. Woods. 2007. "Majority-Minority Districts, Co-Ethnic Candidates, and Mobilization Effects." In *Voting Rights Act Reauthorization of 2006: Perspectives on Democracy, Participation, and Power,* ed. Ana Henderson and Christopher Edley. Berkeley: Berkeley Public Policy Press.

Shafir, Michael. 2000. "The Political Party as National Holding Company: The Hungarian Democratic Federation of Romania." In *The Politics of National Minority Participation in Post-Communist Europe,* ed. Jonathan Stein. Armonk, N.Y.: Sharpe.

Shaw, Daron, Rodolfo O. de la Garza, and Jongho Lee. 2000. "Examining Latino Turnout in 1996: A Three-State, Validated Survey Approach (California, Florida, Texas)." *American Journal of Political Science* 44:338–46.

Shea, Daniel M., and Michael John Burton. 2001. *Campaign Craft: The Strategies, Tactics, and Art of Political Campaign Management.* Westport, Conn.: Praeger.

Sierra, Christine Marie, Teresa Carrillo, Louis DeSipio, and Michael Jones-Correa. 2000. "Latino Immigration and Citizenship." *PS: Political Science and Politics* 33:535–40.

Sonenshein, Raphael. 1993. *Politics in Black and White: Race and Power in Los Angeles.* Princeton: Princeton University Press.

Sonenshein, Raphael. 2003. "Post-Incorporation Politics in Los Angeles." In *Racial Politics in American Cities,* 3rd ed., ed. Rufus Browning, Dale Rogers Marshall, and David Tabb. New York: Longman.

Sonenshein, Raphael, and Susan Pinkus. 2002. "The Dynamics of Latino Political Incorporation: The 2001 Los Angeles Mayoral Election as Seen in *Los Angeles Times* Exit Polls." *PS: Politics and Political Science* 35:67–74.

Sosa, Lionel. 2004. "Communicating to the Latino Voter: What Works, What Doesn't." Paper presented at conference on "From Rhetoric to Reality: Latino Politics in 2004," Tomás Rivera Policy Institute, Los Angeles.

Statewide Survey of Latino Registered Voters. 1996. Claremont, Calif.: Tomás Rivera Policy Institute.

Stokes, Donald. 1963. "Spatial Models of Party Competition." *American Political Science Review* 57:368–77.

Stokes-Brown, Atiya Kai. 2006. "Racial Identity and Latino Vote Choice." *American Politics Research* 34:627–52.

Swain, Carol. 1995. *Black Faces, Black Interests: The Representation of African Americans in Congress.* Cambridge: Harvard University Press.

Tajfel, Henri, and John Turner. 1979. "An Integrative Theory of Intergroup Conflict." In *The Social Psychology of Intergroup Relations,* ed. W. G. Austin and S. Worchel. Monterey, Calif.: Brooks and Cole.

Tam, Wendy K. 1995. "Asians—A Monolithic Voting Bloc?" *Political Behavior* 17:223–49.

Tate, Katherine. 1991. "Black Political Participation in the 1984 and 1988 Presidential Elections." *American Political Science Review* 84:1159–76.

Tate, Katherine. 1993. *From Protest to Politics: The New Black Voters in American Elections.* Cambridge: Harvard University Press.

Tate, Katherine. 2003. *Black Faces in the Mirror.* Cambridge: Harvard University Press.

Tate, Katherine, Ronald Brown, and James Jackson. 1989. *The 1984 National Black Election Study Sourcebook.* Ann Arbor, Mich.: Institute for Social Research.

Taylor, Charles. 1994. "The Politics of Recognition." In *Multiculturalism,* ed. Amy Gutmann. Princeton: Princeton University Press.

Tedin, Kent T., and Richard W. Murray. 1981. "Dynamics of Candidate Choice in a State Election." *Journal of Politics* 43:435–55.

Tolbert, Caroline, and Rodney Hero. 2001. "Dealing with Diversity: Racial/Ethnic Context and Social Policy Change." *Political Research Quarterly* 54:571–604.

Tomas Rivera Policy Institute. 2000. *2000 Presidential Survey of Latino Voters.* Claremont, Calif.

Tomz, Michael, Jason Wittenberg, and Gary King. 2001. CLARIFY: Software for Interpreting and Presenting Statistical Results. Version 2.0. Cambridge: Harvard University, June 1. http://gking.harvard.edu.

Turner, John, M. A. Hogg, P. J. Oakes, S. D. Reicher, and M. S. Wetherell. 1987. *Rediscovering the Social Group: A Self-Categorization Theory.* Oxford: Blackwell

Uhlaner, Carole J. 1989a. "Rational Turnout: The Neglected Role of Groups." *American Journal of Political Science* 33:390–422.

Uhlaner, Carole J. 1989b. "'Relational Goods' and Participation: Incorporating Sociability into a Theory of Rational Action." *Public Choice* 62:253–85.

Uhlaner, Carole J., Bruce Cain, and D. Roderick Kiewiet. 1989. "Political Participation of Ethnic Minorities in the 1980s." *Political Behavior* 11:195–231.

Uhlaner, Carole, and F. Chris Garcia. 2005. "Learning Which Party Fits: Experience, Ethnic Identity, and the Demographic Foundations of Latino Party Identification." In *Diversity in Democracy,* ed. Gary Segura and Shaun Bowler. Charlottesville: University of Virginia Press.

U.S. Immigration and Naturalization Service. 2003. *Statistical Yearbook of the Immigration and Naturalization Service, 2001.* Washington, D.C.: U.S. Government Printing Office.

Valle, Victor M., and Rodolfo D. Torres. 2000. *Latino Metropolis.* Minneapolis: University of Minnesota Press.

Valle, Victor M., and Rodolfo D. Torres. 2003. "Class and Culture Wars in the New Latino

Politics." In *Latino/a Thought,* ed. Francisco H. Vázquez and Rodolfo D. Torres. Lanham, Md.: Rowman and Littlefield.

Vanderleeuw, James M., and Glenn U. Utter. 1993. "Voter Roll-Off and the Electoral Context: A Test of Two Theses." *Social Science Quarterly* 74:664–73.

Verba, Sidney, and Norman H. Nie. 1972. *Participation in America: Political Democracy and Social Equality.* New York: Harper and Row.

Verba, Sidney, Norman H. Nie, and Jae-on Kim 1978. *Participation and Political Equality: A Seven-Nation Comparison.* New York: Cambridge University Press.

Verba, Sidney, Kay Lehman Schlozman, and Henry E. Brady. 1995. *Voice and Equality: Civic Volunteerism in American Politics.* Cambridge: Harvard University Press.

Walton, Hanes, Jr. 1994. *Black Politics and Black Political Behavior: A Linkage Analysis.* Westport, Conn.: Praeger.

Wattenberg, Martin. 1987. "The Hollow Realignment: Partisan Change in a Candidate Centered Era." *Public Opinion Quarterly* 51:58–74.

Wattenberg, Martin P. 1994. *The Decline of American Political Parties, 1952–1992.* Cambridge: Harvard University Press.

Wattenberg, Martin. 1996. *The Decline of American Political Parties, 1952–1994.* Cambridge: Harvard University Press.

Wattenberg, Martin. 2002. *Where Have All the Voters Gone?* Cambridge: Harvard University Press.

Wattenberg, Martin P., and Craig Leonard Brians. 1999. "Negative Campaign Advertising: Demobilizer or Mobilizer?" *American Political Science Review* 93:891–99.

Wattier, M. J. 1983. "Ideological Voting in 1980 Republican Presidential Primaries." *Journal of Politics* 45:1016–26.

Welch, Susan, and John Hibbing. 1984. "Hispanic Representation in the U.S. Congress." *Social Science Quarterly* 65:328–35.

Wesolowsky, G. O. 1976. *Multiple Regression Analysis of Variance: An Introduction for Computer Users in Management and Economics.* New York: Wiley.

Wilhelm, Anthony. 1998. *Closing the Digital Divide: Enhancing Hispanic Participation in the Information Age.* Claremont, Calif.: Tomás Rivera Policy Institute.

Williams, Norma. 1990. *The Mexican American Family: Tradition and Change.* Dix Hills, N.Y.: General Hall.

Wolfinger, Raymond E. 1965. "Development and Persistence of Ethnic Voting." *American Political Science Review* 59:896–908.

Wolfinger, Raymond E., and Steven J. Rosenstone. 1980. *Who Votes?* New Haven: Yale University Press.

Word, David L., and R. Colby Perkins. 1996. *Building a Spanish Surname List for the 1990's—A New Approach to an Old Problem.* Technical Working Paper 13. Washington, D.C.: U.S. Bureau of the Census.

Wrinkle, Robert D., Joseph Stewart Jr., L. Polinard, Kenneth J. Meier, and John R. Arvizu. 1996. "Ethnicity and Nonelectoral Political Participation." *Hispanic Journal of Behavioral Sciences* 18:142–53.

Zax, Jeffrey S. 2002. "Comment on 'Estimating the Extent of Racially Polarized Voting in Multicandidate Contests' by Bernard Grofman and Michael Migalski." *Sociological Methods and Research* 31:75–86.

Zellner, Arnold. 1962. "An Efficient Method for Estimating Seemingly Unrelated Regressions and Tests for Aggregation Bias." *Journal of the American Statistical Association* 57:348–68.

Index